CARMINA GADELICA

ORTHA NAN GAIDHEAL

Alexander Carmichael

CARMINA GADELICA

HYMNS AND INCANTATIONS

WITH ILLUSTRATIVE NOTES ON WORDS, RITES, AND CUSTOMS, DYING AND OBSOLETE: ORALLY COLLECTED IN THE HIGHLANDS AND ISLANDS OF SCOTLAND AND TRANSLATED INTO ENGLISH, BY

ALEXANDER CARMICHAEL

VOLUME I

EDINBURGH

PRINTED FOR THE AUTHOR BY
T. AND A. CONSTABLE, PRINTERS TO HER MAJESTY
AND SOLD BY NORMAN MACLEOD
25 GEORGE IV. BRIDGE
1900

Three hundred copies printed

ORTHA NAN GAIDHEAL

URNAN AGUS UBAGAN

LE SOLUS AIR FACLA GNATHA AGUS
CLEACHDANA A CHAIDH AIR CHUL
CNUASAICHTE BHO BHIALACHAS
FEADH GAIDHEALTACHD NA H-ALBA
AGUS TIONNDAICHTE
BHO GHAIDHLIG GU BEURLA, LE
ALASTAIR MACGILLEMHICHEIL

CONTENTS

CONTENTS

AIMSIRE   SEASONS

CONTENTS

CONTENTS

INTRODUCTION

THIS work consists of old lore collected during the last forty-four years It forms a small part of a large mass of oral literature written down from the recital of men and women throughout the Highlands and Islands of Scotland, from Arran to Caithness, from Perth to St. Kilda.

The greater portion of the collection has been made in the Western Isles, variously called 'Eileana Bride,' Hebrid Isles, Outer Hebrides, Outer Isles, 'Eilean Fada,' 'Innis Fada,' Long Island, and anciently 'Iniscead,' 'Innis Cat,' Isle of the Cat, Isle of the Catey Probably the Catey were the people who gave the name 'Cataibh,' Cat Country, to Sutherland, and 'Caitnis,' Cat Ness, to Caithness

The Long Island is composed of a series of islands, separately known as Barra, South Uist, Benbecula, North Uist, and Harris and Lews. This chain is one hundred and nineteen miles in length, varying from a few yards to twenty-five miles in width. Viewed from the summit of its highest link, the Long Island chain resembles a huge artificial kite stretched along the green Atlantic Ocean, Lews forming the body, the disjointed tail trending away in the blue haze and terminating in Bearnarey of Barra

This long series of islands is evidently the backbone of a large island, perhaps of a great continent, that extended westward beyond the Isle of the Nuns, beyond the Isle of the Monks, beyond the Isle of St Flann, beyond the Isle of St. Kilda, beyond the Isle of Rockal, probably beyond the storied Isle of Rocabarraidh, and possibly beyond the historic Isle of Atlantis

This backbone is now disarticulated like the vertebrata of some huge fossil fish, each section having a life of its own These joints are separated by rills and channels varying from a few feet to eight miles in width.

The Atlantic rushes through these straits and narrows into the Minch, and the Minch rushes through the straits and narrows into the Atlantic, four times every twenty-four hours. The constant rushing to and fro of these mighty waters is very striking

Many of the countless islands comprising the Outer Hebrides are indented with arms of the sea studded with rocks and islands dividing and ramifying into endless mazes, giving in some cases a coast-line of over four hundred miles within their one-mile entrance. No mind could conceive, no imagination could realise, the disorderly distribution of land and water that is to be seen in those Outer Islands, where mountain and moor, sand and peat, rock and morass, reef and shoal, fresh-water lake and salt-water loch, in wildest confusion strive for mastery. Viewing this bewildering scene from the summit of Ruaival in Benbecula, Professor Blackie exclaimed :—

'O God-forsaken, God detested land !
Of bogs and blasts, of moors and mists and rain ;
Where ducks with men contest the doubtful strand,
And shirts when washed are straightway soiled again !' [1]

The formation of the Long Island is Laurentian gneiss, with some outcrops of Cambrian at Aoi, Lews, and four examples of trap at Lochmaddy, Uist. The rocks everywhere show ice action, being smoothed and polished, grooved and striated from hill to sea—the grooves and striæ lying east and west or thereby.

There are no trees in the Long Island except some at Rodail, Harris, and a few at Stornoway, Lews. The wind and spray of the Atlantic are inimical to trees under present climatic conditions. There are evidences, however, that there were trees in historic and prehistoric times.

It is said that a prince of Lews forsook a Norse princess and married a native girl. The princess vowed by Odin, Thor, and Frea, and by all the other gods and goddesses of her fathers, to avenge the insult, and she sent her witch to burn the woods of Lews. The tradition of the burning of these woods is countenanced by the presence of charred trees in peat-moss in many places. It is on record that a Norse prince married a native Barra girl, but whether or not this was the prince of Lews is uncertain.

---

[1] On Sunday, the 21st July 1875, Professor Blackie, Mr. William Jolly, and I ascended the hill of Ruaival, in Benbecula. From the summit of this hill, 409 feet high, we had an extensive view of our extraordinary surroundings, striking to the eye and instructive to the mind. On returning home to Creagorry, where we then lived, Professor Blackie wrote the lines composed on Ruaival on the fly leaf of *Burt's Letters*, which he gave to me. The day that Professor Blackie and Mr Jolly were to have left our house some mishap befell their linens, and these had to be rewashed. Mr. Jolly alleged that I had bribed the servant in charge of the linens to bring about the accident in order to prolong the stay of our well-beloved guests !

There are many evidences that the sea has gained upon the land in the Long Island. In the shore and in the sea, peat-moss, tree-roots, sessile reeds, stone dykes, dwellings and temples may be seen, while pieces of moss, trees and masonry have been brought up from time to time by hooks and anchors in from ten to twenty fathoms of water. I do not know anything more touching yet more fascinating than these submerged memorials of bygone times and of bygone men.

Immense stretches of sandy plains run along the Atlantic border of the Outer Hebrides. These long reaches of sessile sand are locally called machairs—plains. They are singularly bleak, barren, and shelterless in winter, giving rise to the saying :—

' Is luath fear na droch mhnatha	Fast goes the man of the thriftless wife
Air a mhachair Uidhistich '	Upon the machair of Uist.

The inference is that the man is ill clad. In summer, however, these 'machairs' are green and grassy, comforting to the foot, pleasing to the eye, and deliciously fragrant, being covered with strongly aromatic plants and flowers.

But the charm of these islands lies in their people—goodly to see, brave to endure, and pleasing to know.

The population of the Long Island is about forty-four thousand. Of these about forty-four families occupy two-thirds of the whole land, the crofters, cottars, and the poor who exist upon the poor, being confined to the remaining third. These are crowded upon one another like sheep in a pen :—

' Na biasta mor ag itheadh nam biasta beag	The big beasts eating the little beasts,
Na biasta beag a deanamh mar dh'fhaodas iad '	The little beasts doing as best they may.

There are no intermediate farms, no gradation holdings, to which the industrious crofter might aspire, and become a benefit to himself, an example to his neighbour, and a lever to his country.

The people of the Outer Isles, like the people of the Highlands and Islands generally, are simple and law-abiding, common crime being rare and serious crime unknown among them. They are good to the poor, kind to the stranger, and courteous to all. During all the years that I lived and travelled among them, night and day, I never met with incivility, never with rudeness, never with vulgarity, never with aught but courtesy. I never entered a house without the inmates offering me food or apologising for their want of it. I never was asked for charity in the West, a striking contrast to my experience in England, where I was frequently asked for food, for drink, for money, and that by persons whose incomes would have been wealth to the poor men and women of the West. After long experience of his tenants, the late Mr. John Gordon said .—'The Uist people are born gentlemen—Nature's noblemen.'

Gaelic oral literature was widely diffused, greatly abundant, and excellent in quality—in the opinion of scholars, unsurpassed by anything similar in the ancient classics of Greece or Rome.

Many causes contributed towards these attainments — the crofting system, the social customs, and the evening 'ceilidh.' In a crofting community the people work in unison in the field during the day, and discuss together in the house at night. This meeting is called 'ceilidh,'—a word that throbs the heart of the Highlander wherever he be. The 'ceilidh' is a literary entertainment where stories and tales, poems and ballads, are rehearsed and recited, and songs are sung, conundrums are put, proverbs are quoted, and many other literary matters are related and discussed. This institution is admirably adapted to cultivate the heads and to warm the hearts of an intelligent, generous people. Let me briefly describe the 'ceilidh' as I have seen it.

In a crofting townland there are several story-tellers who recite the oral literature of their predecessors. These story-tellers of the Highlands are as varied in their subjects as are literary men and women elsewhere. One is a historian narrating events simply and concisely; another is a historian with a bias, colouring his narrative according to his leanings. One is an inventor, building fiction upon fact, mingling his materials, and investing the whole with the charm of novelty and the halo of romance. Another is a reciter of heroic poems and ballads, bringing the different characters before the mind as clearly as the sculptor brings the figure before the eye. One gives the songs of the chief poets, with interesting accounts of their authors, while another, generally a woman, sings, to weird airs, beautiful old songs, some of them Arthurian. There are various other narrators, singers, and speakers, but I have never heard aught that should not be said nor sung.

The romance school has the largest following, and I go there, joining others on the way. The house of the story-teller is already full, and it is difficult to get inside and away from the cold wind and soft sleet without. But with that politeness native to the people, the stranger is pressed to come forward and occupy the seat vacated for him beside the houseman. The house is roomy and clean, if homely, with its bright peat fire in the middle of the floor There are many present—men and women, boys and girls. All the women are seated, and most of the men Girls are crouched between the knees of fathers or brothers or friends, while boys are perched wherever—boy-like—they can climb.

The houseman is twisting twigs of heather into ropes to hold down thatch, a neighbour crofter is twining quicken roots into cords to tie cows, while another is plaiting bent grass into baskets to hold meal

| 'Ith aran, sniamh muran, | Eat bread and twist bent, |
| Us bi thu am bhadhn mar bha thu'n uraidh.' | And thou this year shalt be as thou wert last. |

The housewife is spinning, a daughter is carding, another daughter is teazing, while a third daughter, supposed to be working, is away in the background conversing in low whispers with the son of a neighbouring crofter. Neighbour wives and neighbour daughters are knitting, sewing, or embroidering. The conversation is general . the local news, the weather, the price of cattle, these leading up to higher themes—the clearing of the glens (a sore subject), the war, the parliament, the effects of the sun upon the earth and the moon upon the tides The speaker is eagerly listened to, and is urged to tell more. But he pleads that he came to hear and not to speak, saying :—

| 'A chiad sgial air tear an taighe, | The first story from the host, |
| Sgial gu la an an aoidh.' | Story till day from the guest. |

The stranger asks the houseman to tell a story, and after a pause the man complies The tale is full of incident, action, and pathos. It is told simply yet graphically, and at times dramatically—compelling the undivided attention of the listener. At the pathetic scenes and distressful events the bosoms of the women may be seen to heave and then silent tears to fall. Truth overcomes craft, skill conquers strength, and bravery is rewarded. Occasionally a momentary excitement occurs when heat and sleep overpower a boy and he tumbles down among the people below, to be trounced out and sent home When the story is ended it is discussed and commented upon, and the different characters praised or blamed according to their merits and the views of the critics

If not late, proverbs, riddles, conundrums, and songs follow. Some of the tales, however, are long, occupying a night or even several nights in recital. 'Sgeul Coise Cein,' the story of the foot of Cian, for example, was in twenty-four parts, each part occupying a night in telling   The story is mentioned by Macnicol in his *Remarks* on Johnson's *Tour*.

The hut of Hector Macisaac, Ceannlangavat, South Uist, stood in a peat-moss.   The walls were of 'riasg,' turf, and the thatch of 'cuilc,' reeds, to the grief of the occupants, who looked upon the reed as banned, because it was used on Calvary to convey the sponge with the vinegar   The hut was about fifteen feet long, ten feet broad, and five feet high.   There was nothing in it that the vilest thief in the lowest slum would condescend to steal.   It were strange if the inmates of this turf hut in the peat-morass had been other than ailing.   Hector Macisaac and his wife were the only occupants, their daughter being at service trying to prolong existence in her parents.   Both had been highly endowed physically, and were still endowed mentally, though now advanced in years   The wife knew many secular runes, sacred hymns, and fairy songs , while the husband had numerous heroic tales, poems, and ballads.

I had visited these people before, and in September 1871, Iain F. Campbell of Islay and I went to see them.   Hector Macisaac, the unlettered cottar who knew no language but his own, who came into contact with no one but those of his own class, his neighbours of the peat-bog, and who had never been out of his native island, was as polite and well-mannered and courteous as Iain Campbell, the learned barrister, the world-wide traveller, and the honoured guest of every court in Europe   Both were at ease and at home with one another, there being neither servility on the one side nor condescension on the other.

The stories and poems which Hector Macisaac went over during our visits to him would have filled several volumes.   Mr. Campbell now and then put a leading question which brought out the story-teller's marvellous memory and extensive knowledge of folklore.

It was similar with blind old Hector Macleod, cottar, Lianacuithe, South Uist, and with old Roderick Macneill, cottar, Miunghlaidh, Barra Each of those men repeated stories and poems, tales and ballads, that would have filled many books.   Yet neither of them told more than a small part of what he knew.   None of the three men knew any letters, nor any language but Gaelic, nor had ever been out of his native island.   All expressed regret in well-chosen words that they had not a better place in which to receive their visitors, and all thanked them in polite terms for coming to see them and for taking an interest in their decried and derided old lore And all were courteous as the courtier

During his visit to us, Mr. Campbell expressed to my wife and to myself his admiration of these and other men with whom we had come in contact. He said that in no other race had he observed so many noble traits and high qualities as in the unlettered, untravelled, unspoiled Highlander.

In 1860, 1861, and 1862, I took down much folk-lore from Kenneth Morrison, cottar, Trithion, Skye Kenneth Morrison had been a mason, but was now old, blind, and poor. Though wholly unlettered, he was highly intelligent. He mentioned the names of many old men in the extensive but now desolate parish of Minngnis, who had been famous story-tellers in his boyhood—men who had been born in the first decade of the eighteenth century Several of these, he said, could recite stories and poems during many nights in succession—some of the tales requiring several nights to relate He repeated fragments of many of these. Some of them were pieces of poems and stories published by Macpherson, Smith, the Stewarts, the MacCallums, the Campbells, and others

Kenneth Morrison told me that the old men, from whom he heard the poems and stories, said that they had heard them from old men in their boyhood That would carry these old men back to the first half of the seventeenth century. Certainly they could not have learnt their stories or poems from books, for neither stories nor poems were printed in their time, and even had they been, those men could not have read them.

Gaelic oral literature has been disappearing during the last three centuries. It is now becoming meagre in quantity, inferior in quality, and greatly isolated.

Several causes have contributed towards this decadence—principally the Reformation, the rebellions, the evictions, the Disruption, the schools, and the spirit of the age Converts in religion, in politics, or in aught else, are apt to be intemperate in speech and rash in action. The Reformation movement condemned the beliefs and cults tolerated and assimilated by the Celtic Church and the Latin Church Nor did sculpture and architecture escape their intemperate zeal. The rebellions harried and harassed the people, while the evictions impoverished, dispirited, and scattered them over the world. Ignorant school-teaching and clerical narrowness have been painfully detrimental to the expressive language, wholesome literature, manly sports, and interesting amusements of the Highland people. Innumerable examples occur.

A young lady said —'When we came to Islay I was sent to the parish school to obtain a proper grounding in arithmetic I was charmed with the schoolgirls and their Gaelic songs. But the schoolmaster—an alien like myself—denounced Gaelic speech and Gaelic songs. On getting out of school one evening the girls resumed a song they had been singing the previous evening I joined willingly, if timidly, my knowledge of Gaelic being small. The schoolmaster heard us, however, and called us back He punished us till the blood trickled from our fingers, although we were big girls, with the dawn of womanhood upon us. The thought of that scene thrills me with indignation '

I was taking down a story from a man, describing how twin giants detached a huge stone from the parent rock, and how the two carried the enormous block of many tons upon their broad shoulders to lay it over a deep gully in order that their white-maned steeds might cross Their enemy, however, came upon them in the night-time when thus engaged, and threw a magic mist around them, lessening their strength and causing them to fail beneath their burden. In the midst of the graphic description the grandson of the narrator, himself an aspirant teacher, called out in tones of superior authority, 'Grandfather, the teacher says that you ought to be placed upon the stool for your lying Gaelic stories.' The old man stopped and gasped in pained surprise. It required time and sympathy to soothe his feelings and to obtain the rest of the tale, which was wise, beautiful, and poetic, for the big, strong giants were Frost and Ice, and their subtle enemy was Thaw. The enormous stone torn from the parent rock is called 'Clach Mhor Leum nan Caorach,' the big stone of the leap of the sheep Truly 'a little learning is a dangerous thing'! This myth was afterwards appreciated by the Royal Society of Edinburgh.

After many failures, and after going far to reach him, I induced a man to come to the lee of a knoll to tell me a tale We were well into the spirit of the story when two men from the hill passed us The story-teller hesitated, then stopped, saying that he would be reproved by his family, bantered by his friends, and censured by his minister. The story, so inauspiciously interrupted and never resumed, was the famous 'Sgeul Coise Cein,' already mentioned.

Having made many attempts, I at last succeeded in getting a shepherd to come to me, in order to be away from his surroundings. The man travelled fifty-five miles, eight of these being across a stormy strait of the Atlantic. We had reached the middle of a tale when the sheriff of the district came to call on me in my rooms. The reciter fled, and after going more than a mile on his way home he met a man who asked him why he looked so scared, and why without his bonnet. The shepherd discovered that he had left his bonnet, his plaid, and his staff behind him in his flight. The remaining half of that fine story, as well as much other valuable Gaelic lore, died with the shepherd in Australia.

Ministers of Lews used to say that the people of Lews were little better than pagans till the Reformation, perhaps till the Disruption If they were not, they have atoned since, being now the most rigid Christians in the British Isles.

When Dr William Forbes Skene was preparing the third volume of *Celtic Scotland*, he asked me to write him a paper on the native system of holding the land, tilling the soil, and apportioning the stock in the Outer Hebrides. Being less familiar with Lews than with the other portions of the Long Island, I visited Lews again. It was with extreme difficulty that I could obtain any information on the subject of my inquiry, because it related to the foolish past rather than to the sedate present, to the secular affairs rather than to the religious life of the people. When I asked about old customs and old modes of working, I was answered, 'Good man, old things are passed away, all things are become new', for the people of Lews, like the people of the Highlands and Islands generally, carry the Scriptures in their minds and apply them in their speech as no other people do. It was extremely disconcerting to be met in this manner on a mission so desirable.

During my quest I went into a house near Ness. The house was clean and comfortable if plain and unpretending, most things in it being home-made. There were three girls in the house, young, comely, and shy, and four women, middle-aged, handsome, and picturesque in their homespun gowns and high-crowned mutches. Three of the women had been to the moorland pastures with their cattle, and had turned in here to rest on their way home.

'Hail to the house and household,' said I, greeting the inmates in the salutation of our fathers 'Hail to you, kindly stranger,' replied the house-wife. 'Come forward and take this seat. If it be not ill-mannered, may we ask whence you have come to-day? You are tired and travel-stained, and probably hungry?' 'I have come from Gress,' said I, 'round by Tolasta to the south, and Tolasta to the north, taking a look at the ruins of the Church of St. Aula, at Gress, and at the ruins of the fort of Dunothail, and then across the moorland.' 'May the Possessor keep you in His own keeping, good man! You left early and have travelled far, and must be hungry.' With this the woman raised her eyes towards her daughters standing demurely silent, and motionless as Greek statues, in the background. In a moment the three fair girls became active and animated. One ran to the stack and brought in an armful of hard, black peats, another ran to the well and brought in a pail of clear spring water, while the third quickly spread a cloth, white as snow, upon the table in the inner room. The three neighbour women rose to leave, and I rose to do the same. 'Where are you going, good man?' asked the housewife in injured surprise, moving between me and the door. 'You must not go till you eat a bit and drink a sip. That indeed would be a reproach to us that we would not soon get over. These slips of lassies and I would not hear the end of it from the men at the sea, were we to allow a wayfarer to go from our door hungry, thirsty, and weary. No! no! you must not go till you eat a bite. Food will be ready presently, and in the meantime you will bathe your feet and dry your stockings, which are wet after coming through the marshes of the moorland' Then the woman went down upon her knees, and washed and dried the feet of the stranger as gently and tenderly as a mother would those of her child. 'We have no stockings to suit the kilt,' said the woman in a tone of evident regret, 'but here is a pair of stockings of the houseman's which he has never had on, and perhaps you would put them on till your own are dry'

One of the girls had already washed out my stockings, and they were presently drying before the bright fire on the middle of the floor. I deprecated all this trouble, but to no purpose. In an incredibly short time I was asked to go 'ben' and break bread.

Through the pressure of the housewife and of myself the other three women had resumed their seats, uneasily it is true. But immediately before food was announced the three women rose together and quietly walked away, no urging detaining them.

The table was laden with wholesome food sufficient for several persons There were fried herrings and boiled turbot fresh from the sea, and eggs fresh from the yard. There were fresh butter and salt butter, wheaten scones, barley bannocks, and oat cakes, with excellent tea, and cream. The woman

apologised that she had no 'aran, coinnich'—moss bread, that is, loaf bread—
and no biscuits, they being simple crofter people far away from the big town.

'This,' said I, taking my seat, 'looks like the table for a "reiteach,"
betrothal, rather than for one man. Have you betrothals in Lews?' I asked,
turning my eyes toward the other room where we had left the three comely
maidens. 'Oh, indeed, yes, the Lews people are very good at marrying
Foolish young creatures, they often marry before they know their responsibilities
or realise their difficulties,' and her eyes followed mine in the direction of her own
young daughters. 'I suppose there is much fun and rejoicing at your marriages
—music, dancing, singing, and merry-making of many kinds?' 'Oh, indeed,
no, our weddings are now quiet and becoming, not the foolish things they were
in my young days. In my memory weddings were great events, with singing
and piping, dancing and amusements all night through, and generally for
two and three nights in succession. Indeed, the feast of the "bord breid,"
kertch table, was almost as great as the feast of the marriage table, all the
young men and maidens struggling to get to it. On the morning after the
marriage the mother of the bride, and failing her the mother of the
bridegroom, placed the "breid tri chearnach," three-cornered kertch, on
the head of the bride before she rose from her bed. And the mother
did this "an ainm na Teoire Beannaichte," in name of the Sacred Three,
under whose guidance the young wife was to walk. Then the bride arose
and her maidens dressed her, and she came forth with the "breid beannach,"
pointed kertch, on her head, and all the people present saluted her and
shook hands with her, and the bards sang songs to her, and recited "ranna-
ghail mhora," great rigmaroles, and there was much rejoicing and merry-
making all day long and all night through. "Gu dearbh mar a b'e fleagh na
bord breid a b'fhearr, cha 'n e gearr bu mheasa"—Indeed, if the feast of the
kertch table was not better, it was not a whit worse

'There were many sad things done then, for those were the days of foolish
doings and of foolish people. Perhaps, on the day of the Lord, when they
came out of church, if indeed they went into church, the young men would
go to throw the stone, or to toss the cabar, or to play shinty, or to run races,
or to race horses on the strand, the young maidens looking on the while, ay,
and the old men and women' 'And have you no music, no singing, no
dancing now at your marriages?' 'May the Possessor keep you! I see
that you are a stranger in Lews, or you would not ask such a question,'

the woman exclaimed with grief and surprise in her tone. 'It is long since
we abandoned those foolish ways in Ness, and, indeed, throughout Lews.
In my young days there was hardly a house in Ness in which there was not
one or two or three who could play the pipe, or the fiddle, or the trump.
And I have heard it said that there were men, and women too, who could play
things they called harps, and lyres, and bellows-pipes, but I do not know what
those things were' 'And why were those discontinued?' 'A blessed change
came over the place and the people,' the woman replied in earnestness, 'and the
good men and the good ministers who arose did away with the songs and the
stories, the music and the dancing, the sports and the games, that were
perverting the minds and ruining the souls of the people, leading them to
folly and stumbling.' 'But how did the people themselves come to discard
their sports and pastimes?' 'Oh, the good ministers and the good elders
preached against them and went among the people, and besought them to
forsake their follies and to return to wisdom. They made the people break
and burn their pipes and fiddles. If there was a foolish man here and there
who demurred, the good ministers and the good elders themselves broke and
burnt their instruments, saying :—

"Is fearr an teine beag a gharas la beag na sithe, Na'n teine mor a loisgeas la mor na feirge "	Better is the small fire that warms on the little day of peace, Than the big fire that burns on the great day of wrath

The people have forsaken their follies and their Sabbath-breaking, and
there is no pipe, no fiddle here now,' said the woman in evident satisfaction.
'And what have you now instead of the racing, the stone-throwing, and the
cabar-tossing, the song, the pipe, and the dance?' 'Oh, we have now
the blessed Bible preached and explained to us faithfully and earnestly, if we
sinful people would only walk in the right path and use our opportunities'

'But what have you at your weddings? How do you pass the time?'
'Oh! the cailes are on one side of the house talking of their crops and their
nowt, and mayhap of the days when they were young and when things were
different And the young men are on the other side of the house talking
about boats, and sailing, and militia, and naval reserve, perhaps of their
own strength, and of many foolish matters besides.'

'And where are the girls? What are they doing?' 'Oh, they, silly
things! are in the "culaist," back-house, perhaps trying to croon over

some foolish song under their breath, perhaps trying to amble through some awkward steps of dancing on the points of their toes, or, shame to tell, perhaps speaking of what diess this or that girl had on at this or that marriage, or worse still, what hat this girl or that girl had on on the Day of the Lord, perhaps even on the Day of the Holy Communion, showing that their minds were on the vain things of the world instead of on the wise things of salvation'

'But why are the girls in the "culaist"?   What do they fear?'

'May the Good Being keep you, good man !   They are in the "culaist" for concealment, "agus eagal am beatha agus am bais oria gu'n cluinnear no gu'm faicear iad"—and the fear of their life and of their death upon them, that they may be heard or seen should the good elder happen to be passing the way'   'And should he, what then?'   'Oh, the elder will tell the minister, and the good minister will scold them from the pulpit, mentioning the girls by name.   But the girls have a blanket on the door and another blanket on the window to deafen the sound and to obscure the light.'

'Do the young maidens allow the young men to join them in the "culaist"?' 'Indeed, truth to tell, the maidens would be glad enough to admit the young men were it not the fear of exposure.   But the young men are so loud of voice, and so heavy of foot, and make so much noise, that they would betray the retreat of the girls, who would get rebuked, while the young men would escape.   The girls would then be ashamed and downcast, and would not lift a head for a year and a day after their well-deserved scolding   They suffer most, for, sad to say, the young men are becoming less afraid of being admonished than they used to be.'

'And do the people have spirits at their marriages?'   'Oh yes, the minister is not so hard as that upon them at all.   He does not interfere with them in that way unless they take too much, and talk loudly and quarrel. Then he is grieved and angry, and scolds them severely.   Occasionally, indeed, some of the carles have a nice "frogan," liveliness, upon them and are very happy together.   But oh, they never quarrel, nor fight, nor get angry with one another.   They are always nice to one another and civil to all around them.'

'Perhaps were the minister to allow the people less drink and more music and dancing, singing and merry-making, they would enjoy it as much. I am sure the young girls would sing better, and dance better, with the help of the young men. And the young men themselves would be less loud of voice and less heavy of heel, among the maidens. Perhaps the happiness of the old people too would be none the less real nor less lasting at seeing the joyousness of the young people'

To this the woman promptly and loyally replied. 'The man of the Lord is untiring in work and unfailing in example for our good, and in guiding us to our heavenly home, constantly reminding us of the littleness of time and the greatness of eternity, and he knows best, and we must do our best to follow his counsel and to imitate his example.'

A famous violin-player died in the island of Eigg a few years ago He was known for his old-style playing and his old-world airs which died with him. A preacher denounced him, saying —'Tha thu shios an sin cul na comhla, a dhuine thruaigh le do chiabhan liath, a cluich do sheann fhiodhla le laimh fhuair a mach agus le teine an diabhoil a steach'—Thou art down there behind the door, thou miserable man with thy grey hair, playing thine old fiddle with the cold hand without, and the devil's fire within. His family pressed the man to burn his fiddle and never to play again A pedlar came round and offered ten shillings for the violin. The instrument had been made by a pupil of Stradivarius, and was famed for its tone. 'Cha b'e idir an rud a fhuaradh na dail a ghoirtich mo chridhe cho cruaidh ach an dealachadh rithe! an dealachadh rithe! agus gu'n tug mi fhein a bho a b'fhearr am buaile m'athar air a son, an uair a bha mi og'—It was not at all the thing that was got for it that grieved my heart so sorely, but the parting with it! the parting with it! and that I myself gave the best cow in my father's fold for it when I was young. The voice of the old man faltered and the tear fell. He was never again seen to smile.

The reciters of religious lore were more rare and more reticent than the reciters of secular lore. Men and women whom I knew had hymns and incantations, but I did not know of this in time. The fragments recalled by their families, like the fragments of Greek or Etruscan vases, indicated the originals.

Before dictating, the reciter went over the tale or poem, the writer making mental notes the while. This was helpful when, in the slow process of dictating, the narrator lost his thread and omitted passages The poems were generally intoned in a low recitative manner, rising and falling in slow modulated cadences charming to hear but difficult to follow.

The music of the hymns had a distinct individuality, in some respects resembling and in many respects differing from the old Gregorian chants of the Church. I greatly regret that I was not able to record this peculiar and beautiful music, probably the music of the old Celtic Church

Perhaps no people had a fuller ritual of song and story, of secular rite and religious ceremony, than the Highlanders. Mirth and music, song and dance, tale and poem, pervaded their lives, as electricity pervades the air. Religion, pagan or Christian, or both combined, permeated everything—blending and shading into one another like the iridescent colours of the rainbow The people were sympathetic and synthetic, unable to see and careless to know where the secular began and the religious ended—an admirable union of elements in life for those who have lived it so truly and intensely as the Celtic races everywhere have done, and none more truly or more intensely than the ill-understood and so-called illiterate Highlanders of Scotland.

If this work does nothing else, it affords incontestable proof that the Northern Celts were endowed, as Renan justly claims for Celts everywhere, with ' profound feeling and adorable delicacy ' in their religious instincts [1]

The Celtic missionaries allowed the pagan stock to stand, grafting their Christian cult thereon. Hence the blending of the pagan and the Christian religions in these poems, which to many minds will constitute their chief charm. Gaelic lore is full of this blending and grafting—nor are they confined to the literature of the people, but extend indeed to their music, sculpture, and architecture. At Rodail, Harris, is a cruciform church of the thirteenth century The church abuts upon a broad square tower of no great height The tower is called ' Tur Chliamain,' tower of Clement, ' Chaman Mor Rodail,' Great Clement of Rodail. Tradition says that the tower is older than the church, and the masonry confirms the tradition.

There are sculptures within the church of much originality of design and of great beauty of execution, but the sculptures without are still more original and interesting. Round the sides of the square tower are the figures of birds and beasts, reptiles and fishes, and of men and women, representing phallic worship Here pagan cult joins with Christian faith, the East with the West, the past with the present. The traveller from India to Scotland can here see, on the cold, sterile rocks of Harris, the petrified symbols of a faith left living behind him on the hot, fertile plains

[1] *Poetry of the Celtic Races, and Other Studies* By Ernest Renan

of Hindustan   He can thus in his own person bridge over a space of eight thousand miles and a period of two thousand years

There are observances and expressions current in the West which savour of the East, such as sun, moon, star, and fire worship, once prevalent, nor yet obsolete.

Highland divinities are full of life and action, local colour and individuality.   These divinities filled the hearts and minds of the people of the Highlands, as their deities filled the hearts and minds of the people of Greece and Rome.   The subject of these genii of the Highlands ought to be investigated and compared with those of other lands   Even yet, on the verge of disappearance, they would yield interesting results.   Though loving their haunts and tenacious of their habitats, the genii of the Highlands are disappearing before the spirit of modernism, as the Red Indian, once bold and courageous, disappears before the white man   Once intrusive, they are now become timid as the mullet of the sea, the shrew of the grass, or the swift of the air—a glimpse, a glint, and gone for ever.   They are startled at the crack of the rifle, the whistle of the steamer, the shriek of the train, and the click of the telegraph   Their homes are invaded and their repose is disturbed, so that they find no rest for their weary feet nor sleep for their heavy eyes; and their native land, so full of their love, so congenial to their hearts, will all too soon know them no more.   Let an attempt be made even yet to preserve their memories ere they disappear for ever

Whatever be the value of this work, it is genuine folk-lore, taken down from the lips of men and women, no part being copied from books.   It is the product of far-away thinking, come down on the long stream of time.   Who the thinkers and whence the stream, who can tell ?   Some of the hymns may have been composed within the cloistered cells of Derry and Iona, and some of the incantations among the cromlechs of Stonehenge and the standing-stones of Callarnis.   These poems were composed by the learned, but they have not come down through the learned, but through the unlearned—not through the lettered few, but through the unlettered many—through the crofters and cottars, the herdsmen and shepherds, of the Highlands and Islands

Although these compositions have been rescued chiefly among Roman Catholics and in the islands, they have been equally common among Protestants and on the mainland.

From one to ten versions have been taken down, differing more or less.

It has been difficult to select. Some examples of these variants are given. Several poems and many notes are wholly withheld, while a few of the poems and all the notes have been abbreviated for want of space.

I had the privilege of being acquainted with Iain F. Campbell of Islay during a quarter of a century, and I have followed his counsel and imitated his example in giving the words and in recording the names of the reciters. Some localisms are given for the sake of Gaelic scholars. Hence the same word may be spelt in different ways through the influence of assonance and other characteristics of Gaelic compositions.

With each succeeding generation Gaelic speech becomes more limited and Gaelic phraseology more obscure. Both reciter and writer felt this when words and phrases occurred which neither knew. These have been rendered tentatively or left untranslated. I can only hope that in the near or distant future some competent scholar may compare these gleanings of mine with Celtic writings at home and abroad, and that light may be shed upon what is to me obscure.

I have tried to translate literally yet satisfactorily, but I am painfully conscious of failure. Although in decay, these poems are in verse of a high order, with metre, rhythm, assonance, alliteration, and every quality to please the ear and to instruct the mind. The translation lacks these, and the simple dignity, the charming grace, and the passionate devotion of the original.

I see faults that I would willingly mend, but it is easier to point to blemishes than to avoid them—

| 'Is furasda dh'an fhear eisdeachd | It is easy for the listening man |
| Beum a thoir dh'an fhear labhairt.' | To give taunt to the speaking man |

Again and again I laid down my self-imposed task, feeling unable to render the intense power and supreme beauty of the original Gaelic into adequate English. But I resumed under the inspiring influence of my wife, to whose unfailing sympathy and cultured ear this work owes much.

My daughter has transcribed the manuscripts and corrected the proofs for press, and has acted as amanuensis throughout, while my three sons have helped in various ways. For deviations in spelling I alone am responsible.

The Celtic letters in the work have been copied by my wife from Celtic MSS., chiefly in the Advocates' Library. This has been a task of extreme

difficulty, needing great skill and patient care owing to the defaced condition
of the originals. The letters have been prepared for the engraver with
feeling and insight by Mr. John Athel Lovegrove, of H.M. Ordnance
Survey.

The Rev. Father Allan Macdonald, Erisgey, South Uist, generously
placed at my disposal a collection of religious folk-lore made by himself. For
this I am very grateful, though unable to use the manuscript, having so much
material of my own.

Mr John Henry Dixon, Inveran, Lochmaree, offered to publish the work
at his own expense That I have not availed myself of his generous appreciation
does not lessen my gratitude for Mr. Dixon's characteristic liberality.

The portrait is the friendly work and generous gift of Mr. W. Skeoch
Cumming, and is inserted at the request of friends outside my family.

Mr. Walter Blaikie's warm interest and extensive knowledge have been
unsparingly given in the printing and issuing of the work.

My dear friend Mr. George Henderson, M.A. Edin., Ph.D. Leipsic,
B Litt. Oxon , has helped and encouraged me throughout.

These, and the many others whose names I regret I am unable to mention
through want of space, I ask to accept my warm, abiding thanks.

Three sacrifices have been made—the sacrifice of time, the sacrifice
of toil, and the sacrifice of means. These I do not regret I have three
regrets—that I had not been earlier collecting, that I have not been more
diligent in collecting, and that I am not better qualified to treat what I
have collected.

These notes and poems have been an education to me. And so have been
the men and women reciters from whose dictation I wrote them down. They
are almost all dead now, leaving no successors. With reverent hand and
grateful heart I place this stone upon the cairn of those who composed and
of those who transmitted the work.

ALEXANDER CARMICHAEL.

EDINBURGH,
St Michael's Day, 1899

I

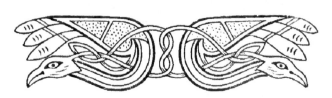

ACHAINE

INVOCATIONS

RANN ROMH URNUIGH [1]

Old people in the Isles sing this or some other short hymn before prayer. Sometimes the hymn and the prayer are intoned in low tremulous unmeasured cadences like the moving and moaning, the soughing and the sighing, of the ever-murmuring sea on their own wild shores.

They generally retire to a closet, to an out-

A mi lubadh mo ghlun
   An sul an Athar a chruthaich mi,
   An sul an Mhic a cheannaich mi,
   An sul an Spioraid a ghlanaich mi,
      Le caird agus caoimh.
  Tre t-Aon Unga fein a Dhe,
  Tabhair duinn tachar n'ar teinn,
      Gaol De,
      Gradh De,
      Gair De,
      Gais De,
      Gras De,
      Sgath De,
      Us toil De,
Dheanamh air talamh nan Tre,
Mar ta ainghlich us naoimhich
A toighe air neamh.
    Gach duar agus soillse,
    Gach la agus oidhche,
    Gach uair ann an caoimhe,
    Thoir duinn do ghne.

RUNE BEFORE PRAYER

house, to the lee of a knoll, or to the shelter of a dell, that they may not be
seen nor heard of men   I have known men and women of eighty, ninety, and
a hundred years of age continue the practice of their lives in going from one to
two miles to the seashore to join their voices with the voicing of the waves and
their praises with the praises of the ceaseless sea

I AM bending my knee
In the eye of the Father who created me,
In the eye of the Son who purchased me,
In the eye of the Spirit who cleansed me,
    In friendship and affection.
Through Thine own Anointed One, O God,
Bestow upon us fulness in our need,
      Love towards God,
      The affection of God,
      The smile of God,
      The wisdom of God,
      The grace of God,
      The fear of God,
      And the will of God
To do on the world of the Three,
As angels and saints
Do in heaven;
      Each shade and light,
      Each day and night,
      Each time in kindness,
      Give Thou us Thy Spirit.

DIA LIOM A LAIGHE [2]

This poem was taken down in 1866 from Mary Macrae, Harris. She came from Kintail when young, with Alexander Macrae, whose mother was one of the celebrated ten daughters of Macleod of Rararsay, mentioned by Johnson and Boswell. Mary Macrae was rather under than over middle height, but strongly and symmetrically formed. She often walked with companions, after the work of the day was done, distances of ten and fifteen miles to a dance, and after dancing all night walked back again to the work of the morning fresh and vigorous as if nothing unusual had occurred. She was a faithful servant and an admirable worker, and danced at her leisure and carolled at her work like 'Fosgag Mhoire,' Our Lady's lark, above her.

The people of Harris had been greatly given to

IA liom a laighe,
Dia liom ag eirigh,
Dia liom anns gach ra soluis.
Us gun mi ra son as aonais,
Gun aon ra as aonais.

Criosda liom a cadal,
Criosda liom a dusgadh,
Criosda liom a caithris,
Gach la agus oidhche,
Gach aon la us oidhche.

Dia liom a comhnadh
Domhnach liom a riaghladh,
Spiorad liom a treoradh,
Gu soir agus siorruidh,
Soir agus siorruidh, Amen.
Triath nan triath, Amen.

GOD WITH ME LYING DOWN

old lore and to the old ways of their fathers, reciting and singing, dancing and merry-making; but a reaction occurred, and Mary Macrae's old-world ways were abjured and condemned

> ' The bigots of an iron time
> Had called her simple art a crime.'

But Mary Macrae heeded not, and went on in her own way, singing her songs and ballads, intoning her hymns and incantations, and chanting her own ' port-a-bial,' mouth music, and dancing to her own shadow when nothing better was available

I love to think of this brave kindly woman, with her strong Highland characteristics and her proud Highland spirit She was a true type of a grand people gone never to return

GOD with me lying down,
God with me rising up,
God with me in each ray of light,
Nor I a ray of joy without Him,
Nor one ray without Him.

Christ with me sleeping,
Christ with me waking,
Christ with me watching,
Every day and night,
Each day and night.

God with me protecting,
The Lord with me directing,
The Spirit with me strengthening,
For ever and for evermore,
Ever and evermore, Amen
Chief of chiefs, Amen

ORA NAM BUADH   [3]

Duncan Maclellan, crofter, Carnan, South Uist, heard this poem from Catherine Macaulay in the early years of this century. When the crofters along the east side of South Uist were removed, many of the more frail and aged left behind became houseless and homeless, moving among and existing upon the crofters left remaining along the west side of the island.

Among these was Catherine Macaulay. Her people went to Cape Breton. She came from Mol-a-deas, adjoining Corradale, where Prince Charlie lived for several weeks when hiding in South Uist after Culloden. Catherine Macaulay had seen the Prince several times, and had many reminiscences of him and of his movements among the people of the district, who entertained him to their best when much in need, and who shielded him to their utmost when sorely harassed.

Catherine Macaulay was greatly gifted in speaking, and was marvellously endowed with a memory for old tales and hymns, runes and incantations, and for unwritten literature and traditions of many kinds.

She wandered about from house to house, and from townland to townland, warmly welcomed and cordially received wherever she went, and remained in each place longer or shorter according to the population and the season, and

ONNLAIME do bhasa

Ann am frasa fiona,

Ann an liu nan lasa,

Ann an seachda siona,

Ann an subh craobh,

Ann am bainne meala,

Us cuirime na naoi buaidhean glana caon,

Ann do ghruaidhean caomha geala,

    Buaidh cruth,

    Buaidh guth,

    Buaidh rath,

    Buaidh math,

    Buaidh chnoc,

    Buaidh bhochd,

THE INVOCATION OF THE GRACES

as the people could spare the time to hear her. The description which Duncan Maclellan gave of Catherine Macaulay, and of the people who crowded his father's house to hear her night after night, and week after week, and of the discussions that followed her recitations, were realistic and instructive. Being then but a child he could not follow the meaning of this lore, but he thought many times since that much of it must have been about the wild beliefs and practices of his people of the long long ago, and perhaps not so long ago either Many of the poems and stories were long and weird, and he could only remember fragments, which came up to him as he lay awake, thinking of the present and the past, and of the contrast between the two, even in his own time.

I heard versions of this poem in other islands and in districts of the mainland, and in November 1888 John Gregorson Campbell, minister of Tiree, sent me a fragment taken down from Margaret Macdonald, Tiree The poem must therefore have been widely known In Tiree the poem was addressed to boys and girls, in Uist to young men and maidens Probably it was composed to a maiden on her marriage The phrase 'eala dhonn,' brown swan, would indicate that the girl was young—not yet a white swan

I BATHE thy palms
In showers of wine,
In the lustral fire,
In the seven elements,
In the juice of the rasps,
In the milk of honey,
And I place the nine pure choice graces
In thy fair fond face,
> The grace of form,
> The grace of voice,
> The grace of fortune,
> The grace of goodness,
> The grace of wisdom,
> The grace of charity,

Buaidh na rogha finne,
Buaidh na fioir eireachdais,
Buaidh an deagh labhraidh.

Is dubh am bail ud thall,
Is dubh na daoine th'ann,
Is tu an eala dhonn,
Ta dol a steach n'an ceann
Ta an cridhe fo do chonn,
Ta an teanga fo do bhonn,
'S a chaoidh cha chan iad bonn,
     Facail is oil leat.

Is dubhar thu ri teas,
Is seasgar thu ri fuachd,
Is suilean thu dha'n dall,
Is crann dha'n deorai thruagh,
Is eilean thu air muir,
Is cuisil thu air tir,
Is fuaran thu am fasach,
     Is slaint dha'n ti tha tinn.

Is tu gleus na Mnatha Sithe,
Is tu beus na Bride bithe,
Is tu creud na Moire mine,
Is tu gniomh na mnatha Greuig,
Is tu sgeimh na h-Eimir aluinn,
Is tu mein na Dearshul agha,
Is tu meanm na Meabha laidir.
     Is tu taladh Binne-bheul.

Is tu sonas gach ni eibhinn.
Is tu solus gath na greine,

The grace of choice maidenliness,
The grace of whole-souled loveliness,
The grace of goodly speech.

Dark is yonder town,
Dark are those therein,
Thou art the brown swan,
Going in among them.
Their hearts are under thy control,
Their tongues are beneath thy sole,
Nor will they ever utter a word
  To give thee offence.

A shade art thou in the heat,
A shelter art thou in the cold,
Eyes art thou to the blind,
A staff art thou to the pilgrim,
An island art thou at sea,
A fortress art thou on land,
A well art thou in the desert,
  Health art thou to the ailing.

Thine is the skill of the Fairy Woman,
Thine is the virtue of Bride the calm,
Thine is the faith of Mary the mild,
Thine is the tact of the woman of Greece.
Thine is the beauty of Emir the lovely,
Thine is the tenderness of Darthula delightful,
Thine is the courage of Maebh the strong,
  Thine is the charm of Binne-bheul.

Thou art the joy of all joyous things,
Thou art the light of the beam of the sun,

B

Is tu dorus flath na feile,
Is tu corra reul an iuil,
Is tu ceum feidh nan ardu,
Is tu ceum steud nam blaru,
Is tu seimh eal an t-snamhu,
    Is tu ailleagan gach run

Cruth aluinn an Domhnuich
Ann do ghnuis ghlain,
An cruth is ailinde
Bha air talamh.

An trath is fearr 's an latha duit,
An la is fearr 's an t-seachdain duit,
An t-seachdain is fearr 's a bhliadhna duit,
A bhliadhn is fearr an domhan Mhic De duit.

Thainig Peadail 's thainig Pol,
Thainig Seumas 's thainig Eoin,
Thainig Muiril us Mun Oigh,
Thainig Uiril uile chorr,
Thainig Airil aill nan og,
Thainig Gabriel fadh na h-Oigh,
Thainig Raphail flath nan seod,
'S thainig Micheal mil air sloigh,
    Thainig 's Iosa Criosda ciuin,
    Thainig 's Spiorad fior an iuil,
    Thainig 's Righ nan righ air stiuir,
    A bhaireadh duit-se graidh us ruin,
        A bhaireadh duit-se graidh us ruin.

Thou art the door of the chief of hospitality,
Thou art the surpassing star of guidance,
Thou art the step of the deer of the hill,
Thou art the step of the steed of the plain,
Thou art the grace of the swan of swimming,
    Thou art the loveliness of all lovely desires.

The lovely likeness of the Lord
Is in thy pure face,
The loveliest likeness that
Was upon earth

The best hour of the day be thine,
The best day of the week be thine,
The best week of the year be thine,
The best year in the Son of God's domain be thine

Peter has come and Paul has come,
James has come and John has come,
Muriel and Mary Virgin have come,
Uiriel the all-beneficent has come,
Ariel the beauteousness of the young has come,
Gabriel the seer of the Virgin has come,
Raphael the prince of the valiant has come,
And Michael the chief of the hosts has come,
    And Jesus Christ the mild has come,
    And the Spirit of true guidance has come,
    And the King of kings has come on the helm,
    To bestow on thee their affection and their love,
        To bestow on thee their affection and their love.

ACHANAIDH CHOITCHEANN   [4]

HE, eisd ri m' urnuigh,
  Lub rium do chluas,
  Leig m' achan agus m' urnuigh
  T' ionnsuidh a suas.
  Thig, a Righ na glorach
  Da m' chomhnadh a nuas,
  A Righ na bith 's na trocair,
  Le comhnadh an Uain,
  A Mhic na Muire Oighe
  Da m' chomhnadh le buadh,
  A Mhic na Muire mine
  Is finne-ghile snuadh.

A GENERAL SUPPLICATION

God, listen to my prayer,
Bend to me Thine ear,
Let my supplications and my prayers
Ascend to Thee upwards,
Come, Thou King of Glory,
To protect me down,
Thou King of life and mercy
With the aid of the Lamb,
Thou Son of Mary Virgin
To protect me with power,
Thou Son of the lovely Mary
Of purest fairest beauty.

DHE BI MAILLE RUINN   [5]

The three poems which follow were obtained from Dr. Donald Munro Morrison in 1889, a few days before he died. Dr. Morrison heard them from an old man known as 'Coinneach Saor'—Kenneth the Carpenter—and his wife, at Obbe, Harris. These aged people were habitually practising quaint religious ceremonies and singing curious religious poems to peculiar music, evidently ancient. In childhood Dr. Morrison lived much with this couple, and in manhood recorded much of their old lore and music. These however he noted in characters and notations of his own invention which he did not live to render intelligible to others. This is extremely regrettable, as Dr. Morrison's wonderfully wide, accurate, and

HE bi maille ruinn
    Air an la an diugh,
            Amen.
[Dhe bi maille ruinn
Air an oidhche nochd,
            Amen.]
    Ruinn agus leinn
    Air an la an diugh,
            Amen.
[Ruinn agus leinn
Air an oidhche nochd,
            Amen.]
    Tha e soilleir duinn ri leirsinn.
    Bho thaine sinn chon an t-saoghail,
    Gu robh sinn toillteanach air t' fhearg,
            Amen.
        O t' fhearg fein
        A Dhe nan dul,
            Amen.
    Tabhair mathanas duinn,
            Amen.

GOD BE WITH US

scientific attainments, deep knowledge of Gaelic of music, and of acoustics, were only surpassed by his native modesty of mind and tender benevolence of heart. He was a distinguished medallist in several subjects at the University of Edinburgh.

A Gaelic proverb says. 'Theid dualchas an aghaidh nan creag'—Heredity will go against the rocks. Dr. Morrison was descended from the famous hereditary brehons of the Isles These Morrisons have been celebrated throughout the centuries for their wit, poetry, music, philosophy, medicine and science, for their independence of mind and sobriety of judgment, and for their benevolence of heart and unfailing hospitality

God be with us
On this Thy day,
        Amen.
[God be with us
On this Thy night,
        Amen.]
To us and with us,
On this Thy day,
        Amen
[To us and with us,
On this Thy night,
        Amen.]
It is clear to be seen of us,
Since we came into the world,
That we have deserved Thy wrath,
        Amen.
O Thine own wrath,
Thou God of all,
        Amen.
Grant us forgiveness,
        Amen

Tabhair mathanas duinn,
           Amen.
Tabhair duinn do mhathanas fein
A Dhe mheinich nan dul,
           Amen.
Ni sam bith is dona duinn,
No thogas fiannis n' ar n-aghaidh
Far am faide am bi sinn,
Suabharaich thus oirnn e,
Duabharaich thus oirnn e,
Fuadaich fein uainn e,
Agus ruaig as ar cridheachan,
Duthainn, suthainn, sior,
     Duthainn, suthainn, sior
           Amen

Grant us forgiveness,

Amen

Grant to us Thine own forgiveness,
Thou merciful God of all,

Amen

Anything that is evil to us,
Or that may witness against us
Where we shall longest be,
Illume it to us,
Obscure it to us,
Banish it from us,
Root it out of our hearts,
Ever, evermore, everlastingly,
Ever, evermore, everlastingly.

Amen

IOS, A MHIC MUIRE [6]

OS, a Mhic Muire
  Dean trocair oirnn,
        Amen.
Ios, a Mhic Muire
Dean siochain ruinne,
        Amen.
Ruinn agus leinn
Far am faide am bi sinn,
        Amen.
Bi ma thus ar slighe,
Bi ma chrich ar saoghail,
        Amen.
Bi aig mosgladh ar beatha,
'S aig dubhradh ar laithean,
        Amen.
Bi ruinn agus leinn
A Dhe mheinich nan dul,
        Amen.

Coisrig sinn
Cor agus crann,
A Re nan re,
A Dhe nan dul,
        Amen.
Coisrig sinn
Coir agus cuid,
A Re nan re,
A Dhe nan dul,
        Amen.

JESU THOU SON OF MARY

Jesu, Thou Son of Mary,
Have mercy upon us,
         Amen
Jesu, Thou Son of Mary,
Make peace with us,
         Amen.
Oh, with us and for us
Where we shall longest be,
         Amen
Be about the morning of our course,
Be about the closing of our life,   [world
         Amen
Be at the dawning of our life,
And oh! at the dark'ning of our day,
         Amen
Be for us and with us,
Merciful God of all,
         Amen.
Consecrate us
Condition and lot,
Thou King of kings,
Thou God of all,
         Amen
Consecrate us
Rights and means,
Thou King of kings,
Thou God of all,
         Amen.

ACHAINE

Coisrig sinn
Cri agus cre,
A Re nan re,
A Dhe nan dul,
Amen.
Gach cri agus cie.
Gach la dhuit fein,
Gach oidhche nan ieir,
A Re nan re,
A Dhe nan dul,
Amen.

Consecrate us
Heait and body,
Thou King of kings,
Thou God of all,
                    Amen
Each heart and body,
Each day to Thyself,
Each night accordingly,
Thou King of kings,
Thou God of all,
                    Amen

ATHAIR NAOMHA NA GLOIR　　[7]

UIDHEACHAS duit, Athair Naomha na Gloir,
　Athair chaomha bhith-bheo, bhith-threin,
　Thaobh gach foghair, gach fabhair, gach foir,
　Tha thu bairigeadh oirnne n' ar feum :
　Ge b'e freasdal thig oirnn mar do chlann,
　N' ar cuibhrionn, n' ar crann, n' ar ceum,
　Tabhair na chuideachd dhuinn soirbhis do laimh
　Agus suilbhireachd saibhir do bheuil.

Ta sinn ciontach us truaillidh a Dhe.
Ann an Spiorad, an cre, us an corp,
Ann an smuain, am focal, am beus.
Tha sinn cruaidh na do leirsinn 's an olc.
Cursa tabhachd do ghraidh dhuinn an ceil.
Bi leum thairis thar sleibhtean ar lochd,
Us nigh sinn am fior-fhuil na reit
Mar chanach an t-sleibh, mar leuig an loch.

An slighe chorraich choitchinn ar gairm,
Biodh i soirbh no doirbh do ar feoil.
Biodh i soilleir no doilleir ri seirm,
Do threorachadh foirfe biodh oirnn.
Bi na d' sgeith dhuinn bho chuilbh an fhir-cheilg,
Bho'n chreach-cheilgneach ta le dheilg air ar toir,
Us anns gach run gheobh ar cnram r'a dheilbh,
Bi-sa fein air ar failm us aig ar sgod.

HOLY FATHER OF GLORY

THANKS be to Thee, Holy Father of Glory,
Father kind, ever-loving, ever-powerful,
Because of all the abundance, favour, and deliverance
That Thou bestowest upon us in our need.
Whatever providence befalls us as thy children,
In our portion, in our lot, in our path,
Seal it to us with the rich gifts of Thine hand
And the joyous blessing of Thy mouth

We are guilty and polluted, O God,
In spirit, in heart, and in flesh,
In thought, in word, in act,
We are hard in Thy sight in sin
Put Thou forth to us the power of Thy love,
Be Thou leaping over the mountains of our transgressions,
And wash us in the true blood of conciliation,
Like the down of the mountain, like the lily of the lake.

In the steep path of our common calling,
Be it easy or uneasy to our flesh,
Be it bright or dark for us to follow,
Thine own perfect guidance be upon us,
Be Thou a shield to us from the wiles of the deceiver,
From the arch-destroyer with his arrows pursuing us,
And in each secret thought our minds get to weave,
Be Thou Thyself on our helm and at our sheet

Ge bhiodh madruich, us gadruich gar sgaradh bho'n chro,
Biodh Aoghar ciodha na gloir air ar sgath
Ge be cuis no cion-fath no cion-sgeoil
Bhios gu leireadh no leoin thoir n' ar dail,
No bheir fianuis n' ar n-aghaidh fa-dheoidh.
Taobh thall abhuinn mhor an dubh-sgail.
O duabharaich thusa sin oirnn.
Us as ar cridhe dean fhogradh gu brath.

Nis dh' an Athair a chruthaich gach creubh,
Nis dh' an Mhac a phaigh eirig a shloigh,
Nis dh' an Spiorad an Comh-fhurtair treun : ─
Bi d' ar dion us d' ar senn bho gach leon,
Bi mu thus us mu dheireadh ar reis,
Bi toir dhuinn a bhi seinn ann an gloir,
Ann an sith, ann am fois, ann an reit,
Far nach silear an deur, far nach eugar ni 's mo.
  Far nach silear an deur, far nach eugar ni 's mo.

Though dogs and thieves would reive us from the fold,
Be Thou the strong Shepherd of glory near us.
Whatever matter or cause or propensity,
That would bring to us grief, or pains, or wounds,
Or that would bear witness against us at the last,
On the other side of the great river of dark shadows,
Oh ! do Thou obscure it from our eyes,
And from our hearts drive it for ever.,

Now to the Father who created each creature.
Now to the Son who paid ransom for His people.
Now to the Holy Spirit, Comforter of might :—
Shield and sain us from every wound ;
Be about the beginning and end of our race,
Be giving us to sing in glory,
In peace, in rest, in reconciliation,
Where we shall shed no tear, where we shall die no more.
    Where we shall shed no tear, where we shall die no more.

UIRNIGH [8]

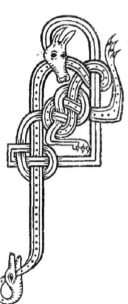

DHIA,

    Ann mo ghniamh,
    Ann mo bhriathar,
    An mo mhiann,
    Ann mo chiall,
    Ann an riarachd mo chail,
    Ann mo shuain,
    Ann mo bhruail,
    Ann mo chluain,
    Ann mo smuain,
    Ann mo chridh agus m'anam a ghnath.
    Biodh an Oigh bheannaichte, Moire,
    Agus Ogan geallaidh na glorach a tamh,
        O ann mo chridh agus m'anam a ghnath,
        Biodh an Oigh bheannaichte, Moire,
        Agus Ogan cubhraidh na glorach a tamh.

A PRAYER

O GOD,
In my deeds,
In my words,
In my wishes,
In my reason,
And in the fulfilling of my desires,
In my sleep,
In my dreams,
In my repose,
In my thoughts,
In my heart and soul always,
May the blessed Virgin Mary,
And the promised Branch of Glory dwell,
    Oh ! in my heart and soul always,
    May the blessed Virgin Mary,
    And the fragrant Branch of Glory dwell.

DUAN NA MUTHAIRN [9]

RIGH na gile,
   A Righ na greine,
   A Righ na rinne,
   A Righ na reula,
   A Righ na crinne,
   A Righ na speura,
   Is aluinn do ghnuis,
   A lub eibhinn.

Da lub shioda
Shios ri d' leasraich
Mhinich, chraicich :
Usgannan buidhe
Agus dolach
As gach sath dhiubh.

RUNE OF THE MUTHAIRN

Thou King of the moon,
Thou King of the sun,
Thou King of the planets,
Thou King of the stars,
Thou King of the globe,
Thou King of the sky.
Oh! lovely Thy countenance,
Thou beauteous Beam.

Two loops of silk
Down by thy limbs,
Smooth-skinned;
Yellow jewels
And a handful
Out of every stock of them.

BEANNAICH, A THRIATH NAM FLATH-FIAL   [10]

EANNAICH, a Thriath nam flath-fial,
   Mi fein 's gach sion a ta na m' choir,
   Beannaich mi na m'uile ghniamh,
   Dean mi tearuinte ri m'bheo,
      Dean mi tearuinte ri m'bheo.

   Bho gach gruagach us ban-sith,
   Bho gach mi-run agus bron,
   Bho gach glaistig us ban-nigh,
   Gach luch-sith agus luch-feoir,
      Gach luch-sith agus luch-feoir.

Bho gach fuath bhiodh feadh nam beann
Bho gach greann bhiodh teann da m'thoir,
Bho gach uruisg measg nan gleann,
Teasruig mi gu ceann mo lo,
   Teasruig mi gu ceann mo lo.

BLESS, O CHIEF OF GENEROUS CHIEFS

BLESS, O Chief of generous chiefs,
Myself and everything anear me,
Bless me in all my actions,
Make Thou me safe for ever,
    Make Thou me safe for ever.

From every brownie and ban-shee,
From every evil wish and sorrow,
From every nymph and water-wraith,
From every fairy-mouse and grass-mouse,
    From every fairy-mouse and grass-mouse.

From every troll among the hills,
From every siren hard pressing me,
From every ghoul within the glens,
Oh ! save me till the end of my day
    Oh ! save me till the end of my day.

SOLUS-IUIL NA SIORRUIDHEACHD　　　[11]

HE, thug mis a fois na h-oidhch an raoir
　　Chon solus aoibh an la an diugh,
　　Bith da mo thoir bho sholus ur an la an diugh,
　　Chon solus iul na siorruidheachd,
　　　　O ! bho sholus ur an la an diugh,
　　　　Gu solus iul na siorruidheachd.

THE GUIDING LIGHT OF ETERNITY

O God, who broughtst me from the rest of last night
Unto the joyous light of this Thy day,
Be Thou bringing me from the new light of this Thy day
Unto the guiding light of eternity.
    Oh! from the new light of this Thy day
    Unto the guiding light of eternity

ACHANAIDH GRAIS [12]

A mi lubadh mo ghlun
 An sul an Athar a chruthaich mi,
 An sul a Mhic a cheannaich mi,
 An sul a Spioraid a ghlanaich mi,
  Le gradh agus run.

Doirt a nuas oirnn a flathas
Trocair shuairce do mhathas ;
Fhir tha 'n uachdar na Cathair,
 Dean-sa fathamas ruinn.

Tabhair duinn, a Shlan'ear Aigh,
Eagal De, gaol De, agus gradh,
Us toil De dheanamh air talamh gach re.
Mar ni ainghlich us naoimhich air neamh,
Gach la agus oidhche thoir duinn do sheimh,
 Gach la agus oidhche thoir duinn do sheimh.

A PRAYER FOR GRACE

I AM bending my knee
In the eye of the Father who created me,
In the eye of the Son who died for me,
In the eye of the Spirit who cleansed me,
    In love and desire.

Pour down upon us from heaven
The rich blessing of Thy forgiveness ;
Thou who art uppermost in the City,
    Be Thou patient with us.

Grant to us, Thou Saviour of Glory,
The fear of God, the love of God, and His affection,
And the will of God to do on earth at all times
As angels and saints do in heaven.
Each day and night give us Thy peace.
    Each day and night give us Thy peace.

ACHANAIDH COMHNADH [13]

HO is tu is Buachaill thar an treuid
    Imain fein sinn do chleidh 's do chaimir,
    Seun sinn fo do bhrot riomhach reidh,
      A Sgeith dhidinn dion ri 'r mairionn.

    Bisa do chlaidh cruaidh, cosgarra,
    Chon sinne dhion a irinn arrais,
Bho fhigeirich us bho fheadaine frinne fuara,
    'S bho dheathach ruadh an aigeil.

    M' anam an urrachd an Ard Righ,
    Micheil murrach an comhdhail m'anama.

PRAYER FOR PROTECTION

As Thou art the Shepherd over the flock
Tend Thou us to the cot and the fold,
Sain us beneath Thine own glorious mantle,
    Thou Shield of protection, guard us for ever

Be Thou a hard triumphant glave
To shield us securely from wicked hell,
From the fiends and from the stieve snell gullies,
    And from the lurid smoke of the abyss

My soul is in the trustance of the High King,
Michael the powerful is in charge of my soul.

EOSAI BU CHOIR A MHOLADH   [14]

THE reciter said that this poem was composed by a woman in Harris. She was afflicted with leprosy, and was removed from the community on the upland to dwell alone on the sea-shore, where she lived on the plants of the plains and on the shell-fish of the strand. The woman bathed herself in the liquid in which she had boiled the plants and shell-fish. All her sores became healed and her flesh became new—probably as the result of the action of the plants and shell-fish.

Leprosy was common everywhere in mediæval times. In Shetland the disease continued till towards the end of last century. Communities erected lazar-houses to safeguard themselves from persons afflicted with leprosy. Liberton, now a suburb of Edinburgh, derives its name from a lazaretto having been established there.

The shrine of St. James of Compostello in Spain was

U cho fus a dh' Iosa
  An crann crion uradh
  'S an crann ur a chrionadh,
  Na'm b'e run a dheanadh.
    Eosai! Eosai! Eosai!
    Eosai 'bu choir a mholadh.

Ni bheil lus an lar
Nach bheil lan d'a thoradh,
Ni bheil cruth an traigh
Nach bheil lan d'a shonas.
    Eosai! Eosai! Eosai!
    Eosai 'bu choir a mholadh.

Ni bheil creubh am fairge,
Ni bheil dearg an abhuinn,

JESU WHO OUGHT TO BE PRAISED

famous for the cure of leprosy. Crowds of leper pilgrims from the whole of Christendom resorted to this shrine, and many of them were healed to the glory of the Saint and the enrichment of his shrine In their gratitude, pilgrims offered costly oblations of silks and satins, of raiments and vestments, of silver and gold, of pearls and precious stones, till the shrine of St. James of Compostello became famous throughout the world The bay of Compostello was famed for fish and shell-fish, and the leper pilgrims who came to pray at the altar of the Saint and to bestow gifts at his shrine were fed on those and were healed—according to the belief of the period, by the miraculous intervention of the Saint As the palm was the badge of the pilgrims to Jerusalem, the scallop-shell was the badge of the pilgrims to Compostello · —

My sandal shoon and scallop-shell '

It were as easy for Jesu
To renew the withered tree
As to wither the new
Were it His will so to do
    Jesu ! Jesu ! Jesu !
    Jesu who ought to be praised.

There is no plant in the ground
But is full of His virtue,
There is no form in the strand
But is full of His blessing.
    Jesu ! Jesu ! Jesu !
    Jesu who ought to be praised

There is no life in the sea,
There is no creature in the river,

Ni bheil cail an fhailbhe,   .
Nach bheil dearbh d'a mhaitheas
    Eosai ! Eosai ! Eosai !
    Eosai 'bu choir a mholadh.

Ni bheil ian air sgeith
Ni bheil reul an adhar,
Ni bheil sian fo'n ghrein
Nach tog sgeul d'a mhaitheas
    Eosai ! Eosai ! Eosai !
    Eosai 'bu choir a mholadh.

There is naught in the firmament,
But proclaims His goodness
    Jesu! Jesu! Jesu!
    Jesu who ought to be praised

There is no bird on the wing,
There is no star in the sky,
There is nothing beneath the sun,
But proclaims His goodness
    Jesu! Jesu! Jesu!
    Jesu who ought to be praised.

CARRAIG NAN AL [15]

THE old man from whom this piece was taken down said
that in his boyhood innumerable hymns and fragments of
hymns of this nature were common throughout the isles of

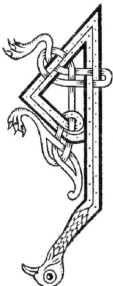

IR Carraig nan al,
　　Sith Pheadail us Phail,
　　Sheumais us Eoin na baigh,
　　Us na lan ionraic Oigh,
　　　　Na lan ionraic Oigh.

　　Sith Athar an aigh,
　　Sith Chriosda na pais,
　　Sith Spiorad nan gras,
　　Duinn fein us do 'n al ta og,
　　　　Duinn fein us do 'n al ta og.

THE ROCK OF ROCKS

Barra   When strangers began to come in they derided the old people and their old lore and their old ways, and the younger generations neglected the ways of their fathers, alike the questionably and the unquestionably good

On the Rock of rocks,
The peace of Peter and Paul,
Of James and John the beloved,
And of the pure, perfect Virgin,
    The pure perfect Virgin

The peace of the Father of peace,
The peace of the Christ of pasch,
The peace of the Spirit of grace,
To ourselves and to our children,
    Ourselves and our children.

SORCHAR NAN REUL   [16]

EUCH Sorchar nan reul,
　Air corbha nan neul,   [corra-bheinn
　Agus ceolra nan speur,
　　Ri luaidh dha.

Tighinn le caithrim a nuas,
Bho an Athair tha shuas,
Clar agus farcha nan duan,
　　Ri seirm dha.

Chriosd a chomaire mo ruin,
Com nach togainn do chliu !
Ainglich us naomhaich chiuil,
　　Ri luaidh dhut.

A Mhic Mhoire nam buadh,
Is fioire finne-ghile snuadh,
Liom bu shon a bhi an cluan,
　　Do shaoibhreis.

A Chriosda mo chaoimhe,
A Chriosda Chro-naoimhe,
Bithim gach la agus oidhche,
　　Ri luaidh ort.

THE LIGHT'NER OF THE STARS

BEHOLD the Light'ner of the stars,
On the crests of the clouds,   [crested mountain clouds
And the choralists of the sky,
        Lauding Him.

Coming down with acclaim,
From the Father above,
Harp and lyre of song,
        Sounding to Him

Christ, Thou refuge of my love,
Why should not I raise Thy fame !
Angels and saints melodious
        Singing to thee

Thou Son of the Mary of graces,
Of exceeding white purity of beauty,
Joy were it to me to be in the fields
        Of Thy riches.

O Christ, my beloved.
O Christ of the Holy Blood,
By day and by night
        I praise Thee.

CROIS NAN NAOMH AGUS NAN AINGEAL   [17]

ROIS nan naomh agus nan aingeal liom,
Bho fhrois m' aodain gu faobhar mo bhonn.

     ✢   ✢   ✢   ✢   ✢

A Mhicheil mhil, a Mhoire ghlorach,
A Bhride mhin nan dualan orach,
Dionaibh mi 's a cholunn bhronach,
Dionadh Tri mi air sligh na corach.
     O! Tri mi air sligh na corach.

Dionaibh mi 's a choich-anama bhochd,
Dionaibh mi 's mi cho diblidh nochd,
Dionaibh mi air sligh gun lochd,   [li
Dionadh Tri air mo thi a nochd.
     O! Tri air mo thi a nochd.

THE CROSS OF THE SAINTS AND THE ANGELS

THE cross of the saints and of the angels with me
From the top of my face to the edge of my soles

.·   .·   .·   .·   .·   .·

O Michael mild, O Mary of glory,
O gentle Bride of the locks of gold,
Preserve Ye me in the weakly body,
The Three preserve me on the just path.
    Oh! Three preserve me on the just path.

Preserve Ye me in the soul-shrine poor,
Preserve Ye me, and I so weak and naked,
Preserve Ye me without offence on the way,   [sea
The preservation of the Three upon me to-night.
    Oh! the Three to shield me to-night.

AN T-AINGHEAL DIONA [18]

INGHIL Dhe a fhuair mo churam
Bho Athair cumh na trocaireachd, [cur
Ciobaireachd caon cro nan naomh
Dheanamh dha mo thaobh a nochd,

Fuad nam gach buar us cunnart
Cuart mi air cuan na dobhachd,
Anns a chunglait, chaimleit, chumhan
Cum mo churach, fein an comhnuidh.

Bi na do lasair leith romham,
Bi na do reuil iuil tharam,
Bi na do ro reidh fotham,
Us na do chiobair caomh mo dheoghann,
An diugh, an nochd agus gu suthann.

Tha mi sgith us mi air m' aineol,
Treoraich mi do thir nan aingheal,
Liom is tim a bhi dol dachaidh
Do chuirt Chriosd, do shith nam flathas.

THE GUARDIAN ANGEL

Thou angel of God who hast charge of me
From the dear Father of mercifulness,   [mighty
The shepherding kind of the fold of the saints
To make round about me this night,

Drive from me every temptation and danger,
Surround me on the sea of unrighteousness,
And in the narrows, crooks, and straits
Keep thou my coracle, keep it always.

Be thou a bright flame before me,
Be thou a guiding star above me,
Be thou a smooth path below me,
And be a kindly shepherd behind me,
To-day, to-night, and for ever.

I am tired and I a stranger,
Lead thou me to the land of angels,
For me it is time to go home
To the court of Christ, to the peace of heaven.

RUIN [19]

ABHRAM gach la a reir do cheartais,
  Gach la taisbim do smachd, a Dhe,
  Labhram gach la a reir do reachd-sa,
  Gach la us oidhche bithim toigh riut fein.

  Gach la cunntam fath do throcair,
  Toirim gach la dha do nosda speis,
  Gach la tionnsgam fein dhut oran,
  Teillim gach la do ghloir, a Dhe.

  Beirim gach la gaol dhut, Iosa,
  Gach oidhche nithim da reir,
  Gach la 's oidhche, duar us soillse,
  Luaidhim do chaoimhneas dhomh, a Dhe.

DESIRES

MAY I speak each day according to Thy justice,
Each day may I show Thy chastening, O God,
May I speak each day according to Thy wisdom,
Each day and night may I be at peace with Thee.

Each day may I count the causes of Thy mercy,
May I each day give heed to Thy laws,
Each day may I compose to Thee a song,
May I harp each day Thy praise, O God.

May I each day give love to Thee, Jesu,
Each night may I do the same,
Each day and night, dark and light,
May I laud thy goodness to me, O God.

ORA CEARTAIS   [20]

PROVERBS anent law and justice abound in Gaelic, as :—'Is cam agus is direach an lagh ' :—Crooked and straight is the law. ' Bheir buidire breith ach co bheir ceartas ? ' —A witling may give judgment, but who will give justice? 'Colach ri ceart a mhadaidh-ruaidh, lugach, liugach, lamalach '—Like the justice of the fox, crooked, cunning, corrupt.

The administration of law and justice throughout the Highlands and Islands has been inadequate—men being too often appointed to administer justice not from their fitness but from their influence. Probably the feeling of distrust engendered by this absence of even-handed justice evoked these poems from the consciousness of the people and led them to appeal their cause to a Higher Court.

The litigant went at morning dawn to a place where three streams met. And as the rising sun gilded the mountain crests, the man placed his two palms edgeways together and filled them with water from the junction of the streams. Dipping his face into this improvised basin, he fervently repeated the prayer, after which he

ONNLAIDH mise m' aodann
   'S na naodh gatha greine,
   Mar a dh' ionnlaid Moire a Mac
     Am bainne brac na breine.

Gaol a bhi na m' aodann,
   Caomh a bhi na m' ghnuis,
   Caora meala na mo theanga,
     M' anail mar an tuis.

Is dubh am bail ud thall,
   Is dubh daoine th' ann,
   Is mis an eala bhan,
     Banruinn os an ceann.

Falbhaidh mi an ainme Dhe,
   An riochd feidh, an riochd each,
   An riochd nathrach, an riochd righ,
     Is treasa liom fin na le gach neach.

INVOCATION FOR JUSTICE

made his way to the court, feeling strong in the justice of his cause   On entering the court and on looking round the room, the applicant for justice mentally, some-times in an undertone, said—

'Dhe, seun an teach	God sain the house
Bho steigh gu fiardh ;	From site to summit ,
M' fheart os cinn gach neach,	My word above every person,
Feart gach neach fo m' thraigh.'	The word of every person below my foot

The ceremonies observed in saying these prayers for justice, like those observed on many similar occasions, are symbolic. The bathing represents purification , the junction of three streams, the union of the Three Persons of the Godhead ; and the spreading rays of the morning sun, divine grace   The deer is symbolic of wariness, the horse of strength, the serpent of wisdom, and the king of dignity

I WILL wash my face
In the nine rays of the sun,
As Mary washed her Son
    In the rich fermented milk.

Love be in my countenance,
Benevolence in my mind,
Dew of honey in my tongue,
    My breath as the incense.

Black is yonder town,
Black are those therein,
I am the white swan,
    Queen above them

I will travel in the name of God,
In likeness of deer, in likeness of horse,
In likeness of serpent, in likeness of king,
    Stronger will it be with me than with all persons

ORA CEARTAIS [21]

HE, tha mi liuthail m' aodainn,
   Anns na naodh gatha greine,
   Mar a liuthail Moire a Mac,
     Am bainne brac breine.

Meile a bhi na m' aodann,
Maon a bhi na m' ghnuis,
Mire meala na mo theanga,
   M' anail mar an tuis.

Is duibh an taigh ud thall,
Is duibhe daoine a th' ann,
Is mis an eala bhan,
   Banruinn os an ceann.

Falbhaidh mi an ainme Dhia,
An riochd fiadh, an riochd each,
An riochd nathar, an riochd righ,
   Is cathar mi na gach neach.

INVOCATION FOR JUSTICE

God, I am bathing my face
In the nine rays of the sun,
As Mary bathed her Son
    In generous milk fermented.

Sweetness be in my face,
Riches be in my countenance,
Comb-honey be in my tongue,
    My breath as the incense.

Black is yonder house,
Blacker men therein,
I am the white swan,
    Queen over them.

I will go in the name of God,
In likeness of deer, in likeness of horse,
In likeness of serpent, in likeness of king,
    More victorious am I than all persons

ORA BUAIDH

IONNLAIDH mi m' aodann
    'S na naoi gatha greine,
    Mar a dh' ionnlaid Moir a Mac,
        Am bainne bragh na breine.

Mil a bhi na m' bheul,
Seirc a bhi na m' aodann,
An gaol thug Moire dha Mac
        Bhi an cridhe gach cairc domhsa.

Gu 'm bu suileach, cluasach, briathrach Dia,
Da m' riarachadh, us da m' neartachadh,
Gu 'm bu dall, bodhar, balbh, sion sior,
        Mo luchd tair us mo luchd taimhlis.

Teanga Chalum-chille na mo cheann,
Agall Chalum-chille na mo chainn,
Foisneachd Mhic bhuadhaich nan gras
        Dhol thugam-sa an lathair sluaigh.

PRAYER FOR VICTORY

I BATHE my face
In the nine rays of the sun,
As Mary bathed her Son
    In the rich fermented milk.

Honey be in my mouth,
Affection be in my face,
The love that Mary gave her Son
    Be in the heart of all flesh for me.

All-seeing, all-hearing, all-inspiring may God be,
To satisfy and to strengthen me,
Blind, deaf, and dumb, ever, ever be
    My contemners and my mockers.

The tongue of Columba in my head,
The eloquence of Columba in my speech,
The composure of the Victorious Son of grace
    Go in me to the presence of the multitude.

H

AN LIUTHAIL   [23]

A mi liuthail m' aodainn
    An caora caon na greine,
    Mar a liuthail Moire Criosd
    Am bainne miamh na h-Eiphit.

    Meile bhi na mo bhial,
    Ciall bhi na mo chainn,
    An gaol thug Moire mhin dha Mac
    Bhi an cridhe gach cairc dhomhsa.

Gradh Chriosd am chom,
Cruth Chriosd am chomhnadh,
Cha 'n 'eil am muir no 'm fonn
Na bheir buaidh air Righ an Domhnuich.

Bas Bhride ma m' mhuineal,
Bas Mhuire ma m' bhraghad,
Bas Mhicheil dha m' liuthail,
Bas Chriosda dha m' thearnadh.

Doigh eile—

    Bith a bhith na m' bhenil,
    Ceil a bhith na m' chainn,
    Blas na sile na mo bhile
    Gon an till mi nall.

THE LUSTRATION

I AM bathing my face
In the mild rays of the sun,
As Mary bathed Christ
In the rich milk of Egypt.

Sweetness be in my mouth,
Wisdom be in my speech,
The love the fair Mary gave her Son
Be in the heart of all flesh for me

The love of Christ in my breast,
The form of Christ protecting me,
There is not in sea nor on land
That can overcome the King of the Lord's Day.

The hand of Bride about my neck,
The hand of Mary about my breast,
The hand of Michael laving me,
The hand of Christ saving me.

Variant—
  Force be in my mouth,
  Sense be in my speech,
  The taste of nectar on my lips,
  Till I return hither.

ORA BOISILIDH   [24]

This poem was taken down at Creagorry, Benbecula, on the 16th of December 1872, from Janet Campbell, nurse, Lochskiport, South Uist. The reciter had many beautiful songs and lullabies of the nursery, and many instructive sayings and fables of the animal world. These she sang and told in the most pleasing and natural manner, to the delight of her listeners. Birds and beasts, reptiles and insects, whales and fishes talked and acted through her in the most amusing

OISILEAG air h-aois,
     Boisileag air h-fhas,
Boisileag air h-ugan,
     Tuilim air a chail.

Air a chuid an chugan dhut,
     Gruidhim agus cal ;
Air a chuid an ghabhail dhut,
     Meal us bainne blath.

Air a chuid an chomaidh dhut,
     Omhan agus ais ;
Air a chuid an chobhartaich
     Le bogha agus gais.

Air a chuid an uidheam dhut,
     Uibhean buidhe Chasg ;
Air a chuid an chuileagan,
     M' ulaidh agus m' agh.

Air a chuid an chuilm dhut,
     Uilim agus can ;
Air a chuid an chuilidh dhut,
     Cuisilin mo ghraidh.

BATHING PRAYER

manner, and in the most idiomatic Gaelic. Her stories had a charm for children, and it was delightful to see a small cluster of little ones pressing round the narrator all eyes, all ears, all mouth, and all attention, listening to what the bear said to the bee, the fox to the lamb, the harrier to the hen, the serpent to the pipet, the whale to the herring, and the brown otter of the stream to the silvery grilse of the current Those fair young heads, now, alas! widely apart, probably remember some of the stories heard at Janet Campbell's knee better than those they afterwards heard in more formal schools

A PALMFUL for thine age,
 A palmful for thy growth,
A palmful for thy throat,
 A flood for thine appetite.

For thy share of the dainty,
 Crowdie and kail ;
For thy share of the taking,
 Honey and warm milk.

For thy share of the supping,
 Whisked whey and milk-product ;
For thy share of the spoil,
 With bow and with spear

For thy share of the preparation,
 The yellow eggs of Easter :
For thy share of the treat,
 My treasure and my joy,

For thy share of the feast
 With gifts and with tribute ;
For thy share of the treasure,
 Pulset of my love.

ACHAINE

Air a chuid an fhaoghaid dhut,
    Ri aghaidh Beinn-a-cheo ;   [Beinn-a-ghlo ?
Air a chuid an fhiadhach dhut,
    Us riaghladh air sloigh.

Air a chuid an luchairt,
    An curtaibh nan righ ;
Air a chuid a fhlathas dhut
    Le mhathas us le shith.

A chuid nach fas 's a chumhanaich,
    Gum fas 's an dubha-thrath ;
A chuid nach fas 's an oidhche dhiot,
    Air dhruim a mheadhon la.

      Tri baslach
      Nan Tri run,
      Dha do chumhn
      Bho gach tnu,
      Sul agus bas ;
      Baslach Ti nan dul
      Baslach Chriosda chumh,
      Baslach Spiorad numh,
        Tri-un
        Nan gras.

Foɪ thy share of the chase
    Up the face of the Beɪnn-a-cheo; [Beinn-a-ghlo ?
For thy share of the hunting
    And the mustering of hosts

For thy share of palaces,
    Iɪ the courts of kings;
For thy share of Paradise
    With its goodness and ɪts peace.

The part of thee that does not grow at dawn,
    May ɪt grow at eventide;
The part of thee that does not grow at night,
    May it grow at ridge of middle-day.

      The three palmfuls
      Of the Secret Three,
      To preserve thee
      From every envy,
      Evil eye and death;
      The palmful of the God of Life,
      The palmful of the Christ of Love,
      The palmful of the Spirit of Peace.
          Triune
          Of Grace.

DHE STIUIR MI   [25]

HE stiuir mi le d' ghliocas,
Dhe smachd mi le d' cheartas,
Dhe foir mi le d' throcair,
Dhe comh'n mi le d' chumhachd.

Dhe lion mi le d' lanachd,
Dhe dion mi le d' sgaileachd,
Dhe lion mi le d' ghrasachd,
Air sgath do Mhic Unga.

Iosa Criosda a shiol Dhaibhidh,
Fear-taghaich an teampuill,
Uan-iobairt a gharaidh,
A bhasaich air mo shon.

GOD GUIDE ME

God guide me with Thy wisdom,
God chastise me with Thy justice,
God help me with Thy mercy,
God protect me with Thy strength.

God fill me with Thy fulness,
God shield me with Thy shade,
God fill me with Thy grace,
For the sake of Thine Anointed Son.

Jesu Christ of the seed of David,
Visiting One of the Temple,
Sacrificial Lamb of the Garden,
Who died for me.

I

BEANNACHADH CADAIL [26]

Tʜᴇ night prayers of the people are numerous. They are called by various names, as: 'Beannachadh Beinge'—Bench-Blessing, 'Beannachadh Bobhstair'—Bolster Blessing, 'Beannachadh Cluasaig'—Pillow Blessing, 'Beannachadh Cuaiche'—Couch Blessing, 'Coich Chuaiche'—Couch Shrining, 'Altachadh Cadail'—Sleep Prayer; and other terms. Many of these prayers are become mere fragments and phrases, supplemented by the people according to their wants and wishes at the time.

IODH do lamh dheas, a Dhe, fo mo cheann,
    Biodh do shoills, a Spioraid, os mo chionn,
    Us biodh crois nan naodh aingeal tharam sios,
    Bho mhullach mo chinn gu iochdar mo bhonn,
        Bho mhullach mo chinn gu iochdar mo bhonn.

O Ios gun lochd, a cheusadh gort,
    Fo bhinn nan olc a sgiursadh Thu,
    A liuthad olc a rinn mo chorp!
    Nach urr' mi nochd a chunntachadh,
        Nach urr' mi nochd a chunntachadh.

A Righ na fola firinnich,
Na dibir mi a d' mhuinntireas,
Na tagair orm mo mhi-cheartan,
Us na di-chuimhnich a d' chunntadh mi,
    Na di-chuimhnich a d' chunntadh mi.

Crois Mhoir us Mhicheil, bhi tharam ann an sith,
M' anam a bhi am firinn, gun mhi-run am chom,
M' anam a bhi an sith aig Sorchair na frithe,
Micheal crodhal an codhail m' anama,
    Moch agus anmoch, la agus oidhche. Amen.

SLEEP BLESSING

It is touching and instructive to hear these simple old men and women in their lowly homes addressing, as they say themselves, 'Dia moi nan dul, Athan nan uile bheo,' the great God of life, the Father of all living. They press upon Him their needs and their desires fully and familiarly, but with all the awe and deference due to the Great Chief whom they wish to approach and to attract, and whose forgiveness and aid they would secure. And all this in language so homely yet so eloquent, so simple yet so dignified, that the impressiveness could not be greater in proudest fane.

Be Thy right hand, O God, under my head,
Be Thy light, O Spirit, over me shining
And be the cross of the nine angels over me down,
From the crown of my head to the soles of my feet,
 From the crown of my head to the soles of my feet.

O Jesu without offence, crucified cruelly,
Under ban of the wicked Thou wert scourged,
The many evils done of me in the body !
That I cannot this night enumerate,
 That I cannot this night enumerate.

O Thou King of the blood of truth,
Cast me not from Thy covenant,
Exact not from me for my transgressions,
Nor omit me in Thy numbering,
 Nor omit me in Thy numbering.

Be the cross of Mary and of Michael over me in peace,
Be my soul dwelling in truth, be my heart free of guile,
Be my soul in peace with thee, Brightness of the mountains,
Valiant Michael, accompany thou my soul,
 Morn and eve, day and night. May it be so.

THIGEAM AN DIUGH

HIGEAM an diugh 'an t-Athair,
Thigeam an diugh 'an Mhac,
Thigeam 'an Spiorad neartor naomh ;
Thigeam an diugh le Dia,
Thigeam an diugh le Criosd,
Thigeam le Spiorad iocshlaint chaomh.

Dia, agus Spiorad, agus Ios,
Bho mhullach mo chinn,
Gu iochdar mo bhonn ;
Thigeam le mo chliu,
Falbham le mo theasd,
Thigeam thugad, Iosa—
    Iosa, dean mo leasd.

COME I THIS DAY

Come I this day to the Father,
Come I this day to the Son,
Come I to the Holy Spirit powerful ;
Come I this day with God,
Come I this day with Christ,
Come I with the Spirit of kindly balm.

God, and Spirit, and Jesus,
From the crown of my head
To the soles of my feet ;
Come I with my reputation,
Come I with my testimony,
Come I to Thee, Jesu—
    Jesu, shelter me.

AN ACHANAIDH ANAMA   [28]

IOS, a nochd,
  Aghair nam bochd,
  Cholann gun lochd,
  Dh-fhuilinn gu gort,
  Fo bhinn nan olc,
  'S a cheusadh.

Saor mi bho olc,
Saor mi bho lochd,
Caomhain mo chorp,
Naomhaich mi nochd,
O Ios, a nochd,
'S na treig mi.

Bairig domh neart,
Aghair nam feart,
Stiuir mi na d' cheart,
Stiuir mi na d' neart,
O Ios, na d' neart
Gleidh mi.

THE SOUL PLAINT

O JESU ! to-night,
Thou Shepherd of the poor,
Thou sinless person
Who didst suffer full sore,
By ban of the wicked,
And wast crucified.

Save me from evil,
Save me from harm,
Save Thou my body,
Sanctify me to-night,
O Jesu ! to-night,
Nor leave me.

Endow me with strength,
Thou Herdsman of might,
Guide me aright,
Guide me in Thy strength,
O Jesu ! in Thy strength
Preserve me.

URNUIGH CHADAIL [29]

A mi cur m' anama 's mo chorp
Air a chomaraig a nochd, a Dhe,
Air a chomaraig, Iosa Criosda,
Air a chomaraig, a Spioraid na firinne reidh,
An Triuir a sheasadh mo chuis,
Us nach cuireadh an cul rium fein,

Thus, Athair, tha caomh agus ceart,
Thus, a Mhic, thug air peacadh buaidh,
Thus, a Spioraid Naoimhe nam feart,
Da mo ghleidheadh an nochd o thruaigh,
An Triuir a dheanadh mo cheart
Mo ghleidheadh an nochd 's gach uair.

SLEEPING PRAYER

I AM placing my soul and my body
On Thy sanctuary this night, O God,
On Thy sanctuary, O Jesus Christ,
On Thy sanctuary, O Spirit of perfect truth,
 The Three who would defend my cause,
 Nor turn Their backs upon me.

Thou, Father, who art kind and just,
Thou, Son, who didst overcome death,
Thou, Holy Spirit of power,
Be keeping me this night from harm,
 The Three who would justify me
 Keeping me this night and always.

K

TIUBHRADH NAN TRI   [30]

PIORAID tiubhir dhomh do phailteas,
   Athair tiubhir dhomh do ghliocas,
   Mhic tiubhir dhomh na m' airceas,
     Iosa fo fhasga do sgeith.

Laigheam sios a nochd,
Le Trithinn mo neart,
Le Athair, le Iosa,
    Le Spiorad nam feart.

THE GIFTS OF THE THREE

Spirit, give me of Thine abundance,
Father, give me of Thy wisdom,
Son, give me in my need,
 Jesus beneath the shelter of Thy shield.

I lie down to-night,
With the Triune of my strength,
With the Father, with Jesus,
 With the Spirit of might.

URNUIGH CHADAIL　　　　[31]

IOS gun lochd,
　A Righ nam bochd,
　A chiosadh gort
　Fo bhinn nan olc,
　Dion-s, an nochd,
　　Bho Iudas mi.

M' anam air do laimh, a Chriosda,
A Righ na Cathrach Neomh,
Is tu cheannaich m' anam, Iosa,
　　Is tu dh' iobair beatha dhomh.

Teasruig mi air sgath mo sprochd,
Air sgath do phais, do lot us d' fhala fein,
Us tabhair tearuint mi an nochd
　　Am fochar Cathair De.

SLEEP PRAYER

O Jesu without sin,
King of the poor,
Who wert sorely subdued
Under ban of the wicked,
Shield Thou me this night
    From Judas.

My soul on Thine own arm, O Christ,
Thou the King of the City of Heaven,
Thou it was who bought'st my soul, O Jesu,
    Thou it was who didst sacrifice Thy life for me.

Protect Thou me because of my sorrow,
For the sake of Thy passion, Thy wounds, and Thy blood,
And take me in safety to-night
    Near to the City of God.

BEANNACHD TAIMH [32]

N ainm an Tighearn Iosa,
 Agus Spiorad iocshlain aigh,
 An ainm Athar Israil,
  Sinim sios gu tamh.

Ma tha musal na dusal,
Na run air bith dhomh 'n dan,
Dhia fuasgail orm us cuartaich orm,
 Us fuadaich uam mo namh.

An ainm Athar priseil,
Us Spiorad iocshlain aigh,
An ainm Tighearn Iosa,
 Sinim sios gu tamh.

* * * * * *

Dhia, cobhair mi us cuartaich mi,
 O 'n uair 's gu uair mo bhais.

RESTING BLESSING

In name of the Lord Jesus,
And of the Spirit of healing balm,
In name of the Father of Israel,
    I lay me down to rest.

If theie be evil threat or quirk,
Or covert act intent on me,
God free me and encompass me,
    And drive from me mine enemy.

In name of the Father precious,
And of the Spirit of healing balm,
In name of the Lord Jesus,
    I lay me down to rest.

*　　*　　*　　*　　*　　*

God, help me and encompass me,
    From this hour till the hour of my death.

COISRIG CADAIL   [33]

UIGHIM sios an nochd
    Le Muire min 's le Mac,
    Le Micheal finn-gheal,
    'S le Bride fo brat.

Luighim sios le Dia,
Us luighidh Dia lium,
Cha luigh mi sios le Briain,
'S cha luigh Briain lium.

A Dhe nam bochd,
Feir orm an nochd,
Na treig mi tort,
A t-ionndastaigh.

Aig meuid nan lot
A reub mi ort,
Cha leir 'omh nochd
An cunntachadh.

A Righ na fola firinnich,
Na dichuimhn mi na d' thuinneachadh,
Na tagair mi 's na mi-cheartan,
Na dibir mi na d' chruinneachadh.
    O na d' chruinneachadh !

SLEEP CONSECRATION

I LIE down to-night
With fair Mary and with her Son,
With pure-white Michael,
And with Bride beneath her corslet.

I lie down with God,
And God will lie down with me,
I will not lie down with Satan,
Nor shall Satan lie down with me.

O God of the poor,
Help me this night,
Omit me not entirely
From Thy treasure-house.

For the many wounds
That I inflicted on Thee,
I cannot this night
Enumerate them.

Thou King of the blood of truth,
Do not forget me in Thy dwelling-place,
Do not exact from me for my transgressions,
Do not omit me in Thine ingathering.
    In Thine ingathering.

BEANNACHADH LEAPA   [34]

AIGHIM sios an nochd mar is coir
    An cluanas Chriosda Mac Oigh nan cleachd,
    An cluanas Athair aigh na gloir,
    An cluanas Spioraid foir nam feart.

    Laighim sios an nochd le Dia,
    Us laighidh Dia an nochd a sios liom,
    Cha laigh mi sios an nochd le olc, 's cha dean
    Olc no fhiamh laighe liom.

    Laighim sios an nochd le Spiorad Naomh,
    Us laighidh Spiorad Naomh an nochd a sios liom,
    Laighim sios le Teoiridh mo chaoimh,
    Us laighidh Teoiridh mo chaoimh a sios liom.

BED BLESSING

I AM lying down to-night as beseems
In the fellowship of Christ, Son of the Virgin golden,
In the fellowship of the gracious Father of glory,
In the fellowship of the Spirit of powerful aid

I am lying down to-night with God,
And God to-night will lie down with me,
I will not lie down to-night with sin, nor shall
Sin nor sin's shadow lie down with me.

I am lying down to-night with the Holy Spirit,
And the Holy Spirit this night will lie down with me,
I will lie down this night with the Three of my love,
And the Three of my love will lie down with me.

AN URNUIGH CHADAIL　　[35]

THA mis a nis a dol dha'n chadal,
Gu mu slan a dhuisgeas mi,
Ma 's a bas domh anns a bhas chadail,
Gu 'n ann air do ghairdean fein
A Dhe nan gras a dhuisgeas mi,
　　O air do ghairdean gradhach fein,
　　A Dhe nan gras a dhuisgeas mi !

M' anam air do laimh dheis, a Dhe,
A Re nan neamha neomh,
Is tu fein a cheannaich mi le t'fhuil.
Is tu thug do bheatha air mo shon,
　　Comraig mis an nochd, a Dhe,
　　Us na h-eireadh dhomh beud no cron.

Am feadh bhios a cholann a tamh 's a chadal,
Biodh an t-anam a snamh an sgath nam flathas,
Micheal cra-gheal an dail an anama,　　　　[crodhal
Moch agus anmoch, oidhche agus latha,
　　Moch agus anmoch, oidhche agus latha.
　　　　　　　　　　　　　　Amen.

THE SLEEP PRAYER

I AM now going into the sleep,
Be it that I in health shall waken,
If death be to me in the death-sleep,
Be it that on Thine own arm,
O God of Grace, I in peace shall waken,
    Be it on Thine own beloved arm,
      O God of Grace, that I in peace shall waken.

My soul is on Thy right hand, O God,
Thou King of the heaven of heavens,
Thou it was who bought'st me with Thy blood,
Thou it was who gavest Thy life for me,
    Encompass Thou me this night, O God,
    That no harm, no evil shall me befall.

Whilst the body is dwelling in the sleep,
The soul is soaring on the steeps of heaven,
Be the red-white Michael in charge of the soul,   [strong
Early and late, night and day,
    Early and late, night and day.
                      Amen.

COISRIG CADAIL [36]

A mise laighe nochd
   Le Athair, le Mac,
   Le Spiorad na firinn,
   Ta 'm dhion o gach lochd.

   Cha laigh mi le olc,
   Cha laigh olc liom,
   Ach laighidh mi le Dia,
   Us laighidh Dia liom.

Dia agus Criosd agus Spiorad naomh,
Us crois nan naodh aingeal fionn,
Da m' dhion mar 'Thri us mar Aon,
Bho chlar mhullach m'aodainn gu faobhar mo bhonn.

A Righ na greine agus na gloire,
Ios a Mhic na h-Oighe cubhra,
Gleidh-sa sinn a glinn nan diar,
Us a taigh nan diamha dubhra,
   Gleidh sinn a glinn nan diar,
   Us a taigh nan diamha dubhra.

SLEEP CONSECRATION

I AM lying down to-night,
With Father, with Son,
With the Spirit of Truth,
Who shield me from harm

I will not lie with evil,
Nor shall evil lie with me,
But I will lie down with God,
And God will lie down with me.

God and Christ and Spirit Holy,
And the cross of the nine white angels,
Be protecting me as Three and as One,
From the top tablet of my face to the soles of my feet.

Thou King of the sun and of glory,
Thou Jesu, Son of the Virgin fragrant,
Keep Thou us from the glen of tears,
And from the house of grief and gloom.
    Keep us from the glen of tears,
    From the house of grief and gloom.

BEANNACHADH LEAPA [37]

LAIGHIM sios an nochd,
Le Moire mhin us le Mac,
Le Mathair mo Righ,
Tha da m' dhion o gach lochd.

Cha laigh mi leis an olc,
Cha laigh an t' olc liom,
Ach laighidh mi le Dia,
Us laighidh Dia liom.

Dia agus Moire agus Micheal caon,
Agus crois nan naodh aingeal fionn
Da m' dhion mar Thri us mar Aon,
Bho chlar m' aodainn gu faobhar mo bhuinn.

Guidheam Peadail, guidheam Pol,
Guidheam Moir Oigh, guidheam am Mac,
Guidheam an da Ostal dochaidh deug
Mo ghleidheadh bho bheud 's bho lochd,
O gun mi a dhol eug a nochd,
Gun mi a dhol eug a nochd !

A Dhia, agus a Mhoire na glorach,
Ios, a Mhic na h-Oighe cubhraidh,
Siantaibh sinn bho phiantaibh siorruidh,
'S bho theine diantaidh dubhraidh,
Sinn bho phiantaidh siorruidh,
'S bho theine diantaidh dubhraidh.

BED BLESSING

I AM lying down to-night,
With Mary mild and with her Son,
With the Mother of my King,
Who is shielding me from harm.

I will not lie down with evil,
Nor shall evil lie down with me,
But I will lie down with God,
And God will lie down with me.

God and Mary and Michael,
And the cross of the nine angels fair
Be shielding me as Three and as One,
From the brow of my face to the edge of my soles.

I beseech Peter, I beseech Paul,
I beseech Mary, I beseech the Son,
I beseech the trustful Apostles twelve
To preserve me from hurt and harm,
    From dying to-night,
    From dying to-night!

O God! O Mary of Glory!
O Jesu! Son of the Virgin fragrant,
Sain Ye us from the pains everlasting,
And from the fire fierce and murky,
    From the pains everlasting,
    And from the fire fierce and murky!

M

A CHOICH ANAMA [38]

THE Soul Shrine is sung by the people as they retire to rest. They say that the angels of heaven guard them in sleep and shield them from harm. Should any untoward

HE tabhair aithne da t' ainghle beannaichte,
 Caim a chumail air an staing-sa nochd,
Comachadh crabhaidh, tabhaidh, teannachaidh,
 Chumas a choich anama-sa bho lochd.

Teasruig a Dhe an t-fhardrach seo a nochd,
 Iad fein 's an cuid 's an cliu,
Tar iad o eug, o ghabhadh, o lochd,
 'S o thoradh na farmaid 's na mi-ruin.

Tabhair duinn, a Dhe na fois,
 Taingealachd an cois ar call,
Bhi coimhlionadh do lagh a bhos,
 'S tu fein a mhealtuinn thall.

THE SOUL SHRINE

event occur to themselves or to their flocks, they avow that the cause was the deadness of their hearts, the coldness of their faith, and the fewness of their prayers

God, give charge to Thy blessed angels,
    To keep guard around this house to-night,
A band sacred, strong, and steadfast,
    That will shield this soul-shrine from harm.

Safeguard Thou, God, this household to-night,
    Themselves and their means and their fame,
Deliver them from death, from distress, from harm,
    From the fruits of envy and of enmity

Give Thou to us, O God of peace,
    Thankfulness despite our loss,
To obey Thy statutes here below,
    And to enjoy Thyself above

COICH-ANAMA [39]

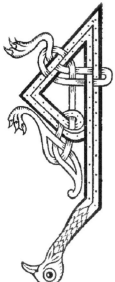

INGHIL Dhe, a fhuair mo churam,
Bho Athair cubhraidh na trocaireachd,
Cuartachadh caon na Cro-Naoimhe
A dheanamh air mo choich-anam a nochd,
O air mo choich-anam a nochd.

Fuadaich uam gach cuar us cunnart,
Cuartaich mi air cnau na corach,
Iarram thu dheanamh solus ur romham,
O ainghil aoibh-ghil, air an oidhche nochd,
O ainghil aoibh-ghil, air an oidhche nochd.

Bi fein a d' reuil-iuil os mo chionn,
Sorchair orm gach foirche us fonn,
Stiuir mo bharc air bharr an liuinn,
Chon cala tamh an samhchair thonn,
Chon cala tamh an samhchair thonn.

SOUL-SHRINE

THOU angel of God who hast charge of me
From the fragrant Father of mercifulness,
The gentle encompassing of the Sacred Heart
To make round my soul-shrine this night,
    Oh, round my soul-shrine this night.

Ward from me every distress and danger,
Encompass my course over the ocean of truth,
I pray thee, place thy pure light before me,
O bright beauteous angel on this very night,
    Bright beauteous angel on this very night.

Be Thyself the guiding star above me,
Illume Thou to me every reef and shoal,
Pilot my barque on the crest of the wave,
To the restful haven of the waveless sea,
    Oh, the restful haven of the waveless sea.

LAIGHIM AM LEABAIDH　　[40]

AIGHIM am leabaidh,
　　Mar a laighinn 's an uaigh,
　　Do ruighe ri m' mhuineal,
　　　　Mhic Mhuire nam buadh.

Bith ainghlean da m' fhaire
'S mi am laighe an suain,
'S bith ainghlean da m' chaithris
　　'S mi 'n cadal na h-uaigh.

Bith Uiril ri m' chasan,
Bith Airil ri m' chul,
Bith Gabrail ri m' bhathais,
　　'S bith Rafal ri m' thubh.

Bith Micheal le m' anam
Sgiath dhaingean mo ruin!
'S bith an Leighe Mac Moire,
Cur na seile ri m' shuil,
　　'S bith an Leighe Mac Moire,
　　Cur na seile ri m' shuil!

I LIE IN MY BED

I LIE in my bed
As I would lie in the grave,
Thine arm beneath my neck,
    Thou Son of Mary victorious.

Angels shall watch me
And I lying in slumber,
And angels shall guard me
    In the sleep of the grave.

Uriil shall be at my feet,
Ariel shall be at my back,
Gabriel shall be at my head,
    And Raphael shall be at my side.

Michael shall be with my soul,
The strong shield of my love!
And the Physician Son of Mary
Shall put the salve to mine eye,
    The Physician Son of Mary
    Shall put the salve to mine eye!

URNIUGH MADUINN

TAING dhut Iosda Criosda,
    Thug mis a nios o 'n oidhche 'n raoir
Chon solas soillse an la 'n diugh,
Chon sonas siorruidh a chosnadh dha m' anam,
An cion na fal a dhoirt thu dhomh.

Cliu dhut fein a Dhe gu brath,
An sgath gach agh a bhairig thu orm—
Mo bhiadh, mo bhriathar, mo ghniomh, mo chail,

    *   *   *   *   *

'S tha mi griosad ort
Mo dhion bho'n olc,
Mo dhion bho lochd,
Mo shian an nochd
'S mi iosal bochd,
O Dhia nam bochd!
O Chriosd nan lot!
Thoir ciall dhomh 'n cois do ghrais.

Gu'n coraich an Ti Naomha mi,
Gu'n comhnaich air muir 's air tir mi,
'S gu'n treoraich o ir gu ir mi
Cho'n sith na Cathair Shiorruiche,
    Sith na Cathair Shiorruiche.

MORNING PRAYER

THANKS be to Thee, Jesus Christ,
Who brought'st me up from last night,
To the gladsome light of this day,
To win everlasting life for my soul,
Through the atoning blood Thou didst shed for me

Praise be to Thee, O God, for ever,
For the blessings Thou didst bestow on me—
My food, my speech, my deeds, my health,
    *   *   *   *   *

And I beseech Thee
To shield me from sin,
To shield me from ill,
To sain me this night,
And I low and poor,
O God of the poor !
O Christ of the wounds !
Give me wisdom along with Thy grace.

May the Holy One claim me,
And protect me on sea and on land,
And lead me on from step to step,
To the peace of the Everlasting City,
    The peace of the Everlasting City !

N

AN TIONNSGANN [42]

AING dhuit, a Dhe
Thug mise bho 'n de
Gu tos an diugh,
Chum solas siorruidh
A chosnadh dha m' chre
Le feum maith.
'S air son gach tiodhlac sith
A dh'iobair thu dhomh,
Mo smuaine, mo bhriathra,
Mo ghniamha, mo thoil,
Tha mi tionnsgann duit.
Tha mi 'g urnuigh riut,
Tha mi griasad ort,
Mo chumail bho lochd,
Mo chomhnadh an nochd,
Air sgath do lot,
Le oifreil do ghrais.

THE DEDICATION

THANKS to Thee, God,
Who brought'st me from yesterday
To the beginning of to-day,
Everlasting joy
To earn for my soul
With good intent.
And for every gift of peace
Thou bestowest on me,
My thoughts, my words,
My deeds, my desires
I dedicate to Thee
I supplicate Thee,
I beseech Thee,
To keep me from offence,
And to shield me to-night,
For the sake of Thy wounds
With Thine offering of grace.

ACHANAIDH TAIMH   [43]

HE, teasruig an tigh, an teine, 's an tan,
    Gach aon ta gabhail tamh an seo an nochd.
    Teasruig mi fein 's mo chroilean graidh,
    Us gleidh sinn bho lamh 's bho lochd,
    Gleidh sinn bho namh an nochd,
    Air sgath Mhic Mhnire Mhathar
    'S an ait-s 's gach ait a bheil an tamh an nochd,
    Air an oidhche nochd 's gach aon oidhche,
        An oidhche nochd 's gach aon oidhche.

A RESTING PRAYER

God shield the house, the fire, the kine,
Every one who dwells herein to-night.
Shield myself and my beloved group,
Preserve us from handling and from harm,
Preserve us from foes this night,
For the sake of the Son of the Mary Mother,
In this place, and in every place wherein they dwell to-night,
On this night and on every night,
    This night and every night.

TEISREADH TAIGHE   [44]

HE, beannaich an ce 's na bheil ann,
  Dhe, beannaich mo cheile us mo chlann,
  Dhe, beannaich an re a ta na m' cheann,
  Us beannaich, a Dhe, laimhseachadh mo laimh,
  An am domh eirigh 's a mhaduinn mhoich,
  Us laighe air leabaidh anamoich,
      Beannaich m' eirigh 's a mhaduinn mhoich,
      Us mo laighe air leabaidh anamoich.

  Dhe, teasruig an teach 's an t-fhardrach,
  Dhe, coistrig a chlann mhathrach,
  Dhe, cuartaich an spreidh 's an t-alach,
  Bi-sa fein na'n deigh 's da'n taladh,
  Duair dhireas ni ri frith 's ri fruan,
  Duair shineas mi a sios an suan,
      Duair dhireas ni ri frith 's ri fruan,
      Duair shineas mi an sith gu suan.

HOUSE PROTECTING

God, bless the world and all that is therein.
God, bless my spouse and my children,
God, bless the eye that is in my head,
And bless, O God, the handling of my hand,
What time I rise in the morning early,
What time I lie down late in bed,

    Bless my rising in the morning early,
    And my lying down late in bed.

God, protect the house, and the household,
God, consecrate the children of the motherhood,
God, encompass the flocks and the young,
Be Thou after them and tending them,
What time the flocks ascend hill and wold,
What time I lie down to sleep,

    What time the flocks ascend hill and wold,
    What time I lie down in peace to sleep.

BEANNACHADH TAIGHE   [45]

HE, beannaich an taigh,
  Bho steidh gu staidh,
  Bho chrann gu fraigh,
  Bho cheann gu saidh,
  Bho dhronn gu traigh,
  Bho sgonn gu sgaith,
  Eadar bhonn agus bhraighe,
      Bhonn agus bhraighe.

BLESSING OF HOUSE

God bless the house,
From site to stay,
From beam to wall.
From end to end,
From ridge to basement.
From balk to roof-tree,
From found to summit,
    Found and summit.

CO DHA DHIOLAS MI CIS   [46]

O dha dhiolas mi cios
   An ainm Mhicheal o'n aird?
   Thugam deachamh dhe m' ni,
   Dha 'n Diobarach Aigh.

Air sgath na chunna mi,
Do shith us d'a bhaigh,
Tog m' anam riut, a Mhic De,
Na treig mi gu brath.

Cuimhnich orm anns an t-sliabh,
Fo do sgiath dean-sa mo sgail,
Charra na firinn na dibir mi'n cian
B'e mo mhiann bhi gu siorruidh na d' dhail.

Tabhair domh trusgan bainnse,
Biodh ainghlean a cainnt rium's gach cas,
Biodh ostail naomha da m' dhion,
Moire mhin us thus, Iosa nan gras,
   Moire mhin us thus, Iosa nan gras.

TO WHOM SHALL I OFFER OBLATION

To whom shall I offer oblation
In name of Michael on high?
I will give tithe of my means
To the Forsaken Illustrious One.

Because of all that I have seen,
Of His peace and of His mercy,
Lift Thou my soul to Thee, O Son of God,
Nor leave me ever.

Remember me in the mountain,
Under Thy wing shield Thou me,
Rock of truth, do not forsake me,
My wish it were ever to be near Thee.

Give to me the wedding garment,
Be angels conversing with me in every need,
Be the holy apostles protecting me,
The fair Mary and Thou Jesu of grace,
    The fair Mary and Thou Jesu of grace.

EARNA MHOIRE [47]

FAILT, a Mhoire! failt, a Mhoire!
  Righinn nan gras, Mathair na trocair;
Failt, a Mhoire, air mhodh gun choimeas,
  Geil ar slainte, fath ar solais.

Riut tha sinne, dh' oidhch 's a latha,
  Sliochd seachranach Adhamh us Eubha,
Togail ar guth 's ag achan,
  An gul 's an gal 's an deura.

Tabhair duinn, a Fhreimh an aigh,
  O 's tu copan nan grasa fial,   [gucag
Creid Eoin, us Pheaid, us Phail,
  Le sgeith Airil an aird nan nial.

Deoin dhuinn, a gheug dhonn,
  Aros ann am Fonn na sith
Tamh o ghabhadh 's o anradh thonn,
  Fo sgath toraidh do bhronn, Ios.

HAIL, MARY

HAIL, Mary! hail, Mary!
    Queen of grace, Mother of mercy;
Hail, Mary, in manner surpassing,
    Fount of our health, source of our joy.

To thee we, night and day,
    Erring children of Adam and Eve,
Lift our voice in supplication,
    In groans and grief and tears.

Bestow upon us, thou Root of gladness,
    Since thou art the cup of generous graces,   [spring
The faith of John, and Peter, and Paul,
    With the wings of Ariel on the heights of the heavens.

Vouchsafe to us, thou golden branch,
    A mansion in the Realm of peace,
Rest from the perils and stress of waves,
    Beneath the shade of the fruit of thy womb, Jesu.

FAILTE A MHOIRE   [48]

AILTE dhuit, a Mhoire Mhathair!
Tha thu lan dheth na grasan caomh,
Tha 'n Tighearna Dia maille riut a ghnath.
Beannaicht thu Mhairi am measg nam mnai,   [thar
Beannaicht toradh do bhronn, Iosa,
Beannaicht thu Righinn an ais;
A Naomh Mhoire, a Mhathair Iosa,
Gnidh air mo shonsa, peacach truagh,
Nis agus aig uair mo bhais,
     Nis agus aig uair mo bhais!

HAIL TO THEE, MARY

HAIL to thee, Mary, Mother !
Thou art full of loving grace,
The Lord God is always with thee,
Blessed art thou Mary among women,   [above
Blessed is the fruit of thy womb, Jesus,
Blessed art thou, Queen of grace ;
Thou holy Mary, thou Mother of Jesus,
Plead for me a miserable sinner,
Now and at the hour of death,
    Now and at the hour of death !

AN CATH NACH TAINIG [49]

OSA Mhic Mhoire eighim air h-ainm,
  Us air ainm Eoin ostail ghradhaich,
  Us air ainm gach naoimh 's an domhan dearg,
  Mo thearmad 's a chath nach tainig,
    Mo thearmad 's a chath nach tainig.

Duair theid am beul a dhunadh,
  Duair theid an t-suil a dhruideadh,
  Duair sguireas an anail da struladh,
  Duair sguireas an cridhe da bhuille,
    Sguireas an cridhe de bhuille.

Duair theid am Breitheamh dha'n chathair,
  Us a theid an tagradh a shuidheach, [tagar
  Iosa Mhic Mhoire cobhair air m' anam,
  A Mhicheil mhin gobh ri mo shiubhal.
    Iosa Mhic Mhoire cobhair air m' anam !
    A Mhicheil mhin gobh ri mo shiubhal !

THE BATTLE TO COME

JESUS, Thou Son of Mary, I call on Thy name,
And on the name of John the apostle beloved,
And on the names of all the saints in the red domain,
To shield me in the battle to come,
    To shield me in the battle to come.

When the mouth shall be closed,
When the eye shall be shut,
When the breath shall cease to rattle,
When the heart shall cease to throb,
    When the heart shall cease to throb.

When the Judge shall take the throne,
And when the cause is fully pleaded,
O Jesu, Son of Mary, shield Thou my soul,
O Michael fair, acknowledge my departure
    O Jesu, Son of Mary, shield Thou my soul!
    O Michael fair, receive my departure!

AM BEANNACHADH BAISTIDH [50]

IT is known that a form of baptism prevailed among the Celts previous to the introduction of Christianity, as forms of baptism prevail among pagan people now. The Gaelic 'baist' may be a metathesis of the Gaelic 'baidse,' rather than from the Latin. 'Baidse' means a gift, a bestowal, a pledge, a musical tribute, largess to a musician. Immediately after its birth the nurse or other person present drops three drops of water on the forehead of the child. The first drop is in the name of the Father, representing wisdom; the second drop is in the name of the Son, representing peace; the third drop is in the name of the Spirit, representing purity. If the child be a male

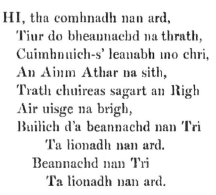

HI, tha comhnadh nan ard,
　Tiur do bheannachd na thrath,
　Cuimhnuich-s' leanabh mo chri,
　An Ainm Athar na sith,
　Trath chuireas sagart an Righ
　Air uisge na brigh,
　Builich d'a beannachd nan Tri
　　Ta lionadh nan ard.
　　Beannachd nan Tri
　　Ta lionadh nan ard.

　　Crath nuas air do ghras,
　　Tabh dha feart agus fas,
　　Tabh dha trein agus treoir,
　　Tabh dha seilbh agus coir,
　　Rian agus ciall gun gho,
　　Gliocas aingeal r'a lo,
　　Chum's gu'n seas e gun sgeo
　　　Na d' lathair.
　　　Gu'n seas e gun sgeo
　　　Na d' lathair.

THE BAPTISM BLESSING

the name 'Maol-domhnuich,' if a female the name 'Griadach,' is applied to it temporarily 'Maol-domhnuich' means tonsured of the Lord, and 'Griadach' is rendered Gertrude When the child is ecclesiastically baptized—generally at the end of eight days—the temporary is superseded by the permanent name. This lay baptism is recognised by the Presbyterian, the Anglican, the Latin, and the Greek Churches If the child were not thus baptized it would need to be carefully guarded lest the fairies should spirit it away before the ecclesiastical baptism took place, when their power over it ceased. The lay baptism also ensured that in the event of death the child should be buried in consecrated ground

THOU Being who inhabitest the heights
Imprint Thy blessing betimes,
Remember Thou the child of my heart,
In Name of the Father of peace,
When the priest of the King
On him puts the water of meaning,
Grant him the blessing of the Three
    Who fill the heights.
  The blessing of the Three
    Who fill the heights.

Sprinkle down upon him Thy grace,
Give Thou to him virtue and growth,
Give Thou to him strength and guidance,
Give Thou to him flocks and possessions,
Sense and reason void of guile,
Angel wisdom in his day,
That he may stand without reproach
    In Thy presence.
  He may stand without reproach
    In Thy presence.

AN TREORAICH ANAMA   [51]

DEATH blessings vary in words but not in spirit. These death blessings are known by various names, as: 'Beannachadh Bais,' Death Blessing, 'Treoraich Anama,' Soul Leading, 'Fois Anama,' Soul Peace, and other names familiar to the people.

The soul peace is intoned, not necessarily by a cleric, over the dying, and the man or the woman who says it is called 'anama-chara,' soul-friend. He or she is held in special affection by the friends of the dying person ever after. The soul peace is slowly sung—all present earnestly joining the soul-friend in beseeching the Three Persons of the Godhead and all the saints of heaven to receive the departing soul of earth. During the prayer the soul-friend makes the sign of the cross with the right thumb over the lips of the dying.

The scene is touching and striking in the extreme, and the man or woman is not to be envied who could witness unmoved the distress of these lovable people of the West taking leave of those who are near and dear to them in their pilgrimage, as they say, of crossing 'abhuinn dubh a bhais'—the black river of death; 'cuan mor na dnibhre'—the great ocean of darkness; and 'beanntaibh na bith-bhuantachd'—the mountains of eternity. The scene may be in a lowly cot begrimed with smoke and

N t-anam-s' air do laimh, a Chriosda,
     A Righ na Cathrach Neomh.
              Amen.

Bho is tus, a Chriosd, a cheannaich an t-anam-s',
Biodh a shith air do theannal fein.
              Amen.

Us biodh Micheal mil, ard righ nan aingeal,
A reiteach an rathaid romh 'n anam-s', a Dhe.
              Amen.

O Micheal mil an sith riut, anaim,
Us a reiteach dhuit rathaid gu flathas Mhic De.
              Amen.

THE SOUL LEADING

black with age, but the heart is not less warm, the tear is not less bitter, and the parting is not less distressful, than in the court of the noble or in the palace of royalty

'Nowhere beats the heart so kindly
As beneath the tartan plaid.'—AYTON

According to the old people.- -

'Duair a bheir an duine suas an ospag chithear an t-anam an cleas meall soluis
ag eiridh a suas anns na neoil Theirear an uair sin ,—

Tha 'n t-anam truagh a nis fo sgaoil
An taobh a muigh dha 'n chaim,
A Chriosd chaoimh nam beannachd saoi
Cuartaich mo ghaol na aim.'

When a person gives up the ghost the soul is seen ascending like a bright ball
of light into the clouds Then it is said —

The poor soul is now set free
Outside the soul-shrine,
O kindly Christ of the free blessings,
Encompass Thou my love in time.

Be this soul on Thine arm, O Christ,
Thou, the King of the City of Heaven

Amen

Since Thou, O Christ, it was who bought'st this soul,
Be its peace on Thine own keeping.

Amen.

And may the strong Michael, high king of the angels,
Be preparing the path before this soul, O God.

Amen.

Oh ! the strong Michael in peace with thee, soul,
And preparing for thee the way to the kingdom of the Son of God.

Amen.

AM BEANNACHADH BAIS   [52]

HIA, na diobair a bhean a d'mhuinntireas, [fear
      Agus a liuth olc a rinn a corp,
    Nach urr i nochd a chunntachas,
        A liuth olc a rinn a corp,
        Nach urr i nochd a chunntachas.

    An t-anam-s' air do laimh, a Chriosda,
    A Righ na Cathrach Neomh.
    Bho's tu a Chriosda cheannaich an t-anam,
    An am tomhas na meidhe,
An am tobhar na breithe,
Biodh e nis air do dheas laimh fein,
    O air do dheas laimh fein.

    Us biodh Naomh Micheal, righ nan aingeal,
    Tighinn an codhail an anama,
    Us ga threorachadh dachaidh
    Gu flathas Mhic De.
        Naomh Micheal, ard righ nan aingeal,
        Tighinn an codhail an anama,
        Us ga threorachadh dachaidh
        Gu flathas Mhic De.

THE DEATH BLESSING

God, omit not this woman from Thy covenant,   [man
And the many evils which she in the body committed,
That she cannot this night enumerate.
        The many evils that she in the body committed,
        That she cannot this night enumerate.

Be this soul on Thine own arm, O Christ,
Thou King of the City of Heaven,
And since Thine it was, O Christ, to buy the soul,
At the time of the balancing of the beam,
At the time of the bringing in the judgment,
Be it now on Thine own right hand,
        Oh ' on Thine own right hand.

And be the holy Michael, king of angels,
Coming to meet the soul,
And leading it home
To the heaven of the Son of God
        The holy Michael, high king of angels,
        Coming to meet the soul,
        And leading it home
        To the heaven of the Son of God.

FOIS ANAMA   [53]

'S tus a Chriosd a cheannaich an t-anam—
Ri linn dioladh na beatha,
Ri linn bruchdadh na falluis,
Ri linn iobar na creadha,
Ri linn dortadh na fala,
Ri linn cothrom na meidhe,
Ri linn sgathadh na h-anal,
Ri linn tabhar na breithe,
Biodh a shith air do theannal fein
Iosa Criosda Mhic Moire mine,
Biodh a shith air do theannal fein,
  O Ios! air do theannal fein.

Us bitheadh Micheal geal caomh,
Ard righ nan aingeal naomh,
An cinnseal an anama ghaoil,
Ga dhion dh'an Triu barra-chaon,
  O! dh'an Triu barra-chaon.

SOUL PEACE

Since Thou Christ it was who didst buy the soul—
At the time of yielding the life,
At the time of pouring the sweat,
At the time of offering the clay,
At the time of shedding the blood,
At the time of balancing the beam,
At the time of severing the breath,
At the time of delivering the judgment,
Be its peace upon Thine own ingathering
Jesus Christ Son of gentle Mary,
Be its peace upon Thine own ingathering,
    O Jesus! upon Thine own ingathering

And may Michael white kindly,
High king of the holy angels,
Take possession of the beloved soul,
And shield it home to the Three of surpassing love,
    Oh! to the Three of surpassing love

A GHEALACH UR   [54]

This little prayer is said by old men and women in the islands of Barra. When they first see the new moon they make their obeisance to it as to a great chief. The women curtsy gracefully and the men bow low, raising their bonnets reverently. The bow of the men is peculiar, partaking somewhat of the curtsey of the women, the left knee being bent and the right drawn forward towards the middle of the left leg in a curious but not inelegant manner.

This fragment of moon-worship is now a matter of custom rather than of belief, although it exists over the whole British Isles.

N ainm Spiorad Naomh nan gras,
   An ainm Athar na Cathrach aigh,
   An ainm Iosa thug dhinn am bas,
   O! an ainm na Tri tha da'r dion's gach cas,
   Ma's math a fhuair thu sinn an nochd,
   Seachd fearr gum fag thu sinn gun lochd,
      A Ghealach gheal nan trath,
      A Ghealach gheal nan trath.

The following versification is by Mr. John Henry Dixon of Inveran :—

In name of the Father Almighty,
In name of the Glorious Son,
In name of the Holy Spirit,
By grace of the Three-in-One.

If to-night, O moon, thou hast found us
   In peaceful, happy rest,

THE NEW MOON

In Cornwall the people nod to the new moon and turn silver in their pockets   In Edinburgh cultured men and women turn the rings on their fingers and make their wishes.   A young English lady told the writer that she had always been in the habit of bowing to the new moon, till she had been bribed out of it by her father, a clergyman, putting money in her pocket lest her lunar worship should compromise him with his bishop   She naively confessed, however, that among the free mountains of Loch Etive she reverted to the good customs of her fathers, from which she derived great satisfaction !

In name of the Holy Spirit of grace,
In name of the Father of the City of peace,
In name of Jesus who took death off us,
Oh ! in name of the Three who shield us in every need,
If well thou hast found us to-night,
Seven times better mayest thou leave us without harm,
Thou bright white Moon of the seasons,
Bright white Moon of the seasons.

May thy laving lustre leave us
Seven times still more blest

O moon so fair,
May it be so,
As seasons come,
And seasons go

II

AIMSIRE

SEASONS

NUALL NOLLAIG   [55]

CHRISTMAS chants were numerous and their recital common throughout Scotland. They are now disappearing with the customs they accompanied. Where they still linger their recital is relegated to boys. Formerly on Christmas Eve bands of young men went about from house to house and from townland to townland chanting Christmas songs. The band was called 'goisearan,' guisers, 'fir-duan,' song men; 'gillean Nollaig,' Christmas lads, 'nuallairean,' rejoicers, and other names. The 'rejoicers' wore long white shirts for surplices, and very tall white hats for mitres, in which they made a picturesque appearance as they moved along singing their loudest. Sometimes they went about as one band, sometimes in sections of twos and threes. When they entered a dwelling they took possession of a child, if there was one in the house. In the absence of a child, a lay figure was improvised. The child was called 'Crist, Cristean'—Christ, Little Christ. The assumed Christ was placed on a skin, and carried three times round the fire, sunwise, by the 'ceann-snaodh'—head of the band, the song men singing the Christmas Hail. The skin on which the symbolic Christ was carried was that of a white male lamb without spot or blemish and consecrated to this service. The skin was called 'uilim.' Homage and offerings and much rejoicing were made to the symbolic Christ. The people of the house gave the guisers bread, butter, crowdie, and other eatables, on which they afterwards feasted.

The three poems which follow were taken down from Angus Gunn, Ness, Lews, then over eighty-four years of age. Angus Gunn had been a strong man physically and was still a strong man mentally. He had lived for many years in the island of North Roney, and gave a graphic description of it, and of his life there. He had much oral lore which he told with great

O Ri, ho Ri,
   Beannaicht e, beannaicht e,
        Ho Ri, ho Ri,
   Beannaicht e, thainig 's an am,
        Ho Ri, ho Ri,
   Beannaicht an tigh 's na bheil ann,
        Ho Ri, ho Ri,
   Eadar chuall, us chlach, us chrann,
        Ho Ri, ho Ri,
   Iomair do Dhia, eadar bhrat us aodach,

CHRISTMAS HAIL

dramatic power. The following tale is one of those related by him.—'Ronan came to Lews to convert the people to the Christian faith. He built himself a prayer-house at Eorabay. But the people were bad and they would not give him peace. The men quarrelled about everything, and the women quarrelled about nothing, and Ronan was distressed and could not say his prayers for their clamour. He prayed to be removed from the people of Eorabay, and immediately an angel came and told him to go down to the "laimrig," natural landing-rock, where the "cionaran-cro," cragen, was waiting him. Ronan arose and hurried down to the sea-shore shaking the dust of Eorabay off his feet, and taking nothing but his "pollaire," satchel, containing the Book, on his breast. And there, stretched along the rock, was the great "cionaran-cro," his great eyes shining like two stars of night. Ronan sat on the back of the "cionaran-cro," and it flew with him over the sea, usually wild as the mountains, now smooth as the plains, and in the twinkling of two eyes reached the remote isle of the ocean. Ronan landed on the island, and that was the land full of "nathair bheumnaich, gribh mich, nathair nimhe, agus leomhain bheucaich"—biting adders, taloned griffins, poisonous snakes, and roaring lions. All the beasts of the island fled before the holy Ronan and rushed backwards over the rocks into the sea. And that is how the rocks of the island of Roney are grooved and scratched and lined with the claws and the nails of the unholy creatures. The good Ronan built himself a prayer-house in the island where he could say his prayers in peace'

Roney is a small, precipitous island in the North Atlantic, sixty miles from the Butt of Lews and sixty miles from Cape Wrath, forming the apex of a triangle between the two promontories. It is inaccessible except in a smooth sea, which is rare there. The rocks of Roney are much striated. The island is now uninhabited. St. Ronan lived in the end of the seventh century

HAIL to the King, hail to the King,
Blessed is He, blessed is He,
    Hail to the King, hail to the King,
Blessed is He who has come betimes,
    . Hail to the King, hail to the King,
Blessed be the house and all therein,
    Hail to the King, hail to the King,
'Twixt stock and stone and stave,
    Hail to the King, hail to the King,
Consign it to God from corslet to cover,

Slainte dhaoine gu 'n robh ann,
  Ho Ri, ho Ri,
Beannaicht e, beannaicht e,
  Ho Ri, ho Ri,
Beannaicht e, beannaicht e,
  Ho Ri, ho Ri,
Gu'm bu buan mu'n tulach sibh,
  Ho Ri, ho Ri,
Gu'm bu slan mu'n teallach sibh
  Ho Ri, ho Ri,
Gu'm bu liuth crann 's an tigh,
Daoine tamh 's a' bhunntair,
  Ho Ri, ho Ri,
Beannaicht e, beannaicht e,
  Ho Ri, ho Ri,
Beannaicht e, beannaicht e.

  Ho Ri, ho Ri,
Nochd oichdhe Nollaige moire,
  Ho Ri, ho Ri,
Beannaicht e, beannaicht e,
  Ho Ri, ho Ri,
Rugadh Mac na Moir Oighe,
  Ho Ri, ho Ri,
Beannaicht e, beannaicht e,
  Ho Ri, ho Ri,
Rainig a bhonnaibh an lar,
  Ho Ri, ho Ri,
Beannaicht e, beannaicht e,
  Ho Ri, ho Ri,
Shoillsich grian nam beann ard,
  Ho Ri, ho Ri,
Beannaicht e, beannaicht e.

Be the health of men therein,
> Hail to the King, hail to the King,

Blessed is He, blessed is He,
> Hail to the King, hail to the King,

Blessed is He, blessed is He,
> Hail to the King, hail to the King,

Lasting round the house be ye,
> Hail to the King, hail to the King,

Healthy round the hearth be ye,
> Hail to the King, hail to the King,

Many be the stakes in the house,
And men dwelling on the foundation,
> Hail to the King, hail to the King,

Blessed is He, blessed is He,
> Hail to the King, hail to the King,

Blessed is He, blessed is He.

> Hail to the King, hail to the King,

This night is the eve of the great Nativity,
> Hail to the King, hail to the King,

Blessed is He, blessed is He,
> Hail to the King, hail to the King,

Born is the Son of Mary the Virgin,
> Hail to the King, hail to the King,

Blessed is He, blessed is He,
> Hail to the King, hail to the King,

The soles of His feet have reached the earth,
> Hail to the King, hail to the King,

Blessed is He, blessed is He,
> Hail to the King, hail to the King,

Shone the sun of the mountains high,
> Hail to the King, hail to the King,

Blessed is He, blessed is He.

R

Shoillsich fearann, shoillsich fonn,
  Ho Ri, ho Ri,
Beannaicht e, beannaicht e,
  Ho Ri, ho Ri,
Chualas an tonn air an traigh,
  Ho Ri, ho Ri.
Beannaicht e, beannaicht e,
Beannaicht e, beannaicht e,
  Ho Ri, ho Ri.
Beannaicht an Righ,
Gun tus, gun chrich,
Gu suthainn, gu sior,
Gach linn gu brath.

Shone the earth, shone the land,
    Hail to the King, hail to the King,
Blessed is He, blessed is He,
    Hail to the King, hail to the King,
Heard was the wave upon the strand,
    Hail to the King, hail to the King,
Blessed is He, blessed is He,
Blessed is He, blessed is He,
    Hail to the King, hail to the King,
Blessed the King,
Without beginning, without end.
To everlasting, to eternity,
To all ages, to all time

DUAN NOLLAIG [56]

OIRE ! hoire ! beannaicht e ! beannaicht e !
  Hoire ! hoire ! beannaicht e ! beannaicht e !
  Hoire ! hoire ! beannaicht e'n Righ dh'am bi sinn
      Ho ! ro ! biodh aoibh !   [a' seinn,

Nochd oidhche Nollaige moire,
Rugadh Mac na Moir Oighe,
Rainig a bhonnaibh an lar,
Mac nam buadh a nuas o'n ard,
Dhealraich neamh us cruinne dha,
    Ho ! ro ! biodh aoibh !

Seimh saoghal dha, sona neamh dha,
  Feuch rainig a bhonn an lar,
  Fodhail Righ dha, failt Uain dha,
Righ nam buadh, Uan nan agh,
Shoillsich cluan agus cuanta dha,
    Ho ! ro ! biodh aoibh !

Shoillsich frith dha, shoillsich fonn dha,
Nuall nan tonn le fonn nan tragh,
Ag innse dhuinne gu'n d' rugadh Criosda
Mac Righ nan righ a tir na slaint,
Shoillsich grian nam beannaibh ard dha,
    Ho ! ro ! biodh aoibh !

Shoillsich ce dha us cruinne comhla,
Dh' fhosgail De an Domhnaich Dorus,
A Mhic Mhuir Oighe greas ga'm chomhnadh,
A Chriosd an dochais, a Chomhla 'n t-sonais,
Oradh Ghreine shleibh us mhonaidh,
    Ho ! ro ! biodh aoibh !

CHRISTMAS CAROL

Hail King! hail King! blessed is He! blessed is He!
Hail King! hail King! blessed is He! blessed is He!
Hail King! hail King! blessed is He, the King of whom
      All hail! let there be joy!   [we sing,

This night is the eve of the great Nativity,
Born is the Son of Mary the Virgin,
The soles of His feet have reached the earth,
The Son of glory down from the height,
Heaven and earth glowed to Him,
      All hail! let there be joy!

The peace of earth to Him! the joy of heaven to Him,
Behold His feet have reached the world,
The homage of a King be His, the welcome of a Lamb be His,
King all victorious, Lamb all glorious,
Earth and ocean illumed to Him,
      All hail! let there be joy!

The mountains glowed to Him, the plains glowed to Him,
The voice of the waves with the song of the strand,
Announcing to us that Christ is born,
Son of the King of kings from the land of salvation,
Shone the sun on the mountains high to Him,
      All hail! let there be joy!

Shone to Him the earth and sphere together,
God the Lord has opened a Door,
Son of Mary Virgin, hasten Thou to shield us,
Thou Christ of hope, Thou Door of joy,
Golden Sun of hill and mountain,
      All hail! let there be joy!

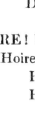

DUAN NOLLAIG [57]

OIRE! hoire! beannaicht e! beannaicht e!
Hoire! hoire! beannaicht e! beannaicht e!
   Ho! hi! beannaicht an Righ!
   Ho! hi! biodh aoibh.

Buaidh biodh air an tulaich seo,
Na chualas leibh 's na chunnas leibh,
Air na leaca loma loinnear lair.
'S air na clacha corrach cuimir clair,
   Hoire! hoire! beannaicht e! beannaicht e!

Beannaich an taigh 's na bheil ann,
Eadar chuaill us chlach us chrann,
Imir do Dhia eadar bhrat us aodach,
Slainte dhaoine gu'n robh ann,
   Hoire! hoire! beannaicht e! beannaicht e!

Gu mu buan mu'n tulach sibh,
Gu mu slan mu'n teallach sibh,
Gu mu liuth dul 's ceann sguilb 's an aros,
Daoine tamh 's a bhunntair,
   Hoire! hoire! beannaicht e! beannaicht e!

CHRISTMAS CHANT

Hail King! hail King! blessed is He! blessed is He!
Hail King! hail King! blessed is He! blessed is He '
    Ho, hail! blessed the King!
    Ho, hi! let there be joy!

Prosperity be upon this dwelling,
On all that ye have heard and seen,
On the bare bright floor stones,
On the shapely standing stone staves,
    Hail King! hail King! blessed is He! blessed is He!

Bless this house and all that it contains,
From rafter and stone and beam,
Deliver it to God from pall to cover,
Be the healing of men therein,
    Hail King! hail King! blessed is He! blessed is He!

Be ye in lasting possession of the house,
Be ye healthy about the hearth,
Many be the ties and stakes in the homestead,
People dwelling on this foundation,
    Hail King! hail King! blessed is He! blessed is He!

Iobair dha'n Ti eadar bhonn agus bhrat,
Eadar chuaill agus chlach agus chrann,
Iobair a ris eadar shlat agus aodach,
Slanadh shaoghal, a dhaoine th' ann,
　　Hoire! hoire! beannaicht e! beannaicht e!
　　Hoire! hoire! beannaicht e! beannaicht e!
　　　Ho, hi, beannaicht an Righ,
　　　　Ho, hi, biodh aoibh!

　　　Beannaicht an Righ,
　　　Gun tus gun chrich,
　　　Gu suth, gu sior,
　　　Gach linn gu brath,
　　　　Ho! hi! biodh aoibh!

Offer to the Being from found to cover,
Include stave and stone and beam,
Offer again both rods and cloth,
Be health to the people therein,
　　Hail King! hail King! blessed is He! blessed is He!
　　Hail King! hail King! blessed is He! blessed is He!
　　　　Ho, hail! blessed the King!
　　　　　Let there be joy!

　　　　Blessed the King,
　　　　Without beginning, without ending,
　　　　To everlasting, to eternity,
　　　　　Every generation for aye,
　　　　　Ho! hi! let there be joy!

HEIRE, BANNAG   [58]

THESE carols were sung by a band of men who went about from
house to house in the townland. The band selected a leader for
their singing and for their actions throughout the night. This
leader was called 'fear-duan,' song-man, and the others were

EIRE Bannag, hoire Bannag,
  Heire Bannag, air a bheo.

Chaidh Muire mhin gheal air a glun,
Is e Righ nan dul a bha na h-uchd.

Taobh an t-sorcain, taobh an t-searcain,
Buailtear boicionn air an spar.

'G innse duinn gu 'n do rugadh Criosd,
Righ nan righ, a tir na slaint.

Chi mi tulach, chi mi traigh,
Chi mi ullaim air an t-snamh.

Chi mi ainghlean air an luinn,
Tighinn le cimh us cairdeas duinn.

ı

HEY THE GIFT

called 'fir-funn,' chorus-men. When they had sung their carols at a house, two or three bannocks were handed out to them through a window

The song-man got half of every bannock so received, and the other half went to the chorus-men

Hey the Gift, ho the Gift,
Hey the Gift on the living.

The fair Mary went upon her knee,
It was the King of glory who was on her breast.

The side of the sack (?) the side of the sark (?)
The hide is struck upon the spar.

To tell to us that Christ is born,
The King of kings of the land of salvation

I see the hills, I see the strand,
I see the host upon the wing.

I see angels on clouds,   [waves
Coming with speech and friendship to us.

HEIRE BANNAG, HOIRE BANNAG [59]

EIRE Bannag, hoire Bannag,
Heire Bannag, air a bheo.

Mac na niula, Mac na neula,
Mac na runna, Mac na reula,
Heire Bannag, etc.

Mac na dile, Mac na deire,
Mac na spire, Mac na speura,   [spisʀe
Heire Bannag, etc.

Mac na lasa, Mac na leusa,
Mac na cruinne, Mac na ce,
Heire Bannag, etc.

Mac nan dula, Mac nan neamha,
Mac na gile, Mac na greine,
Heire Bannag, etc.

Mac Moire na De-meine,
Us Mac De tus gach sgeula,
Heire Bannag, etc.

HEY THE GIFT, HO THE GIFT

Hey the Gift, ho the Gift,
Hey the Gift, on the living.

Son of the dawn, Son of the clouds,
Son of the planet, Son of the star,
    Hey the Gift, etc.

Son of the rain, Son of the dew,
Son of the welkin, Son of the sky,
    Hey the Gift, etc.

Son of the flame. Son of the light,
Son of the sphere, Son of the globe,
    Hey the Gift, etc.

Son of the elements, Son of the heavens,
Son of the moon, Son of the sun,
    Hey the Gift, etc.

Son of Mary of the God-mind,
And the Son of God first of all news,
    Hey the Gift, etc.

BANNAG NAM BUADH [60]

S mise Bannag, is mise Bochd,
Is mise Fear na h-oidhche nochd.

Is mise Mac De anns an dorus,
Di-luain air thuaradh nam bannag.

Is uasal Bride mhin-gheal air a glun,
Is uasal Righ nan dul na h-uchd.

Mac na gile, Mac na greine,
Mac Moire mor na De-meine,

Crois air gach guala dheis,
Mis is dorus, fosgail thusa.

Is leir 'omh tulach, is leir 'omh traigh,
Is leir 'omh ainghlean tighinn air snamh.

Is leir 'omh calaman, cuimir, caon,
Tighinn le caomh us cairdeas duinn.

THE GIFT OF POWER

I AM the Gift, I am the Poor,
I am the Man of the night.

I am the Son of God in the door,
On Monday seeking the gifts.

Noble is Bride the gentle fair on her knee,
Noble the King of glory on her breast.

Son of the moon, Son of the sun,
Son of great Mary of God-like mind.

A cross on each right shoulder,
I am in the door, open thou

I see the hills, I see the strands,
I see angels heralding on high.

I see the dove shapely, benign,
Coming with kindness and friendship to us

HUNNACAS an Oigh a teachd,
Criosda gu h-og na h-uchd.

A Mhoir Oighe, agus a Mhic,
Beannaich an taigh agus a luchd.

Beannaich am biadh, beannaich am bord,
Beannaich an dias, an triall 's an stor.

An trath bha oirnn an raidhe gann,
Is tu fein Oighe bu mhathair dhuinn.

Is gil thu na ghealach earra-gheal
Ag eirigh air an tulaich.

Is gil thu na ghrian cheit-ghil,
Fo eibhneas subhach.

Bho nach faod am bard fuireach,
Cuiribh uilim 's a bhalg le beannachd.

Mise gille Mhic De an cois an doruis,
A uchd De, eirich fein us fosgail domh e.

THE VIRGIN AND CHILD

BEHOLD the Virgin approaching,
Christ so young on her breast

O Mary Virgin ! and O Holy Son !
Bless Ye the house and all therein.

Bless Ye the food, bless Ye the board,
Bless Ye the corn, the flock and the store.

What time to us the quarter was scarce,
It is thou thyself, Virgin, who wast mother to us.

Thou art brighter than the waxing moon
Rising over the mountains.

Thou art brighter than the summer sun.
Under his fulness of joy.

Since the bard must not tarry,
Place ye alms in the bag with a blessing.

Servant am I of God the Son at the door,
From the bosom of God, arise thyself and open to me

T

RUGADH BUACHAILLE NAN TREUD [62]

IDHCHE sin a dhealraich an reult,
Rugadh Buachaille nan treud,
Le Oigh nan ceudaibh beus,
    Moire Mhathar.

An Trianaid shiorruidh r'a taobh,
Ann am frasach fuar, faoin,
Thig 's thoir deachamh de d' mhaoin,
    Dha 'n t-Slan-Fhear.

An cobhrach, ciochrach, caomh,
Gun aon dachaidh fo 'n t-saoghal,
Am Fogaran naomha, maoth,
        'Manul !

A thri ainglibh nam buadh   [tha shuas
Thigibh, thigibh a nuas,
Do Chriosd an t-sluaigh
        Thugaibh failte.

Pogaibh a bhasa,
Tioramaichibh a chasa
Le falt bhur cinn,
'S O ! Thi na cruinne,
'S Iosa, Mhicheil, Mhuire,
        Na fagaibh sinn.

THE SHEPHERD OF THE FLOCK WAS BORN

THAT night the star shone
Was born the Shepherd of the Flock,
Of the Virgin of the hundred charms,
    The Mary Mother.

The Trinity eternal by her side,
In the manger cold and lowly,
Come and give tithes of thy means
    To the Healing Man.

The foam-white breastling beloved,
Without one home in the world,
The tender holy Babe forth driven,
    Immanuel!

Ye three angels of power   [above
Come ye, come ye down,
To the Christ of the people
    Give ye salutation.

Kiss ye His hands,
Dry ye His feet
With the hair of your heads,
And O! Thou world-pervading God,
And Ye, Jesu, Michael, Mary,
    Do not Ye forsake us.

CALLUINN A BHUILG　　　　[63]

Calluinn Ho!—This rune is still repeated in the Isles. Rarely, however, do two persons recite it alike. This renders it difficult to decide the right form of the words.

The walls of the old houses in the West are very thick—from five to eight feet. There are no gables, the walls being of uniform height throughout. The roof of the house being raised from the inner edge of the wall, a broad terrace is left on the outside. Two or three stones project from the wall at the door, forming steps. On these the inmates ascend for purposes of thatching and securing the roof in time of storm.

ALLUINN a bhuilg,
　　Calluinn a bhuilg,
　　　　Buail am boicionn,
　　　　Buail am boicionn.
　　Calluinn a bhuilg,
　　Calluinn a bhuilg,
　　　　Buail an craicionn,
　　　　Buail an craicionn.
　　Calluinn a bhuilg,
　　Calluinn a bhuilg,
　　　　Sios e! suas e!
　　　　Buail am boicionn.
　　Calluinn a bhuilg,
　　Calluinn a bhuilg,
　　　　Sios e! suas e!
　　　　Buail an craicionn.
　　Calluinn a bhuilg,
　　Calluinn a bhuilg.

HOGMANAY OF THE SACK

The 'gillean Callaig' carollers or Hogmanay lads perambulate the townland at night   One man is enveloped in the hard hide of a bull with the horns and hoofs still attached.   When the men come to a house they ascend the wall and run round sunwise, the man in the hide shaking the horns and hoofs, and the other men striking the hard hide with sticks.   The appearance of the man in the hide is gruesome, while the din made is terrific.   Having descended and recited their tunes at the door, the Hogmanay men are admitted and treated to the best in the house

The performance seems to be symbolic, but of what it is not easy to say, unless of laying an evil spirit   That the rite is heathen and ancient is evident.

HOGMANAY of the sack,
Hogmanay of the sack,
    Strike the hide,
    Strike the hide.
Hogmanay of the sack,
Hogmanay of the sack,
    Beat the skin,
    Beat the skin.
Hogmanay of the sack,
Hogmanay of the sack,
    Down with it! up with it!
    Strike the hide.
Hogmanay of the sack,
Hogmanay of the sack,
    Down with it! up with it
    Beat the skin
Hogmanay of the sack,
Hogmanay of the sack

CAIRIOLL CALLAIG 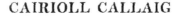 [64]

IS tha mis air tighinn dha 'r duthaich
A dh-urachadh dhuibh na Callaig,
Cha leig mi leas a dhol ga innse,
Bha i ann ri linn ar seanar.

Dirim ris an ardorus,
Teurnam ris an starsach,
Mo dhuan a ghabhail doigheil,
Modhail, moineil, maineil.

Caisean Callaig na mo phoca,
Is mor an ceo thig as an ealachd
     *   *   *   *

Gheibh fear an taighe na dhorn e,
Cuiridh e shron anns an teallach,
Theid e deiseil air na paisdean,
Seachd ar air bean an taighe.   [neo-r-thaing

Bean an taighe is i is fhiach e,
Lamh a riarach oirnn na Callaig,
Sochair bheag a bhlath an t-samhraidh,
Tha mi 'n geall air leis an arain.

Tabhair duinn ma dh-fhaodas,
Mar a faod na cum maill oirnn,
Mise gille Mhic De 's an dorus,
Eirich fein us fosgail domh e.

HOGMANAY CAROL

I AM now come to your country,
To renew to you the Hogmanay,
I need not tell you of it,
It was in the time of our forefathers.

I ascend by the door lintel,
I descend by the doorstep,
I will sing my song becomingly,
Mannerly, slowly, mindfully.

The Hogmanay skin is in my pocket,
Great will be the smoke from it presently,
   *   *   *   *

The house-man will get it in his hand,
He will place its nose in the fire,
He will go sunwards round the babes,
And for seven verities round the housewife

The housewife it is she who deserves it,
The hand to dispense to us the Hogmanay,
A small gift of the bloom of summer,
Much I wish it with the bread.

Give it to us if it be possible,
If you may not, do not detain us,
I am the servant of God's Son at the door,
Arise thyself and open to me.

DUAN CALLAIG [65]

IST o thaine sinn dh' an duthaich,
Dh' urachadh dhuibh na Callaig,
Cha ruig uine dhuinn bhi g' innse,
   Bha i ann ri linn ar seanar.

A direadh ri tobht an taighe,
A teurnadh aig an dorus,
Mo dhuan a ghabhail modhail,
   Mar b' eol domh aig a Challaig.

Caisein Callaig na mo phocaid,
Is mor an ceo thig as an fhear ud,
Cha' n' eil aon a gheobh de aile,
   Nach bi gu brath de fallain.

Gheobh fear an taighe na dhorn e,
Cuiridh e shron anns an teallach ;
Theid e deiseil air na paisdean,
   Us seachd araid bean an taighe.

Gheobh a bhean e, is i 's t-fhiach e,
Lamh a riarachadh na Callaig,
Lamh a bhairig cais us im duinn,
   Lamh gun spiocaireachd, gun ghainne.

THE SONG OF HOGMANAY

Now since we came to the country
To renew to you the Hogmanay,
Time will not allow us to explain,
It has been since the age of our fathers.

Ascending the wall of the house,
Descending at the door,
My carol to say modestly,
As becomes me at the Hogmanay

The Hogmanay skin is in my pocket,
Great the fume that will come from that,
No one who shall inhale its odour,
But shall be for ever from it healthy.

The house-man will get it in his grasp,
He will put its point in the fire,
He will go sunwise round the children,
And very specially round the goodwife.

The wife will get it, she it is who deserves it,
The hand to distribute the Hogmanay,
The hand to bestow upon us cheese and butter,
The hand without niggardliness, without meanness

Bho 'n ta tart air tighinn an duthaich,
Us nach bi duil againn ri annas,
Rud beag a shugh an t-samhraidh,
　　B' annsa leinn e leis an aran.

Mur bheil sin againn ri fhaotainn,
Ma dh-fhaodas tu, na cum maill oirnn,
Mise gille-Mhic-De air Chollaig,
　　Eirich fein us fosgail dorus.
　　　　Callain seo! Callain seo!

Since drought has come upon the land,
And that we do not expect rarity,
A little of the substance of the summer,
    Would we desire with the bread.

If that we are not to have it,
If thou mayest, do not detain us,
I am the servant of God's Son on Hogmanay,
    Arise thyself and open the door.
        Hogmanay here ! Hogmanay here !

OIDHCHE CHALLAIG [66]

HAINE sinne chon an doruis,
Feuch am feairde sinn an turas,
Dh' innis a mhnathan coir a bhaile,
Gur e maireach La Cullaig.

After being entertained the guisers go sunwise round

Gu'm beannaicheadh Dia an t-fhardach,
Eadar chlach, us chuaille, us chrann,
Eadar bhithe, bhliochd, us aodach,
Slainte dhaoin bhi daonnan ann,

Should the guisers be inhospitably treated, they file round the fire withershins and walk out, and raise a cairn in or near the door, called ' carnan mollachd,' cairn of malison, ' carnan cronachd,' scath cairn.

Mallachd Dhe us Challaig oirbh,
'S cronachd chlaimhein chiuchaich,
Fioinn, fithich agus fiolair,
'S cronachd sionnaich liugaich.

Cronachd chon us chat oirbh,
Thorc us bhroc us bhrugha,
Mhaghain mais 's mhadaidh-alla,
'S cronachd thaghain tutaidh.

HOGMANAY

WE are come to the door,
To see if we be the better of our visit,
To tell the generous women of the townland
That to-morrow is Calenda Day.

the fire singing—

May God bless the dwelling,
Each stone, and beam, and stave,
All food, and drink, and clothing,
May health of men be always there.

They tramp loudly, shaking the dust of the place off their feet, and intoning with a deep voice the following and other maledictions—

The malison of God and of Hogmanay be on you,
And the scath of the plaintive buzzard,
Of the hen-harrier, of the raven, of the eagle,
And the scath of the sneaking fox.

The scath of the dog and of the cat be on you,
Of the boar, of the badger, and of the ' brugha,'
Of the hipped bear and of the wild wolf,
And the scath of the foul foumart.

BEANNACHADH BLHADHNA UIR   [67]

This poem was repeated the first thing on the first day of the year.   It was common

HE, beannaich dhomh an la ur,
   Nach do thuradh dhomh roimhe riamh,
   Is ann gu beannachadh do ghnuis,
   Thug thu 'n uine seo dhomh, a Dhia.

Beannaich thusa dhomh mo shuil,
Beannaicheadh mo shuil na chi,
Beannaichidh mise mo nabaidh,
Beannaicheadh mo nabaidh mi.

Dhe tabhair dhomh-sa cridhe glan,
Na leig a seall do shula mi,
Beannaich dhomh mo ghin 's mo bhean,
'S beannaich domh mo nearc 's mo ni.

THE BLESSING OF THE NEW YEAR

throughout the Highlands and Islands The writer has heard versions of it in many places

God, bless to me the new day,
Never vouchsafed to me before,
It is to bless Thine own presence
Thou hast given me this day, O God.

Bless Thou to me mine eye,
May mine eye bless all it sees,
I will bless my neighbour,
May my neighbour bless me.

God, give me a clean heart,
Let me not from sight of Thine eye,
Bless to me my children and my wife,
And bless to me my means and my cattle

CRIOSDA CLEIREACH OS AR CIONN   [68]

RIOSDA Cleireach os ar cionn,
    Dh' orduich Ti nan dul do gach duil a t' ann.
        Criosda Cleireach os ar cionn.

Nochd oidhch a chrochaidh chruaidh,
    Crann cruaidh ris na chrochadh Criosd.
        Criosda Cleireach os ar cionn.

Is uasal Bannag, is uasal Bochd,
    Is uasal Fear na h-oidhche nochd.
        Criosda Cleireach os ar cionn.

Is i Bride mhin chaidh air a glun,
Is e Righ nan dul a ta na h-uchd,
        Criosda Cleireach os ar cionn.

Chluinn mi tulach, chluinn mi traigh,
Chluinn mi ainghlean air an t-snamh,
        Criosda Cleireach os ar cionn.

Chluinn mi Cairbre cuimir, cruinn,
Tighinn cluimh le cairdeas duinn.
        Criosda Cleireach os ar cionn.

Is ioma tionailt air an tulaich,
Gun farmad duine ri cheile.
        Criosda Cleireach os ar cionn.

Is mise gille Mic De is an dorus,
Eirich fein us fosgail domh e.
        Criosda Cleireach os ar cionn.

CHRIST THE PRIEST ABOVE US

CHRIST the Priest above us,
Ordained of God for all living.
     Christ the Priest above us

To-night, the night of the cross of agony,
The cross of anguish to which Christ was crucified.
     Christ the Priest above us.

Noble the Gift! noble the Poor!
Noble the Man of this night.
     Christ the Priest above us.

It was Bride the fair who went on her knee,
It is the King of glory who is in her lap.
     Christ the Priest above us.

I hear the hills, I hear the seas,
I hear the angels heralding to earth
     Christ the Priest above us.

I hear Cairbre of the shapely, rounded limbs,
Coming softly in friendship to us.
     Christ the Priest above us.

Great the assemblage upon this knoll,
Without the envy of man to another.
     Christ the Priest above us.

I am servant of God the Son at the door,
Oh! arise thou thyself and open to me.
     Christ the Priest above us.

LA CHALUIM-CHILLE [69]

Diardaoin, Didaoirn—the day between the fasts—Thursday, was St. Columba's Day—Diardaoin Chaluim-chille, St. Columba's Thursday—and through him the day of many important events in the economy of the people. It was a lucky day for all enterprises—for warping thread, for beginning a pilgrimage, or any other undertaking. On Thursday eve the mother of a family made a bere, rye, or oaten cake into which she put a small silver coin. The cake was toasted before a fire of rowan, yew, oak, or other sacred wood. On the morning of Thursday the father took a keen-cutting knife and cut the cake into as many sections as there were children in the family, all the sections being equal. All the pieces were then placed in a 'ciosan'— a bee-hive basket—and each child blindfold drew a piece of cake from the basket in name of the Father, Son, and Spirit. The child who got the coin got the crop of lambs for the year. This was called 'sealbh uan'—lamb luck. Sometimes it was arranged that the person who got the coin got a certain number of the lambs, and the others the rest of the lambs among them. Each child had a separate mark, and there was much emulation as to who had most lambs, the best lambs, and who took best care of the lambs.

Maunday Thursday is called in Uist 'Diardaoin a brochain,' Gruel Thursday, and in Iona 'Diardaoin a brochain mhoir,' Great Gruel Thursday. On this day people in maritime districts

AORN Chalum-chille chaomh
  La chur chaorach air seilbh,
  La chur ba air a laogh,
  La chur aodach an deilbh.

  La chur churach air sal,
  La chur gais chon a meirgh,
  La chon breith, la chon bais,
  La chon ardu a sheilg.

  La chur ghearran an eil,
  La chur feudail air raon,
  La chur urnuigh chon feum,
  La m' eudail an Daorn.
    La m' eudail an Daorn.

THE DAY OF ST. COLUMBA

made offerings of mead, ale, or gruel to the god of the sea. As the day merged from Wednesday to Thursday a man walked to the waist into the sea and poured out whatever offering had been prepared, chanting :—

' A Dhe na mara	O God of the sea,
Cuir todhar 's an tarruinn	Put weed in the drawing wave
Chon tachan an talaimh	To enrich the ground,
Chon baileidh dhuinn biaidh '	To shower on us food.

Those behind the offerer took up the chant and wafted it along the sea-shore on the midnight air, the darkness of night and the rolling of the waves making the scene weird and impressive. In 1860 the writer conversed in Iona with a middle-aged man whose father, when young, had taken part in this ceremony. In Lews the custom was continued till this century. It shows the tolerant spirit of the Columban Church and the tenacity of popular belief, that such a practice should have been in vogue so recently.

The only exception to the luck of Thursday was when Beltane fell on that day

' 'D uair is Ciadaoineach an t-Samhain	When the Wednesday is Hallowmas
Is iurganach fir an domhain,	Restless are the men of the universe,
Ach 's meirg is mathair dha'n mhac bhaoth	But woe the mother of the foolish son
'D uair is Daorn dha 'n Bhealltain '	When Thursday is the Beltane

THURSDAY of Columba benign,
Day to send sheep on prosperity,
Day to send cow on calf,
Day to put the web in the warp

Day to put coracle on the brine,
Day to place the staff to the flag,
Day to bear, day to die,
Day to hunt the heights.

Day to put horses in harness,
Day to send herds to pasture,
Day to make prayer efficacious,
Day of my beloved, the Thursday,
    Day of my beloved, the Thursday.

SLOINNTIREACHD BHRIDE [70]

The Genealogy of Bride was current among people who had a latent belief in its efficacy Other hymns to Bride were sung on her festival, but nothing now remains except the names and fragments of the words. The names are curious and suggestive, as 'Ora Bhride,' Prayer of Bride, 'Lorg Bhride,' Staff of Bride, 'Luireach Bhride,' Lorica of Bride, 'Lorg Bhride,' Mantle of Bride, 'Brot Bhride,' Corslet of Bride, and others. La Feill Bhride, St. Bridget's Day, is the first of February, new style, or the thirteenth according to the old style, which is still much in use in the Highlands. It was a day of great rejoicing and jubilation in olden times, and gave rise to innumerable sayings, as .—

' Feill na Bride, feis na finne '	Feast of the Bride, feast of the maiden
' Bride binn nam bas ban '	Melodious Bride of the fair palms
' A Bhride chaoin cheanail, Is caoimh liom anail do bheoil, 'D uair reidhinn air m' aineol Bu tu fein ceann eisdeachd mo sgeoil '	Thou Bride fair charming, Pleasant to me the breath of thy mouth, When I would go among strangers Thou thyself wert the hearer of my tale

There are many legends and customs connected with Bride. Some of these seem inconsistent with one another, and with the character of the Saint of Kildare. These seeming inconsistencies arise from the fact that there were several Brides, Christian and pre-Christian, whose personalities have become confused in the course of centuries—the attributes of all being now popularly ascribed to one. Bride is said to preside over fire, over art, over all beauty, 'fo cheabhar agus fo chuan,' beneath the sky and beneath the sea And man being the highest type of ideal beauty, Bride presides at his birth and dedicates him to the Trinity She is the Mary and the Juno of the Gael She is much spoken of in connection with Mary, —generally in relation to the birth of Christ She was the aid-woman of the Mother of Nazareth in the lowly stable, and she is the aid-woman of the mothers of Uist in their humble homes

It is said that Bride was the daughter of poor pious parents, and the serving-maid in the inn of Bethlehem. Great drought occurred in the land, and the

GENEALOGY OF BRIDE

master of the hostel went away with his cart to procure water from afar, leaving with Bride 'faircil buirn agus breacag arain,' a stoup of water and a bannock of bread to sustain her till his return The man left injunctions with Bride not to give food or drink to any one, as he had left only enough for herself, and not to give shelter to any one against his return

As Bride was working in the house two strangers came to the door. The man was old, with brown hair and grey beard, and the woman was young and beautiful, with oval face, straight nose, blue eyes, red lips, small ears, and golden brown hair, which fell below her waist   They asked the serving-maid for a place to rest, for they were footsore and weary, for food to satisfy their hunger, and for water to quench their thirst   Bride could not give them shelter, but she gave them of her own bannock and of her own stoup of water, of which they partook at the door ; and having thanked Bride the strangers went their way, while Bride gazed wistfully and sorrowfully after them   She saw that the sickness of life was on the young woman of the lovely face, and her heart was sore that she had not the power to give them shade from the heat of the sun, and cover from the cold of the dew   When Bride returned into the house in the darkening of the twilight, what was stranger to her to see than that the bannock of bread was whole, and the stoup of water full, as they had been before ! She did not know under the land of the world what she would say or what she would do   The food and the water of which she herself had given them, and had seen them partake, without a bit or a drop lacking from them !   When she recovered from her wonderment Bride went out to look after the two who had gone their way, but she could see no more of them   But she saw a brilliant golden light over the stable door, and knowing that it was not ' dreag a bhais,' a meteor of death, she went into the stable and was in time to aid and minister to the Virgin Mother, and to receive the Child into her arms, for the strangers were Joseph and Mary, and the child was Jesus Christ, the Son of God, come to earth, and born in the stable of the hostel of Bethlehem ''D uair a rugadh an leanabh chuir Bride tri braona burna fuarain fion-uisge air clar a bhathais ann an ainm De, ann an ainm Iosa, ann an ainm Spioraid '   When the Child was born Bride put three drops of water from the spring of pure water on the tablet of His forehead, in name of God, in name of Jesus, in name of Spirit   When the master of the inn was returning home, and ascending the hill on which his house stood, he heard the murmuring music of a stream flowing past his house, and he saw the light of a bright star above his stable door He knew from these signs that the Messiah was come and that Christ was born, 'oir bha e ann an dailgneachd nan daome gu'm beirte Iosa Criosda Mac De ann am Betlehem baile Dhaibhidh '—for it was in the seership of the people that Jesus Christ, the Son of God, would be born in Bethlehem, the town of David And the man rejoiced with exceeding joy at the fulfilment of the prophecy, and he went to the stable and worshipped the new Christ, whose infant cradle was the manger of the horses.

Thus Bride is called 'ban-chuideachaidh Moire,' the aid-woman of Mary. In this connection, and in consequence thereof, she is called 'Muime Chriosa,' foster-mother of Christ; 'Bana-ghoistidh Mhic De,' the god-mother of the Son of God, 'Bana-ghoistidh Iosda Criosda nam bann agus nam beannachd,' god-mother of Jesus Christ of the bindings and blessings Christ again is called 'Dalta Bride,' the foster-son of Bride, 'Dalta Bride bith nam beannachd,' the foster-son of Bride of the blessings; 'Daltan Bride,' little fosterling of Bride, a term of endearment.

John the beloved is called 'Dalta Moire,' foster-son of Mary, and 'Comhdhalta Chriosda,' the foster-brother, literally co-foster, of Christ Fostership among the Highlanders was a peculiarly close and tender tie, more close and more tender even than blood. There are many proverbs on the subject, as, 'Fuil gu fichead, comhdhaltas gu ceud,' blood to the twentieth, fostership to the hundredth degree. A church in Islay is called 'Cill Daltain,' the Church of the Fosterling

When a woman is in labour, the midwife or the woman next her in importance goes to the door of the house, and standing on the 'fad-buinn,' sole-sod, door-step, with her hands on the jambs, softly beseeches Bride to come .

' Bhride ! Bhride ! thig a steach	Bride ! Bride ! come in,
Tha do bheatha deanta,	Thy welcome is truly made,
Tabhair cobhair dha na bhean,	Give thou relief to the woman,
'S tabh an gein dh'an Triana '	And give the conception to the Trinity

When things go well, it indicates that Bride is present and is friendly to the family ; and when they go ill, that she is absent and offended Following the action of Bride at the birth of Christ, the aid-woman dedicates the child to the Trinity by letting three drops of clear cold water fall on the tablet of his forehead (See page 114)

The aid-woman was held in reverence by all nations Juno was worshipped with greater honour than any other deity of ancient Rome, and the Pharaohs paid tribute to the aid-women of Egypt. Perhaps, however, appreciation of the aid-woman was never more touchingly indicated than in the reply of two beautiful maidens of St Kilda to John Macdonald, the kindly humorist, and the unsurpassed seaman and pilot of Admiral Otter of the West Coast Survey 'O ghradhanan an domhain agus an t-saoghail, carson a Righ na gile 's na greine! nach 'eil sibh a posadh us sibh cho briagh?' 'A ghaol nan daona, ciamar a phosas sinne? nach do chaochail a bhean-ghlun!' 'Oh! ye loves of the domain and of the universe, why, King of the moon and of the sun! are ye not marrying and ye so beautiful?' 'Oh! thou love of men, how can we marry? has not the knee-wife died!'

On Bride's Eve the girls of the townland fashion a sheaf of corn into the likeness of a woman They dress and deck the figure with shining shells, sparkling crystals, primroses, snowdrops, and any greenery they may obtain In the mild climate of the Outer Hebrides several species of plants continue in flower during winter, unless the season be exceptionally severe. The gales of March are there the destroyers of plant-life. A specially bright shell or crystal is placed over the heart of the figure This is called 'reul-iuil Bride,' the guiding star of Bride, and typifies the star over the stable door of Bethlehem, which led Bride to the infant Christ The girls call the figure 'Bride,' 'Brideag,' Bride, Little Bride, and carry it in procession, singing the song of 'Bride bhoidheach oigh nam mile beus,' Beauteous Bride, virgin of a thousand charms The 'banal Bride,' Bride maiden band, are clad in white, and have their hair down, symbolising purity and youth They visit every house, and every person is expected to give a gift to Bride and to make obeisance to her The gift may be a shell, a spar, a crystal, a flower, or a bit of greenery to decorate the person of Bride Mothers, however, give 'bonnach Bride,' a Bride bannock, 'cabag Bride,' a Bride cheese, or 'rolag Bride,' a Bride roll of butter Having made the round of the place the girls go to a house to make the 'feis Bride,' Bride feast They bar the door and secure the windows of the house, and set Bride where she may see and be seen of all. Presently the young men of the community come humbly asking permission to honour Bride. After some parleying they are admitted and make obeisance to her

Much dancing and singing, fun and frolic, are indulged in by the young men and maidens during the night. As the grey dawn of the Day of Bride breaks they form a circle and sing the hymn of 'Bride bhoidheach muime chorr Chriosda,' Beauteous Bride, choice foster-mother of Christ. They then distribute 'fuidheal na feisde,' the fragments of the feast—practically the whole, for they have par-taken very sparingly, in order to have the more to give—among the poor women of the place

A similar practice prevails in Ireland. There the churn staff, not the corn sheaf, is fashioned into the form of a woman, and called 'Brideog,' little Bride The girls come clad in their best, and the girl who has the prettiest dress gives it to Brideog. An ornament something like a Maltese cross is affixed to the breast of the figure The ornament is composed of straw, beautifully and artistically inter-laced by the deft fingers of the maidens of Bride It is called 'rionnag Brideog,' the star of little Bride. Pins, needles, bits of stone, bits of straw, and other things are given to Bride as gifts, and food by the mothers

Customs assume the complexion of their surroundings, as fishes, birds, and beasts assimilate the colours of their habitats The seas of the ' Garbh Chriocha,' Rough Bounds in which the cult of Bride has longest lived, abound in beautiful iridescent shells, and the mountains in bright sparkling stones, and these are utilised to adorn the ikon of Bride. In the districts of Ireland where the figure of Bride is made, there are no shining shells, no brilliant crystals, and the girls decorate the image with artistically interlaced straw

The older women are also busy on the Eve of Bride, and great preparations are made to celebrate her Day, which is the first day of spring. They make an oblong basket in the shape of a cradle, which they call ' leaba Bride,' the bed of Bride It is embellished with much care Then they take a choice sheaf of corn, generally oats, and fashion it into the form of a woman They deck this ikon with gay ribbons from the loom, sparkling shells from the sea, and bright stones from the hill. All the sunny sheltered valleys around are searched for primroses, daisies, and other flowers that open their eyes in the morning of the year This lay figure is called Bride, ' dealbh Bride,' the ikon of Bride. When it is dressed and decorated with all the tenderness and loving care the women can lavish upon it, one woman goes to the door of the house, and standing on the step with her hands on the jambs, calls softly into the darkness, ' Tha leaba Bride deiseil,' Bride's bed is ready. To this a ready woman behind replies, ' Thigeadh Bride steach, is e beatha Bride,' Let Bride come in, Bride is welcome The woman at the door again addresses Bride, ' A Bhride! Bhride thig a steach, tha do leaba deanta Gleidh an teach dh'an Triana,' Bride! Bride, come thou in, thy bed is made. Preserve the house for the Trinity. The women then place the ikon of Bride with great ceremony in the bed they have so carefully prepared for it They place a small straight white wand (the bark being peeled off) beside the figure This wand is variously called ' slatag Bride,' the little rod of Bride, ' slachdan Bride,' the little wand of Bride, and ' barrag Bride,' the birch of Bride. The wand is generally of birch, broom, bramble, white willow, or other sacred wood, ' crossed ' or banned wood being carefully avoided. A similar rod was given to the kings of Ireland at their coronation, and to the Lords of the Isles at their instatement It was straight to typify justice, and white to signify peace and purity—bloodshed was not to be needlessly caused The women then level the ashes on the hearth, smoothing and dusting them over carefully Occasionally the ashes, surrounded by a roll of cloth, are placed on a board to safeguard them against disturbance from draughts or other contingencies In the early morning the family closely scan the ashes. If they find the marks of the wand of Bride they rejoice, but if they find ' loirg Bride,' the footprint of Bride, their joy is very great, for this is a sign that Bride was present with them during the night, and is favourable to them, and that there is increase in family, in flock, and in field during the coming year Should there be no marks on the ashes, and no traces of Bride's presence, the family are dejected. It is to them a sign that she is offended, and will not hear their call To propitiate her and gain her ear the family offer oblations and burn incense The oblation generally is a cockerel, some say a pullet, buried alive near the junction of three streams, and the incense is burnt on the hearth when the family retire for the night

In the Highlands and Islands St Bride's Day was also called 'La Cath Choileach,' Day of Cock-fighting The boys brought cocks to the school to fight. The most successful cock was called 'coileach buadha,' victor cock, and its proud owner was elected king of the school for the year. A defeated bird was called 'fuidse,' craven, 'coileach fuidse,' craven cock All the defeated, maimed, and killed cocks were the perquisites of the schoolmaster. In the Lowlands 'La Coinnle,' Candlemas Day, was the day thus observed

It is said in Ireland that Bride walked before Mary with a lighted candle in each hand when she went up to the Temple for purification. The winds were strong on the Temple heights, and the tapers were unprotected, yet they did not flicker nor fail From this incident Bride is called 'Bride boillsge,' Bride of brightness This day is occasionally called 'La Fheill Bride nan Coinnle,' the Feast Day of Bride of the Candles, but more generally 'La Fheill Moire nan Coinnle,' the Feast Day of Mary of the Candles—Candlemas Day

The serpent is supposed to emerge from its hollow among the hills on St Bride's Day, and a propitiatory hymn was sung to it. Only one verse of this hymn has been obtained, apparently the first. It differs in different localities.—

'Moch maduinn Bhride,
Thig an nimhir as an toll,
Cha bhoin mise ris an nimhir,
Cha bhoin an nimhir rium '

To-day is the Day of Bride,
The serpent shall come from the hole,
I will not molest the serpent,
Nor will the serpent molest me

Other versions say ·—

' La Feill na Bride,
Thig nighean Imhir as a chnoc,
Cha bhean mise do nighean Imhir,
'S cha dean i mo lochd '

The Feast Day of the Bride,
The daughter of Ivor shall come from the knoll,
I will not touch the daughter of Ivor,
Nor shall she harm me.

' La Fheill Bride brisgeanach
Thig an ceann de 'n chaiteanach,
Thig nighean Iomhair as an tom
Le fonn feadalaich.'

On the Feast Day of Bride,
The head will come off the 'caiteanach,'
The daughter of Ivor will come from the knoll
With tuneful whistling.

'Thig an nathair as an toll
La donn Bride,
Ged robh tri traighean dh' an t-sneachd
Air leachd an lair.'

The serpent will come from the hole
On the brown Day of Bride,
Though there should be three feet of snow
On the flat surface of the ground.

The 'daughter of Ivor' is the serpent; and it is said that the serpent will not sting a descendant of Ivor, he having made 'tabhar agus tuis,' offering and incense, to it, thereby securing immunity from its sting for himself and his seed for ever.

' La Bride nam brig ban	On the day of Bride of the white hills
Thig an rigen ran a tom,	The noble queen will come from the knoll,
Cha bhoin mise ris an rigen ran,	I will not molest the noble queen,
'S cha bhoin an rigen ian rium '	Nor will the noble queen molest me.

These lines would seem to point to serpent-worship One of the most curious customs of Bride's Day was the pounding of the serpent in effigy. The following scene was described to the writer by one who was present:—'I was one of several guests in the hospitable house of Mr John Tolmie of Uignis, Skye. One of my fellow-guests was Mrs Macleod, widow of Major Macleod of Stein, and daughter of Flora Macdonald. Mrs Macleod was known among her friends as "Major Ann" She combined the warmest of hearts with the sternest of manners, and was the admiration of old and young for her wit, wisdom, and generosity When told that her son had fallen in a duel with the celebrated Glengarry—the Ivor MacIvor of *Waverley*—she exclaimed, "Math thu fein mo ghiullan ! math thu fein mo ghiullan ! gaol geal do mhathar fein ! Is fearr bas saoidh na gras daoidh, cha bhasaich an gaisgeach ach an aon turas, ach an gealtair iomadaidh uair !'"—"Good thou art my son ! good thou art my son ! thou the white love of thine own mother ! Better the hero's death than the craven's life, the brave dies but once, the coward many times" In a company of noblemen and gentlemen at Dunvegan Castle, Mrs Macleod, then in her 88th year, danced the reel of Tulloch and other reels, jigs, and strathspeys as lightly as a girl in her teens. Wherever she was, all strove to show Mrs Macleod attention and to express the honour in which she was held She accepted all these honours and attentions with grace and dignity, and without any trace of vanity or self-consciousness. One morning at breakfast at Uignis some one remarked that this was the Day of Bride. "The Day of Bride," repeated Mrs Macleod meditatively, and with a dignified bow of apology rose from the table. All watched her movements with eager curiosity Mrs Macleod went to the fireside and took up the tongs and a bit of peat and walked out to the doorstep She then took off her stocking and put the peat into it, and pounded it with the tongs And as she pounded the peat on the step, she intoned a ' rann," rune, only one verse of which I can remember :—

"An diugh La Bride,	This is the day of Bride,
Thig an righinn as an tom,	The queen will come from the mound,
Cha bhean mise ris an righinn,	I will not touch the queen,
Cha bhean an righinn rium."	Nor will the queen touch me.

'Having pounded the peat and replaced her stocking, Mrs Macleod returned to the table, apologising for her remissness in not remembering the Day earlier in the morning I could not make out whether Mrs Macleod was serious or acting, for she was a consummate actress and the delight of young and old. Many curious ceremonies and traditions in connection with Bride were told that morning, but I do not remember them '

The pounding in the stocking of the peat representing the serpent would indicate destruction rather than worship perhaps the bruising of the serpent's head Probably, however, the ceremony is older, and designed to symbolise something now lost.

Gaelic lore is full of sayings about serpents These indicate close observation 'Tha cluas nathraeh aige,'—he has the ear of a serpent (he hears keenly but does not speak); 'Tha a bhana-bhuitseach lubach mar an nathair,'—the witch-woman is crooked as the serpent; 'Is e an t-iorball is neo-chronail dhiot, cleas na nathrach nimhe,'—the tail is the least harmful of thee, the trick of the serpent venomous

'Ge min do chraicionn Is nimheil gath do bheuil, Tha thu mar an nathair lachdann, Gabh do rathad fein.'	Though smooth be thy skin Venomous is the sting of thy mouth, Thou art like the dun serpent, Take thine own road
'Bean na maise te neo-fhialaidh, 'S i lan do na briathra blath Tha i mar an nathan riabhach, 'S gath na spiocaireachd na dail '	The beauteous woman, ungenerous, And she full of warm words, Is like the brindled serpent, And the sting of greed is in her.

The people of old practised early retiring, early rising, and diligent working :—

'Suipeir us soillse Oidhch Fheill Bride, Cadal us soillse Oidhch Fheill Parnig '	Supper and light the Night of St. Bride, Sleep and light the Night of St. Patrick

The dandelion is called 'bearnan Bride,' the little notched of Bride, in allusion to the serrated edge of the petal The linnet is called 'bigein Bride,' little bird of Bride In Lismore the oyster-catcher is called 'gille Bride,' page of Bride :—

'Gille Bride bochd, Gu de bhigil a th' ort ?'	Poor page of Bride, What cheeping ails thee ?

In Uist the oyster-catcher is called 'Bridein,' bird of Bride. There was once an oyster-catcher in Uist, and he was so elated with his own growing riches that he thought he would like to go and see something of the great world around him He went away, leaving his three beautiful, olive-brown, blotched black-and-grey eggs in the rough shingle among the stones of the seashore Shortly after he left the grey crow came hopping round to see what was doing in the place. In her pecking she saw the three eggs of the oyster-catcher in the hollow among the rocks, and she thought she would like to try the taste of one of them, as a variant upon the refuse of land and shore. So she drove her strong bill through the broad end of an egg, and seizing it by the shell, carried it up to the mossy holm adjoining. The quality of the egg was so pleasing to the grey crow that she went back for the second, and then for the third egg. The grey crow was taking the last suck of the last egg when the oyster-catcher was heard returning with his usual fuss and flurry and hurry-scurry. He looked at his nest, but there were no eggs there—no, not one, and the oyster-catcher knew not what to do or say He flew about to and fro, hither and thither in great distress, crying out in the bitterness of his heart, ' Co dh' ol na h-uibhean? Co dh' ol na h-uibhean? Cha chuala mi riamh a leithid! Cha chuala mi riamh a leithid!' Who drank the eggs? Who drank the eggs? I never heard the like! I never heard the like! The grey crow listened now on this side and now on that, and gave two more precautionary wipes to her already well-wiped bill in the fringy, friendly moss, then looked up with much affected innocence and called out in deeply sympathetic tones, ' Cha chuala na sinne sin fhein sin, ged is sinn is sine 's an aite,' No, nor heard we ourselves that, though we are older in the place

Bride is said to preside over the different seasons of the year and to bestow their functions upon them according to their respective needs Some call January ' am mios marbh,' the dead month, some December, while some apply the terms, ' na tri miosa marbh,' the three dead months, ' an raidhe marbh,' the dead quarter, and ' raidhe marbh na bliadhna,' the dead quarter of the year, to the winter months when nature is asleep Bride with her white wand is said to breathe life into the mouth of the dead Winter and to bring him to open his eyes to the tears and the smiles, the sighs and the laughter of Spring. The venom of the cold is said to tremble for its safety on Bride's Day and to flee for its life on Patrick's Day There is a saying:—

' Chuir Bride miar 's an abhuinn	Bride put her finger in the river
La na Feill Bride	On the Feast Day of Bride
Us dh' fhalbh mathair ghuir an fhuachd,	And away went the hatching mother of the cold,
Us nigh i basan anns an abhuinn	And she bathed her palms in the river
La na Feill Padruig	On the Feast Day of Patrick
Us dh' fhalbh mathair ghin an fhuachd.'	And away went the conception mother of the cold,

Another version says —

' Chuir Brighid a bas ann,	Bride put her palm in it,
Chuir Moire a cas ann,	Mary put her foot in it,
Chuir Padruig a chlach fhuar ann.' (·)	Patrick put the cold stone in it,

alluding to the decrease in cold as the year advances. In illustration of this is— ' Chuir Moire meoirean anns an uisge La Fheill Bride us thug i neimh as, 's La Fheill Padruig nigh i lamhan ann 's dh' fhalbh am fuachd uil as,' Mary put her fingers in the water on Bride's Feast Day and the venom went out of it, and on Patrick's Feast Day she bathed her hands in it and all the cold went out of it

Poems narrating the events of the seasons were current That mentioning the occurrences of Spring begins —

'La Bride breith an earraich	The Day of Bride, the birthday of Spring,
Thig an dearras as an tom,	The serpent emerges from the knoll,
Theirear "tri bliadhnaich" ri aighean,	'Three-year olds' is applied to heifers,
Bheirear gearrain chon nam fonn '	Garrons are taken to the fields

In Uist the flocks are counted and dedicated to Bride on her Day

'La Fheill Bride boidheach	On the Feast Day of beautiful Bride
Cunntar spreidh air monnteach	The flocks are counted on the moor.
Cuirear fitheach chon na nide,	The raven goes to prepare his nest,
'S cuirear rithis rocais '	And again goes the rook

'Nead air Bhrighit, ugh air Inid, ian air Chasg,	Nest at Brigit, egg at Shrove, chick at Easter,
Mar a bith aig an fhitheach bithidh am bas.'	If the raven has not he has death

The raven is the first bird to nest, closely followed by the mallard and the rook It is affirmed that—

'Co fad 's a theid a ghaoth 's an dorus	As far as the wind shall enter the door
La na Feill Bride,	On the Feast Day of Bride,
Theid an cabhadh anns an dorus	The snow shall enter the door
La na Feill Paruig '	On the Feast Day of Patrick.

In Barra, lots are cast for the 'iolachan iasgaich,' fishing-banks, on Bride's Day. These fishing-banks of the sea are as well known and as accurately defined by the fishermen of Barra as are the qualities and boundaries of their crofts on land, and they apportion them with equal care. Having ascertained among themselves the number of boats going to the long-line fishing, the people divide the banks accordingly All go to church on St Bride's Day. After reciting the virtues and blessings of Bride, and the examples to be drawn from her life, the priest reminds his hearers that the great God who made the land and all thereon, also made the sea and all therein, and that 'murachan na mara agus tachar na tire,' 'cuilidh Chaluim agus cuilidh Mhoire,' the wealth of sea and the plenty of land, the treasury of Columba and the treasury of Mary, are His gift to them that follow Him and call upon His name, on rocky hill or on crested wave. The priest urges upon them to avoid disputes and quarrels over their fishing, to remember the dangers of the deep and the precariousness of life, and in their fishing to remember the poor, the widow and the orphan, now left to the fatherhood of God and to the care of His people. Having come out of church, the men cast lots for the fishing-banks at the church door. After this, they disperse to their homes, all talking loudly and discussing their luck or unluck in the drawing of the lots A stranger would be apt to think that the people were quarrelling. But it is not so The simultaneous talking is their habit, and the loudness of their speaking is the necessity of their living among the noise of winds and waves, whether on sea or on shore Like the people of St Kilda, the people

of Barra are warmly attached to one another, the joy of one and the grief of
another being the joy and grief of all.

The same practice of casting lots for their fishing-banks prevails among the
fisher-folks of the Lofodin Islands, Norway.

LOINNEADH na Ban-naomh Bride,
     Lasair dhealrach oir, muime chorr Chriosda.
Bride nighinn Dughaill duinn,
Mhic Aoidh, mhic Airt, mhic Cuinn,
Mhic Crearair, mhic Cis, mhic Carmaig, mhic
     Carruinn.

Gach la agus gach oidhche
Ni mi sloinntireachd air Bride,
Cha mharbhar mi, cha spuillear mi,
Cha charcar mi, cha chiurar mi,
Cha mhu dh' fhagas Chriosd an dearmad mi.

Cha loisg teine, grian, no gealach mi,
Cha bhath luin, li, no sala mi,
Cha reub saighid sithich, no sibhich mi,
Us mi fo chomaraig mo Naomh Muire
Is i mo chaomh mhuime Bride.

From these traditional observations, it will be seen that Bride and her services are near to the hearts and lives of the people In some phases of her character she is much more to them than Mary is

Dedications to Bride are common throughout Great Britain and Ireland.

THE genealogy of the holy maiden Bride,
Radiant flame of gold, noble foster-mother of Christ.
Bride the daughter of Dugall the brown,
Son of Aodh, son of Art, son of Conn,
Son of Crearar, son of Cis, son of Carmac, son of
    Carruin.

Every day and every night
That I say the genealogy of Bride,
1 shall not be killed, 1 shall not be harried,
I shall not be put in cell, I shall not be wounded,
Neither shall Christ leave me in forgetfulness

No fire, no sun, no moon shall burn me,
No lake, no water, nor sea shall drown me,
No arrow of fairy nor dart of fay shall wound me,
And I under the protection of my Holy Mary,
And my gentle foster-mother is my beloved Bride.

BRIDE BAN-COBHAIR   [71]

HAINIG thugam cobhair,
    Moire gheal us Bride;
    Mar a rug Anna Moire,
    Mar a rug Moire Criosda,
    Mar a rug Eile Eoin Baistidh
    Gun mhar-bhith dha dhi,
    Cuidich thusa mise 'm asaid,
        Cuidich mi a Bhride!

Mar a gheineadh Criosd am Moire
    Comhliont air gach laimh,
    Cobhair thusa mise, mhoime,
    An gein a thoir bho 'n chnaimh,
    'S mar a chomhn thu Oigh an t-solais,
    Gun or, gun odh, gun ni,
    Comhn orm-sa, 's mor m' orrais,
        Comhn orm a Bhride!

BRIDE THE AID-WOMAN

THERE came to me assistance,
Mary fair and Bride;
As Anna bore Mary,
As Mary bore Christ,
As Eile bore John the Baptist
Without flaw in him,
Aid thou me in mine unbearing,
    Aid me, O Bride!

As Christ was conceived of Mary
Full perfect on every hand,
Assist thou me, foster-mother,
The conception to bring from the bone,
And as thou didst aid the Virgin of joy,
Without gold, without corn, without kine,
Aid thou me, great is my sickness,
    Aid me, O Bride!

MANUS MO RUIN [72]

Magnus was descended from Malcolm Canmore, King of the Scots. Earl Magnus and his half-brother Earl Hakon ruled the Northern Isles, and while they were in agreement with one another there was peace and plenty within those isles. But dissensions arose. Magnus was eminently handsome, beneficent, and beloved. Hakon was lacking in these qualities, and he became morose and jealous of his brother.

The two brothers met at the Thingstead in Lent, Hakon being there for offensive, and Magnus for defensive, purposes. Wisdom prevailed, however, and war was averted. To confirm the peace Hakon invited Magnus to meet him in Pasch week in the church of Egilsey, the brothers agreeing to limit their retinue to two warships each. Magnus observed the agreement and came with two ships, but Hakon brought eight, with their full complement of armed men.

His people wished to defend Magnus, but he refused to allow the spilling of blood, or the perilling of souls. Magnus submitted to his brother three proposals. First, that he should go to his relative, the King of the Scots, and never return ; second, that he should go to Rome or to Jerusalem and never return ; or third, that he would submit to be maimed, gouged, or slain. Hakon spurned all the proposals save the last, and Magnus was put to death on the 14th of April, 1115, to the great grief of his people.

MHANUIS mo ruin,
Is tu dheanadh dhuinn iul,
A chuirp chubhraidh nan dul,
    Cuimhnuich oirnn.

Cuimhnuich a naoimh nam buadh,
A chomraig 's a chomhn an sluagh,
Cobhair oirnne n' ar truaigh,
    'S na treig sinn.

Tog ar seilbh mach ri leirg,
Casg coin ghioirr us coin dheirg,
Cum uainn fuath, fath, feirg,
    Agus foirne.

MAGNUS OF MY LOVE

The place where Magnus was slain had been a rough, sterile moor of heath and moss, but immediately Magnus was put to death the moor became a smiling grassy plain, and there issued a heavenly light and a sweet odour from the holy ground.

Those who were in peril prayed to Magnus and were rescued, and those who were sick came to his grave and were healed. Pilgrims flocked to his tomb to keep vigil at his shrine, and be cured of their leprosy of body or of soul

St. Magnus had three burials—the first in the island of Egilsey where he was slain, and the second at the intercession of his mother, Thora, in Christ Church in the island of Birsa During imminent peril at sea Earl Rognovald prayed to Magnus for deliverance, and vowed that he would build a minster to his memory more beautiful than any church in those lands The prayer was heard, and Rognovald built and endowed, to the memory of the holy Magnus, the cathedral church of Kirkwall Thither the relics of the saint were brought and interred, and the cathedral became the resort of pilgrims who sought the aid of St. Magnus.

At the battle of Anglesea, between Magnus Barefoot, his brother Ireland, his cousin Haco, and the Earls of Chester and Shrewsbury, Magnus recited the Psalter during the conflict The victory of his northern kinsmen was attributed to the holy Magnus

> O Magnus of my love,
> Thou it is who would'st us guide,
> Thou fragrant body of grace,
> Remember us.
>
> Remember us, thou Saint of power,
> Who didst encompass and protect the people,
> Succour thou us in our distress,
> Nor forsake us.
>
> Lift our flocks to the hills,
> Quell the wolf and the fox,
> Ward from us spectre, giant, fury,
> And oppression.

Cuartaich tan agus buar,
Cuartaich caor agus uan,
Cum uap an fhamh-bhual,
    'S an luch-fheoir.

Crath an druchd o'n speur air crodh,
Thoir fas air feur, deis, agus snodh,
Dubhrach, lus-feidh, ceis, meacan-dogh,
    Agus neoinean.

O Mhanuis nan glonn,
Air bharca nan sonn,
Air bharra nan tonn,
Air sala no fonn,
    Comhn agus gleidh sinn.

Surround cows and herds,
Surround sheep and lambs,
Keep from them the water-vole,
    And the field-vole.

Sprinkle dew from the sky upon kine,
Give growth to grass, and corn, and sap to plants,
Water-cress, deer's-grass, 'ceis,' burdock,
    And daisy.

O Magnus of fame,
On the barque of the heroes,
On the crest of the waves,
On the sea, on the land,
    Aid and preserve us

AM BEANNACHADH BEALLTAIN [73]

BEALLTAIN, Beltane, is the first day of May. On May Day all the fires of the district were extinguished and 'tein eigin,' need-fire, produced on the knoll. This fire was divided in two, and people and cattle rushed through for purification and safe-guarding against 'ealtraigh agus dosgaidh,' mischance and murrain, during the year. The people obtained fires for their homes from this need-fire. The practice of pro-ducing the need-fire came down in the Highlands and Islands to the first quarter of this century. The writer found traces of it in such distant places as Arran, Uist, and Sutherland. In 1895 a woman in Arran said that in

EANNAICH, a Thrianailt fhioir nach gann,
  Mi fein, mo cheile agus mo chlann,
  Mo chlann mhaoth 's am mathair chaomh na' ceann,
  Air chlar chubhr nan raon, air airidh chaon nam beann,
    Air chlar chubhr nan raon, air airidh chaon nam beann.

    Gach ni na m' fhardraich, no ta na m' shealbh,
    Gach buar us barr, gach tan us tealbh,
    Bho Oidhche Shamhna chon Oidhche Bheallt;
    Piseach maith, agus beannachd mallt,
    Bho mhuir gu muir, agus bun gach allt,
      Bho thonn gu tonn, agus bonn gach steallt.

  Tri Pears a gabhail sealbh anns gach ni na m' stor,
  An Trianailt dhearbha da m' dhion le coir,
  O m' anam riaraich am briathra Phoil,
  Us dion mo chiallain fo sgiath do ghloir,
    Dion mo chiallain fo sgiath do ghloir.

THE BELTANE BLESSING

the time of her father the people made the need-fire on the knoll, and then rushed
home and brought out their 'creatan ean,' creatures, and put them round the fire to
safeguard them, 'bho 'n bhana bhuitsich mhoir Nic-creafain,' from the arch-witch
Crawford

The ordeal of passing through the fires gave rise to a proverb which I heard used by
an old man in Lewis in 1873 —'A Mhoire! mhicean bu dora dhomhsa sin a dheanamh
dhuit na dhol eadar dha theine mhoir Bheaill,' Ah Mary ! sonnie, it were worse for
me to do that for thee, than to pass between the two great fires of Beall.

Bless, O Threefold true and bountiful,
Myself, my spouse, and my children,
My tender children and their beloved mother at their head.
On the fragrant plain, on the gay mountain sheiling,
    On the fragrant plain, on the gay mountain sheiling.

Everything within my dwelling or in my possession,
All kine and crops, all flocks and corn,
From Hallow Eve to Bealtane Eve,
With goodly progress and gentle blessing,
From sea to sea, and every river mouth,
    From wave to wave, and base of waterfall.

Be the Three Persons taking possession of all to me belonging,
Be the sure Trinity protecting me in truth,
Oh ! satisfy my soul in the words of Paul,
And shield my loved ones beneath the wing of Thy glory,
    Shield my loved ones beneath the wing of Thy glory.

Beannaich gach ni, agus gach aon,
Ta 's an teaghlach bheag ri m' thaobh,
Cuir Crois Chriosd oirnn le buaidh baigh,
Gu 'n am faic sinn tir an aigh,
    Gu 'n am faic sinn tir an aigh.

Trath threigeas buar am buabhal bho,
Trath threigeas cuanal an cual chro,
Trath dh' eireas ceigich ri beinn a cheo,
Treoir na Trianaid bhi triall n' an coir,
    O treoir na Trianaid bhi triall n' an coir.

A Thi a chruthaich mi air tus,
Eisd us fritheil rium aig lubadh glun,
Moch us anamoch mar is iul,
A d' lathair fein a Dhe nan dul,
    A d' lathair fein a Dhe nan dul.

Bless everything and every one,
Of this little household by my side,
Place the cross of Christ on us with the power of love,
Till we see the land of joy,
    Till we see the land of joy.

What time the kine shall forsake the stalls,
What time the sheep shall forsake the folds,
What time the goats shall ascend to the mount of mis ,
May the tending of the Triune follow them,
    May the tending of the Triune follow them.

Thou Being who didst create me at the beginning,
Listen and attend me as I bend the knee to Thee,
Morning and evening as is becoming in me,
In Thine own presence, O God of life,
    In Thine own presence, O God of life.

AM BEANNACHD BEALLTAIN   [74]

MHOIRE, a mhathair nan naomh,
Beannaich an t-al 's an crodh-laoigh,
Na leig fuath na foirne, n'ar gaoith,
Fuadaich oirnne doigh nan daoi.

Cum do shuil gach Luan us Mart,
Air crodh-laoigh 's air aighean dair,
Iomachair leinn o bheinn gu sal,
Tionail fein an treud 's an t-al.

Gach Ciadaon agus Daorn bi leo,
Biodh do lamh chaon a chaoidh na'n coir,
Cuallaich buar d'am buabhal bho,
Cuallaich cuanal d'an cual chro.

Gach Aona bisa a Naomh n'an ceann,
Treoraich caoraich a aodann bheann,
Le 'n al beag ba as an deigh,
Cuartaich 'ad le cuartachd Dhe.

Gach Sathurna bith leo mar chach,
Tabhair gobhair a steach le 'n al,
Gach meann us maos gu taobh sal,
Us Lioc a h-Eigir gu h-ard,
Le biolair uaine shuas m'a barr.

THE BELTANE BLESSING

Mary, thou mother of saints,
Bless our flocks and bearing kine,
Hate nor scath let not come near us,
Drive from us the ways of the wicked.

Keep thine eye every Monday and Tuesday
On the bearing kine and the pairing queys,
Accompany us from hill to sea,
Gather thyself the sheep and their progeny.

Every Wednesday and Thursday be with them,
Be thy gracious hand always about them,
Tend the cows down to their stalls,
Tend the sheep down to their folds!

Every Friday be thou, O Saint, at their head,
Lead the sheep from the face of the bens,
With their innocent little lambs following them,
Encompass them with God's encompassing

Every Saturday be likewise with them,
Bring the goats in with their young,
Every kid and goat to the sea side,
And from the Rock of Aegir on high,
With cresses green about its summit.

Treoir na Trianailt d' ar dian 's gach cas,
Treoir Chriosda le shith 's le Phais,
Treoir an Spioraid, Ligh na slaint,
Us Athar priseil, Righ nan gras.

    *   *   *   *

'S gach naomh eile bha nan deigh
'S a choisinn suamhnas rioghachd De.

Beannaich sinn fein agus ar cloinn,
Beannaich gach creubh a thig o'r loinn,
Beannaich am fear sin air an sloinn,
Beannaich a Dhe, an te a rug o'n bhroinn.

Gach naomhachd, beannachd agus buaidh,
Bhi 'g aomadh leinn gach am 's gach uair,
An ainm Trithinn Naomha shuas,
Athar, Mic, us Spiorad buan.

Crois Chriosd bhi d' ar dion a nuas,
Crois Chriosd bhi d' ar dion a suas,
Crios Chriosd bhi d' ar dion mu 'r cuart,
Gabhail beannachd Bealltain uainn,
    Gabhail beannachd Bealltain uainn

The strength of the Triune our shield in distress,
The strength of Christ, His peace and His Pasch,
The strength of the Spirit, Physician of health,
And of the priceless Father, the King of grace

     *   *   *   *   *

And of every other saint who succeeded them
And who earned the repose of the kingdom of God.

Bless ourselves and our children,
Bless every one who shall come from our loins,
Bless him whose name we bear,
Bless, O God, her from whose womb we came.

Every holiness, blessing and power,
Be yielded to us every time and every hour,
In name of the Holy Threefold above,
Father, Son, and Spirit everlasting.

Be the Cross of Christ to shield us downward,
Be the Cross of Christ to shield us upward,
Be the Cross of Christ to shield us roundward,
Accepting our Beltane blessing from us,
    Accepting our Beltane blessing from us

LAOIDH AN TRIALL   [75]

On the first day of May the people of the crofter townland are up betimes and busy as bees about to swarm. This is the day of migrating, 'bho baile gu beinn,' from townland to moorland, from the winter homestead to the summer sheiling The summer of their joy is come, the summer of the sheiling, the song, the pipe, and the dance, when the people ascend the hill to the clustered bothies, overlooking the distant sea from among the fronded ferns and fragrant heather, where neighbour meets neighbour, and lover meets lover. All the families of the townland bring their different flocks together at a particular place and drive the whole away This miscellaneous herd is called 'triall,' procession, and is composed of horses, cattle, sheep, and goats In the 'triall' the sheep lead, the cattle follow according to their ages; then come the goats, and finally the horses, with creels slung across their backs laden with domestic gear of various kinds The men carry burdens of spades, sticks, pins, ropes, and other things that may be needed to repair their summer huts, while the women carry bedding, meal, and dairy utensils About their waists the women wear a cord of wool, or a belt of leather called 'crios-feile,' kilt girdle, underneath which their skirts are drawn up and fastened, to enable them to walk the moor with greater ease. These crofter women appear like Leezie Lindsay in the old song—

'She kilted her coats of green satin,
And she kilted them up to the knee '

When the people meet, they greet each other with great cordiality, as if they had not seen one another for months or even years, instead of probably only a few days before. There are endless noises in the herd · sheep bleat for their lambs, lambs for their mothers, cows low for their calves, and the calves respond, mares neigh for their foals, and foals whinny in reply to their dams as they lightly skip and scamper, curveting in and out, little dreaming of coming work and hard fare. The men give directions, several at a time; the women knit their stockings and sing their songs, walking free and erect as if there were no burdens on their backs or on their hearts, nor any sin or sorrow in the world so far as they are concerned

Ranged along on either side of the procession are barefooted, bareheaded comely girls, and sturdy boys, and sagacious dogs, who every now and then, and every here and there, have a neck-and-neck race with some perverse young beast, unwillingly driven from his home, for, unlike his elders, the animal does not know or does not remember the pleasures of the heathery knoll, the grassy dell or

HYMN OF THE PROCESSION

fronded glen, and the joyous freedom of the summer sheiling. All who meet them on the way bless the 'triall,' and invoke upon it a good day, much luck and prosperity, and the safe shepherding of the Son of Mary on man and beast When the grazing ground is reached, the loads are laid down, the huts repaired, fires kindled and food made ready The people bring forward their stock, each man his own, and count them into the fold. The herdsman of the townland and one or two more men stand within the gateway and count the flocks as they enter Each crofter is restricted in his stock on the common grazing of the townland. He may, however, vary the number and the ages of the species and thus equalise a deficit in one species by an excess in another Should a man have a 'barr-suma,' oversoum, he may arrange with a man who has a 'di-suma,' undersoum, or with the townland at large, for his extra stock. Every facility is given to a man in straits, the consideration of these intelligent crofting people towards one another being most pleasing The grazing arrangements of the people, complex to a stranger, but simple to themselves, show an intimate knowledge of animal and pastoral life. Having seen to their flocks and to the repairing of their huts, the people resort to their sheiling feast. This feast consists principally of a male lamb, without spot or blemish, killed that day. Formerly this lamb was sacrificed, now it is eaten The feast is shared with friends and neighbours, all wish each other luck and prosperity, with increase in their flocks .—

' Aun an coir gach fireach	Beside each knoll
Piseach crodh na h-airidh '	The progeny of the sheiling cows.

The frugal feast being finished and the remains divided among the dogs, who are not the least interested or interesting actors in the day's proceedings, every head is uncovered and every knee is bent as they invoke on man and beast the 'shepherding of Abraham, of Isaac, and of Jacob '

Protestantism prevails in Lews, Harris, and North Uist, and the people confine their invocations to the Trinity .—

' Feuch an feai coimhead Israil	The Shepherd that keeps Israel
Codal cha 'n aom no suain '	He slumbers not nor sleeps

Roman Catholicism prevails in Benbecula, South Uist, and Barra, and in their dedicatory hymn the people of these islands invoke, besides the Trinity, St Michael of the

three-cornered shield and flaming sword, patron of their horses; St. Columba of the
holy deeds, guardian of their cattle; Bride of the clustering hair, the foster-mother
of Christ; and the golden-haired Virgin, mother of the White Lamb.

HICHEIL mhil nan steud geala,
Choisinn cios air Dragon fala,
Ghaol Dia 's pian Mhic Muire,
Sgaoil do sgiath oirnn, dion sinn uile,
    Sgaoil do sgiath oirnn, dion sinn uile.

Mhoire ghradhach! Mhathair Uain ghil,
Cobhair oirnne ghlan Oigh na h-uaisleachd,
Bhride bhuaidheach, bhuachaille nan treud.
Cum ar cuallach, cuartaich sinn le cheil,
    Cum ar cuallach, cuartaich sinn le cheil.

A Chaluim-chille, chairdeil, chaoimh,
An ainm Athar, us Mic, us Spiorad Naoimh,
Trid na Trithinn, trid na Triaid
Comaraig sinn fein, gleidh ar triall,
    Comaraig sinn fein, gleidh ar triall.

Athair! a Mhic! a Spioraid Naoimh!
Biodh an Trithinn leinn a la 's a dh' oidhche,
'S air machair loim no air roinn nam beann
Bidh an Trithinn leinn 's bidh a lamh mu 'r ceann,
    Bidh an Trithinn leinn 's bidh a lamh mu 'r ceann!

As the people intone their prayers on the lonely hill-side, literally in the wilderness, the music of their evensong floats over glen and dell, loch and stream, and is echoed from corrie and cliff till it is lost on the soft evening air.

VALIANT Michael of the white steeds,
Who subdued the Dragon of blood,
For love of God, for pains of Mary's Son,
Spread thy wing over us, shield us all,
    Spread thy wing over us, shield us all.

Mary beloved! Mother of the White Lamb,
Shield, oh shield us, pure Virgin of nobleness,
And Bride the beauteous, shepherdess of the flocks,
Safeguard thou our cattle, surround us together,
    Safeguard thou our cattle, surround us together

And Columba, beneficent, benign,
In name of Father, and of Son, and of Spirit Holy,
Through the Three-in-One, through the Trinity,
Encompass thou ourselves, shield our procession,
    Encompass thou ourselves, shield our procession

O Father! O Son! O Spirit Holy!
Be the Triune with us day and night,
On the machair plain or on the mountain ridge
Be the Triune with us and His arm around our head,
    Be the Triune with us and His arm around our head.

Iasgairean Bharrai—

Athair! a Mhic! a Spioraid Naoimh!
Bi-sa, Thrithinn leinn a la 's a dh' oidhche,
S air chul nan tonn no air thaobh nam beann
Bidh ar Mathair leinn 's bidh a lamh fo 'r ceann,
    'S air chul nan tonn no air thaobh nam beann
    Bidh ar Mathair leinn 's bidh a lamh fo 'r ceann!

BARRA FISHERMEN—

O Father! O Son! O Spirit Holy!
Be thou Three-One with us day and night,
And on the back of the wave as on the mountain side
Thou our Mother art there with thine arm under our head
    And on the back of the wave as on the mountain side
    Thou our Mother art there with thine arm under our head.

LA-FEILL MOIRE [76]

The Feast-Day of Mary the Great is the 15th day of August. Early in the morning of this day the people go into their fields and pluck ears of corn, generally bere, to make the 'Moilean Moire.' These ears are laid on a rock exposed to the sun, to dry. When dry, they are husked in the hand, winnowed in a fan, ground in a quern, kneaded on a sheep-skin, and formed into a bannock, which is called 'Moilean Moire,' the fatling of Mary. The bannock is toasted before a fire of fagots of rowan, or some other sacred wood. Then the husbandman breaks the bannock and gives a bit to his wife and to each of his children, in order according to their ages, and the family raise the 'Iollach Mhoire Mhathar,' the Pæan of Mary Mother who promised to shield

A feill Moire cubhr,
 Mathair Buachaille nan treud,
 Bhuain mi beum dhe'n toradh ur,
 Chruadhaich mi e caon ri grein,
  Shuath mi e gu geur dhe 'n rusg,
   Le mo bhasa fein.

  Mheil mi e air brath Di-aoine,
  Dh' fhuin mi e air cra na caoire,
  Bhruich mi e ri aine caorain,
  S' phairtich mi e'n dail mo dhaoine.

  Chaidh mi deiseil m' fhardrach,
  An ainm Mhoire Mhathar,
  A gheall mo ghleidheadh,
  A rinn mo ghleidheadh,
  A ni mo ghleidheadh,
  Ann an sith, ann an ni,
  Ann am fireantas cri,

THE FEAST-DAY OF MARY

them, and who did and will shield them from scath till the day of death   While
singing thus, the family walk sunwise round the fire, the father leading, the mother
following, and the children following according to age.

After going round the fire, the man puts the embers of the fagot-fire, with bits
of old iron, into a pot, which he carries sunwise round the outside of his house, sometimes round his steadings and his fields, and his flocks gathered in for the purpose.
He is followed without as within by his household, all singing the praise of Mary
Mother the while

The scene is striking and picturesque, the family being arrayed in their brightest
and singing their best

On the feast-day of Mary the fragrant,
Mother of the Shepherd of the flocks,
I cut me a handful of the new corn,
I dried it gently in the sun,
I rubbed it sharply from the husk,
    With mine own palms.

I ground it in a quern on Friday,
I baked it on a fan of sheep-skin,
I toasted it to a fire of rowan,
And I shared it round my people

I went sunways round my dwelling,
In name of the Mary Mother,
Who promised to preserve me,
Who did preserve me,
And who will preserve me,
In peace, in flocks,
In righteousness of heart,

Ann an gniomh, ann an gradh,
Ann am brìgh, ann am baigh,
Air sgath Do Phais.
A Chriosd a ghrais
Gu la mo bhais
Gu brath nach treig mi!
  O gu la mo bhais
  Gu brath nach treig mi!

In labour, in love,
In wisdom, in mercy,
For the sake of Thy Passion.
Thou Christ of grace
Who till the day of my death
Wilt never forsake me!
  Oh, till the day of my death
  Wilt never forsake me!

MICHEAL NAM BUADH   [77

St Michael is spoken of as 'brian Micheal,' god Michael.

' Bu tu gaisgeach na misnich	Thou wert the warrior of courage
Dol air astar na fiosachd,	Going on the journey of prophecy,
Is tu nach siubhladh air criplich,	Thou wouldst not travel on a cripple,
Ghabh thu steud brian Micheil,	Thou didst take the steed of the god Michael,
E gun chabstar na shliopan,	He was without bit in his mouth,
Thu 'g mharcachd air iteig,	Thou didst ride him on the wing,
Leum thu thairis air hosrachadh Naduir	'Thou didst leap over the knowledge of Nature.

St Michael is the Neptune of the Gael.   He is the patron saint of the sea, and of maritime lands, of boats and boatmen, of horses and horsemen throughout the West.   As patron saint of the sea St. Michael had temples dedicated to him round the coast wherever Celts were situated   Examples of these are Mount St Michael in Brittany and in Cornwall, and Aird Michael in South and in North Uist, and elsewhere.   Probably Milton had this phase of St. Michael's character in view.   As patron saint of the land St Michael is represented riding a milk-white steed, a three-pronged spear in his right hand and a three-cornered shield in his left.   The shield is inscribed 'Quis ut Deus,' a literal translation of the Hebrew Mi-cha-el Britannia is substituted for the archangel on sea and St George on land

On the 29th of September a festival in honour of St Michael is held throughout the Western Coasts and Isles   This is much the most imposing pageant and much the most popular demonstration of the Celtic year.   Many causes conduce to this—causes which move the minds and hearts of the people to their utmost tension.   To the young the Day is a day of promise, to the old a day of fulfilment, to the aged a day of retrospect.   It is a day when Pagan cult and Christian doctrine meet and mingle like the lights and shadows on their own Highland hills

The Eve of St. Michael is the eve of bringing in the carrots, of baking the 'struan,' of killing the lamb, of stealing the horses   The Day of St Michael is the day of the early mass, the day of the sacrificial lamb, the day of the oblation 'struan,' the day of the distribution of the lamb, the day of the distribution of the 'struan,' the day of the pilgrimage to the burial-ground of their fathers, the day of the burial-ground service, the day of the burial-ground circuiting, the day of giving and receiving the carrots with their wishes and acknowledgments, and the day of the 'oda'—the athletics of the men and the racing of the horses   And the Night of Michael is the night of the dance and the song, of the merry-making, of the love-making, and of the love-gifts

MICHAEL, THE VICTORIOUS

Several weeks previously the people begin to speak of St. Michael's Day, and to prepare for St Michael's Festival Those concerned count whose turn it will be to guard the crops on St. Michael's Day and to circuit the townland on St. Michael's Night. The young men upon whom these duties fall arrange with old men to take their place on these occasions As the time approaches the interest intensifies, culminating among the old in much bustle, and among the young in keen excitement

Three plants which the people call carrots grow in Uist—the 'daucus carota,' the 'daucus maritimus,' and the 'conium' The 'daucus carota' is the original of the cultivated carrot The 'daucus maritimus' is a long slender carrot, much like the parsnip in appearance and in flavour, and is rare in the British Isles The 'conium,' hemlock, resembles the carrot, for which it is occasionally mistaken It is hard, acrid, and poisonous.

Some days before the festival of St. Michael the women and girls go to the fields and plains of the townland to procure carrots The afternoon of the Sunday immediately preceding St Michael's Day is specially devoted to this purpose, and on this account is known as 'Domhnach Curran'—Carrot Sunday. When the soil is soft and friable, the carrots can be pulled out of the ground without digging When, however, the soil is hard, a space is dug to give the hand access to the root This space is made in the form of an equal-sided triangle, technically called 'torcan,' diminutive of 'torc,' a cleft The instrument used is a small mattock of three prongs, called 'tri-meurach,' three-fingered, 'shopag,' 'shobhag.' The three-sided 'torcan' is meant to typify the three-sided shield, and the three-fingered 'shopag,' the trident of St. Michael, and possibly each to symbolise the Trinity The many brightly-clad figures moving to and fro, in and out, like the figures in a kaleidoscope, are singularly pretty and picturesque Each woman intones a rune to her own tune and time irrespective of those around her The following fragment was intoned to me in a soft, subdued voice by a woman who had gathered carrots eighty years previously —

'Torcan torrach, torrach, torrach,
Sonas curran corr orm,
Micheal mil a bhi dha m' chonuil,
Bride gheal dha m' chonradh

Piseach lium gach piseach,
Piseach dha mo bhronn,
Piseach lium gach piseach,
Piseach dha mo chloinn '

Cleft fruitful, fruitful, fruitful,
Joy of carrots surpassing upon me,
Michael the brave endowing me,
Bride the fair be aiding me

Progeny pre-eminent over every progeny,
Progeny on my womb,
Progeny pre-eminent over every progeny,
Progeny on my progeny

Should a woman find a forked carrot, she breaks out into a more exultant strain that brings her neighbours round to see and to admire her luck.

'Fhorca shona, shona, shona,   Fork joyful, joyful, joyful,
Fhorca churran mor orm,   Fork of great carrot to me,
Conuil curian corr orm,   Endowment of carrot surpassing upon me,
Sonas curran moi dhomh '   Joy of great carrot to me

There is much rivalry among the women who shall have most and best carrots They carry the carrots in a bag slung from the waist, called 'crioslachan,' little girdle, from 'crios,' a girdle. When the 'earrasaid' was worn, the carrots were carried in its ample folds The women wash the carrots and tie them up in small bunches, each of which contains a 'glac,' handful The bunches are tied with three-ply thread, generally scarlet, and put in pits near the houses and covered with sand till required

The people do not retire to rest on the Eve of St. Michael. The women are engaged all night on baking 'struain,' on household matters, and on matters personal to themselves and to others, while the men are out and in watching their horses in the fields and stables It is permissible on this night to appropriate a horse, where-ever found and by whatever means, on which to make the pilgrimage and to perform the circuiting

'Meirle eich na Feill Micheil,   Theft of horse of the Feast of Michael,
Meirle nach do dhiteadh riamh '   Theft that never was condemned.

The people act upon this ancient privilege and steal horses without compunction, owners and stealers watching and outwitting and circumventing one another It is obligatory to leave one horse with the owner to carry himself and his wife on the pilgrimage and to make the circuiting, but this may be the worst horse in the townland No apology is offered or expected for this appropriation provided the horse be returned uninjured; and even if it be injured, no adequate redress is obtained. The Eve of St Michael is thus known as 'feasgar faire nan steud,' the evening of watching the steeds; 'feasgar furachaidh nan each,' the evening of guarding the horses ; 'oidhche crothaidh nan capull,' the night of penning the mares ; 'oidhche glasadh nan each,' the night of locking the horses—hence also 'glasadh na Feill Micheil,' the locking of the Feast of Michael. A male lamb, without spot or blemish, is slain This lamb is called 'Uan Micheil,' the Michael Lamb

A cake called 'struan Micheil' is made of all the cereals grown on the farm during the year It represents the fruits of the field, as the lamb represents the fruits of the flocks. Oats, bere, and rye are the only cereals grown in the Isles These are fanned on the floor, ground in the quern, and their meal in equal parts used in the struan The struan should contain a peck of meal, and should be baked on ' imicinn,' a lamb-skin. The meal is moistened with sheep's milk, the sheep being deemed the most sacred animal. For this purpose the ewes are retained in milk till St Michael's Eve, after which they are allowed to remain in the hill and to run dry. The struan is baked by the eldest daughter of the family, guided by her mother, and assisted by her eager sisters   As she moistens the meal with the milk the girl softly says—

'Ruth agus rath an treo,	Progeny and prosperity of family,
Run Mhicheil, dion an Teor.'	Mystery of Michael, protection of Trinity

A 'leac struain,' struan flag, brought by the young men of the family from the moorland during the day, is securely set on edge before the fire, and the 'struan' is set on edge against it   The fire should be of 'cnonach caon,' sacred fagots, such as the fagots of the oak, the rowan, the bramble, and others   The blackthorn, wild fig, trembling aspen, and other 'crossed' wood are avoided   As the 'struan' gains consistency, three successive layers of a batter of cream, eggs, and butter are laid on each side alternately. The batter ought to be put on with three tail feathers of a cockerel of the year, but in Uist this is generally done with 'badan murain,' a small bunch of bent-grass   This cake is called 'struan treo,' family struan; 'struan mor,' large struan, and 'struan comachaidh,' communal struan   Small struans are made for individual members of the family by mothers, daughters, sisters, and trusted servants   These are known as 'struain beag,' little struans, 'struain cloinne,' children's struans, and by the names of those for whom they are made   If a member of the family be absent or dead, a struan is made in his or her name. This struan is shared among the family and special friends of the absent one in his or her name, or given to the poor who have no corn of their own   In mixing the meal of the individual struan, the woman kneading it mentions the name of the person for whom it is being made

'Ruth agus rath Dhomhnuill,	Progeny and prosperity to Donald,
Run Mhicheil, dion an Domhnaich.'	Mystery of Michael, shielding of the Lord

The individual struans of a family are uniform in size but irregular in form, some being three cornered, symbolic of the Trinity; some five, symbolic of the Trinity, with Mary and Joseph added; some seven, symbolic of the seven mysteries; some nine, symbolic of the nine archangels; and some round, symbolic of eternity   Various ingredients are introduced into the small struans, as cranberries, bilberries, brambleberries, carraway seed, and wild honey. Those who make them and those for whom they are made vie with their friends who shall have the best and most varied ingredients   Many cautions are given to her who is making the struan to take exceptional care of it   Ills and evils innumerable would befall herself and her house should any mishap occur to the struan   Should it break before being fired, it betokens ill to the girl baking it, if after being fired and before being used, to the household   Were the struan flag to fall and the struan with it, the omen is full of evil augury to the family   A broken struan is not used   The 'fallaid,' dry meal remaining on the baking-board after the struan is made, is put into a 'mogan,' footless stocking, and dusted over the flocks on the following day —being the Day of Michael—to bring them 'piseach agus pailteas agus pionntachd,' progeny and plenty and prosperity, and to ward from them 'suileachd agus ealtraidh agus dosgaidh,' evil-eye, mischance, and muriam Occasionally the 'fallaid' is preserved for a year and a day before being used.

On the morning of the Feast of Michael all within reach go to early mass. They take their struans with them to church to be blessed of the 'pears eaglais,' priest. At this festal service the priest exhorts the people to praise their guardian angel Michael for his leading and their Father God for His corn and wool, fruits of the field and fruits of the flocks, which He has bestowed on them, while the foodless and the fatherless among them are commended to the fatherhood of God and to the care of His people

On returning from mass the people take the 'biadh Micheil,' Michael food, 'biadh maidne Micheil,' Michael morning food The father of the family places the struan 'air bord co gile ri caile na fuinn no ii sneachda nam beann'—on a board as white as the chalk of the rock or the snow of the hill. He then takes

'Sgian gheur, ghlan,	A knife keen, true,
Gun smal, gun smur,	Without stain, without dust,
Gun sal, gun sur,	Without smear, without flaw,
Gun mhur, gun mheirg,'	Without grime, without rust,

and having made the sign of the cross of Christ on the tablet of his face, the man cuts the struan into small sections, retaining in the parts the form of the whole And he cuts up the lamb into small pieces He places the board with the bread and the flesh on the centre of the table Then the family, standing round, and holding a bit of struan in the left hand and a piece of lamb in the right, raise the 'Iolach Micheil,' triumphal song of Michael, in praise of Michael, who guards and guides them, and in praise of God, who gives them food and clothing, health, and blessing withal The man and his wife put struan into one 'crosan,' beehive basket, and lamb into another, and go out to distribute them among the poor of the neighbourhood who have no fruits nor flocks themselves Nor is this all 'Ta e iunachaidh gu'n toireadh gach tuathanach anns a bhaile La na Feill Micheil peic mine, ceathramh struain, ceathramh uanail, ceathramh caise agus platar ime dha na buichd, agus dha na deoiridh, agus dha na diolacha-deirce truagha, agus dha na diblidh agus dha na dilleachdain gun chli, gun treoir, cruthaichte ann an cruth an Athar shioriiudh Agus tha an duine a toir so seachad air mhodh Mhicheil mar nasga deirce do Dhia treun nan dul a thug dha ni agus ciob, ith agus iodh, buaidh agus pais, fas agus cinneas a chum agus gu'm bi e roimh anam diblidh tiuagh an tiath theid e null Agus togaidh na buichd agus na deoiridh agus na diolacha-deirce truagha, agus na dilleachdain gun chli, gun treoir, agus togaidh na truaghain an Iolach Micheil a toir chu agus moladh do Mhicheil min-gheal nam buadh agus do'n Athair uile-bheannaichte, uile-chumhachdach, a beannachadh an duine agus na mnatha n' am mic agus n' an nighean n' an ciud nan chu n' an crannachai n' an m agus n' an ciob, ann an toradh an tan agus ann an toradh an talamhan Is iad so am muinntir ris an canair "na feara fiala," "na feara cneasda," agus "na mnathan matha" "na mnathan coire," a ta deanamh comhnadh agus trocair air na boichd, agus air na deonidh, air na dibhdh, agus air na dimbidh, air na diolacha-deirce truagha, agus air na dilleachdain gun chli, gun treoir, gun chul-tacsa, gun loig bhrollaich, gun sgoia-cuil, ciuthaichte ann an cruth an Athar uile-chruthachaidh Agus tha ainglean gile-ghil De agus an cas ii barracha biod, an suil ri bunnacha bachd, an cluas ri fonnacha fuinn, an sgiathan a sgaireanaich an colann a ciitheanaich a feitheamh ri fios a chur mu'n ghniomh le buille dhe 'n sgeith a chon Righ na Cathair shiorriudh '

'It is proper that every husbandman in the townland should give, on the day of the St. Michael Feast, a peck of meal, a quarter of struan, a quarter of lamb, a quarter of cheese, and a platter of butter to the poor and forlorn, to the despised and dejected, to the alms-deserving, and to the orphans without pith, without power, formed in the image of the Father everlasting And the man is giving this on the beam of Michael as an offering to the great God of the elements who gave him cattle and sheep, bread and coin, power and peace, growth and prosperity, that it may be before his abject, contrite soul when it goes thither. And the miserable, the poor the tearful, the alms-deserving helpless ones, and the orphan, will raise the triumphal song of Michael, giving fame and laud to Michael, the fair hero of power, and to the Father all-blessed and powerful, blessing the man and the woman in their sons and in their daughters, in their means, fame, and lot, in their cattle, and in their sheep, in the produce of their herds, and in the produce of their lands These are the people who are called "the humane men," "the compassionate men," and "the generous women," "the good women," who are taking mercy and compassion on the poor, and on the tearful, on the dejected and the despised, on the miserable alms-deserving. and on the orphans without pith, without power, without support, without breast-staff, without leaning-rod, formed in the image of the Father all-creative. And the surpassingly white angels of God, with their foot on tiptoe, their eye on the horizon, their ear on the ground, their wings flapping, their bodies trembling, are waiting to send announcement of the deed with a beat of their wings to the King of the throne everlasting.'

After the father and mother have distributed their gifts to the poor. the family mount their horses and set out on their pilgrimage to perform the circuiting of St Michael's burying-ground None remain at home save the very old and the very young, to whom is assigned for the day the duty of tending the sheep, herding the cattle, and guarding the corn The husband and wife ride on one horse, with probably a boy astride before the father and a girl sideways beside the mother filling up the measure of the horse's capacity A girl sits 'culag' behind her brother, or occasionally behind the brother of another girl, with her arm round him to steady her A little girl sits 'bialag' in front of a brother, with his hand lovingly round her waist, while with his other hand he guides the horse A little brother sits 'culag' behind his elder brother, with his two arms round him The people of the different hills, glens, islands, and townlands join the procession on the way, and all travel along together, the crowded cavalcade gaily clad in stuffs and stripes and tartans whose fineness of texture and brilliancy of colouring are charming to see, if impossible to describe. The air is full of salutations and cordialities Even the whinnying, neighing, restive horses seem to know and to feel that this is the Day of their patron saint the holy archangel,

'Michael mil nan steuda geala   The valiant Michael of the white steeds
Choisin cios air dragon fala.'   Who subdued the dragon of blood.

On reaching their destination the people crowd into and round the simple prayer-house. The doors and windows of the little oratory are open, and the people kneeling without join those kneeling within in earnest supplication that all may go well with them for the day. And commending themselves and their horses to the leading of the valiant, glorious archangel of the cornered shield and flaming sword, the people remount their horses to make 'cuartachadh a chlaidh,' the circuiting of the burial ground. The great crowd starts from the east and follows the course of the sun in the name of God, in the name of Christ, in the name of Spirit. The priest leads the way riding on a white horse, his grey hair and white robe waving in the autumn breeze Should there be more than one priest present they ride abreast. Should there be higher dignitaries they ride in front of, or between the priests The people follow in a column from two to ten abreast Those on horseback follow immediately behind the priest, those on foot behind these The fathers of the different townlands are stationed at intervals on either side of the procession, to maintain regularity and to guard against accidents All are imbued with a befitting reverence for the solemnity of the proceedings and of the occasion Families, friends, and neighbours try to keep together in the processional circuiting As they move from left to right the people raise the 'Iolach Micheil,' song of Michael the victorious, whose sword is keen to smite, and whose arm is strong to save. At the end of the circuit the 'culag' gives to her 'bialag,' 'glac churran,' a handful of carrots, saying —

'Rath agus rath air a laighe 's eiridh'   Progeny and prosperity on thy lying and rising

The 'bialag' acknowledges the gift in one of the many phrases common on the occasion —

'Piseach agus pais air an lamh a thug.   Progeny and peace on the hand that gave
Por agus pais dha mo ghradh a thug   Issue and peace on my love who gave
Piseach agus pailteas gun an aire na   Progeny and plenty without scarcity in thy
   d'chomhnuidh   dwelling.
Banas agus brioghas dha mo nighinn duinn   Wifehood and motherhood on my brown maid
Baireas agus buaidh dha mo luaidh a thug.'   Endowment and prosperity to my love who gave

Greetings, courtesies, and gifts are exchanged among the people, many of whom have not met since they met at the circuiting The most prized courtesy however, is a 'culag' round the burial-ground, and the most prized gift is a carrot with its customary wishes and acknowledgments Those who have no horses readily obtain them to make the circuiting, the consideration of those who have for those who have not being native and habitual

Having performed the processional pilgrimage round the graves of their fathers, the people hasten to the 'oda'—the scene of the athletics of the men and the racing of the horses The games and races excite much interest The riders in the races ride without bonnet, without shoes, clothed only in a shirt and 'triubhais bheag,' small trews like football trousers All ride without saddle, some without bridle, guiding and driving their horses with 'steamhag chaol chruaidh,' a hard slender tangle in each hand Occasionally girls compete with one another and sometimes with men They sit on either side as may be most convenient in mounting. They have no saddle, and how they retain their seat is inconceivable Some circuiting goes on all day, principally among the old and the young—the old teaching the young the mysteries of the circuiting and the customs of the olden times Here and there young men and maidens ride about and wander away, converting the sandy knolls and grassy dells of the fragrant 'machair' into Arcadian plains and Eden groves

On the night of St Michael a 'cuideachd,' ball, is held in every townland The leading piper selects the place for the ball, generally the house of largest size and of evenest floor Every man present contributes a sixpence, or its equivalent in farm produce, usually in grain, towards paying the piper if he be a married man, if not, he accepts nothing Several pipers, fiddlers, and players of other instruments relieve one another during the night. The small bets won at the 'oda' during the day are spent at the ball during the night, no one being allowed to retain his luck

The women put their bunches of carrots into white linen bags with the mark of the owner Having filled their 'crioslachain,' they leave the bags in some house convenient to the 'taigh dannsa,' dance-house. As their 'crioslachain' become empty during the night they replenish them from the 'falachain,' hidden store When a woman comes into the dance-house after refilling her 'crioslachan,' she announces her entrance with a rhyme, the refrain of which is—

' 'S ann agam fein a bhiodh na currain,	It is I myself that have the carrots,
Ga be co bhuinneadh bhuam iad '	Whoever he be that would win them from me
' 'S ann agam fein a bhiodh an ulaidh,	It is I myself that have the treasure,
Ge be 'n curaidh bheneadh bhuam e '	Whoso the hero could take them from me

At the circuiting by day and at the ball at night, youths and maidens exchange simple gifts in token of good feeling The girls give the men bonnets, hose, garters, cravats, purses, plaids, and other things of their own making, and the men give the girls brooches of silver, brass, bronze, or copper, knives, scissors, snoods, combs, mirrors, and various other things Some of these gifts are mentioned in the following verses :—

'N A GEALLAIDH	THE PROMISES
'Thug mo leannan dhomh sgian bheag A ghearradh am meangan goid, A ghearradh am bog 's an cruaidh, Saoghal buan dh 'an laimh a thug.	My lover gave to me a knife That would cut the sapling withe, That would cut the soft and hard, Long live the hand that gave.
Gheall mo leannan dhomh-sa stiom Gheall, agus braiste 's cir, 'S gheall mise comneamh ris Am bun a phris mu'n eireadh grian.	My lover promised me a snood, Ay, and a brooch and comb, And I promised, by the wood, To meet him at rise of sun
Gheall mo leannan dhomh-sa sgathan Anns am faicinn m'aille fein, Gheall, agus breid us fainne, Agus clarsach bhinn nan teud	My lover promised me a mirror That my beauty I might see, Yes, and a coif and ring, And a dulcet harp of choids.
Gheall e sid dhomh 's buaile bha, Agus falaire nan steud, Agus biulainn bheannach bhan, Readhadh slan thar chuan nam beud	He vowed me those and a fold of kine, And a palfrey of the steeds, And a barge, pinnacled white, That would safely cross the perilous seas.
Mile beannachd, mile buaidh Dha mo luaidh a dh'fhalbh an de, Thug e dhomh-sa 'n gealladh buan, Gu 'm b'e Bhuachaill-san Mac Dhe.'	A thousand blessings, a thousand victories To my lover who left me yestreen, He gave to me the promise lasting, Be his Shepherd God's own Son.

The song and the dance, the mirth and the merriment, are continued all night, many curious scenes being acted, and many curious dances performed, some of them in character. These scenes and dances are indicative of far-away times, perhaps of far-away climes. They are evidently symbolic One dance is called, 'Cailleach an Dudain,' cailin of the mill-dust This is a curious character-dance. The writer got it performed for him several times

It is danced by a man and a woman The man has a rod in his right hand, variously called 'slachdan druidheachd,' druidic wand, 'slachdan geasachd,' magic wand The man and the woman gesticulate and attitudinise before one another, dancing round and round, in and out, crossing and recrossing, changing and exchanging places. The man flourishes the wand over his own head and over the head of the woman, whom he touches with the wand, and who falls down, as if dead, at his feet He bemoans his dead 'carlin,' dancing and gesticulating round her body. He then lifts up her left hand, and looking into the palm, breathes upon it, and touches it with the wand. Immediately the limp hand becomes alive and moves from side to side and up and down The man rejoices, and dances round the figure on the floor. And having done the same to the right hand, and to the left and right foot in succession, they also become alive and move But although the limbs are living, the body is still inert The man kneels over the woman and breathes into her mouth and touches her heart with the wand. The woman comes to life and springs up, confronting the man. Then the two dance vigorously and joyously as in the first part. The tune varies with the varying phases of the dance It is played by a piper or a fiddler, or sung as a 'port-a-bial,' mouth tune, by a looker-on, or by the performers themselves The air is quaint and irregular, and the words are curious and archaic

In his *West Highland Tales*, Iain F. Campbell of Islay mentions that he saw 'cailleach an dudain' danced in the house of Lord Stanley of Alderley He does not say by whom it was danced, but probably it was by the gifted narrator himself. In October 1871, Mr Campbell spent some time with the writer and his wife in Uist When driving him to Lochmaddy, at the conclusion of his stay, I mentioned that there were two famous dancers of 'cailleach an dudain' at Clachan-a-ghluip We went to their bothy, but they were away. The neighbours told us that they were in the direction of Lochmaddy. When we reached there we went in search of them, but were unsuccessful Some hours afterwards, as I was coming up from the shore after seeing Mr. Campbell on board the packet for Dunvegan, I saw the two women racing down the hill, their long hair and short dresses flying wildly in the wind They had heard that we had been inquiring for them But it was too late. The packet, with Mr. Campbell on board, was already hoisting her sails and heaving her anchor

Another dance is called 'cath nan coileach,' the combat of the cocks, another, 'turraban nan tunnag,' waddling of the ducks, another, 'ruidhleadh nan coileach dubha,' reeling of the black-cocks; another, 'cath nan curaidh,' contest of the warriors, where a Celtic Saul slays his thousands, and a Celtic David his tens of thousands Many dances now lost were danced at the St. Michael ball, while those that still remain were danced with much more artistic complexity The sword-dance was performed in eight sections instead of in four, as now The reel of Tulloch was danced in eight figures with side issues, while 'seann triubhas' contained much more acting than it does now. Many beautiful and curious songs, now lost, were sung at these balls.

The young people who have individual 'strūans' give and receive and share them the night through, till sleep overcomes all.

Chiefs and chieftains, tacksmen and tenants, men and women, old and young, rich and poor, mingle in the pilgrimage, in the service, in the circuiting, in the games and races, in the dancing and the merry-making. The granddame of eighty and the granddaughter of eight, the grandsire of ninety and the grandson of nine, all take much interest in the festival of St. Michael. The old and the young who do not go to the ball entertain one another at their homes, exchanging 'strūans' and carrots and homely gifts in token of friendship and neighbourliness The pilgrimage, the service, the circuiting, and the games and races of the 'oda,' once so popular in the Western Isles, are now become obsolete. The last circuiting with service was performed in South Uist in 1820. It took place as usual round Cladh

Mhicheil, the burial-ground of Michael, near the centre of the island. The last great 'oda' in North Uist was in 1866, and took place on the customary spot, 'Traigh Mhoire,' the strand of Mary, on the west side of the island.

' Ach dh'fhalbh sud uile mar bhruadar,	But all that has gone like a vision,
Mar bhriseadh builgean air uachdar nan tonn.'	Like the breaking of a bubble on the surface of the sea.

　　The Michael lamb is sometimes slain, the Michael 'strūan' is sometimes baked, and the carrots are occasionally gathered, but the people can give no account of their significance. Probably the lamb and the 'strūan' represented the first-fruits of the flock and the fields, the circuiting and the sun-warding, ancestor-worship and sun-worship, and the carrots of the west the mandrakes of the east, ' given in the time of the wheat-harvest.'

　　The wives of husbandmen carried 'strūans' to the castles of the chiefs, and to the houses of the gentlemen in their neighbourhood, as marks of good-will. This was one of the many links in the social chain which bound chief and clansmen, proprietor and tenant together. In the past the chiefs and gentlemen and their families joined the people in their festivals, games and dances, secular amusements and religious observances, joys and sorrows, to the great good of all and to the stability of society. In the present, as a rule, the proprietors and gentlemen of the Highlands and Islands are at the best but temporary residents, if so much, and generally strangers in blood and speech, feeling and sympathy, more prone to criticise than to help, to scoff than to sympathise. As a result, the observances of the people have fallen into disuse, to the loss of the spiritual life of the country, and of the patriotic life of the nation.

HICHEAL nam buadh,
　　Cuartam fo d' dhion,
　　A Mhicheal nan stend geal,
　　'S nan leug lanna liomh,
　　Fhir bhuadhaich an dreagain,
　　Bi fein ri mo chul,
　　Fhir-chuartach nan speura,
　　Fhir-feuchd Righ nan dul,
　　　　A Mhicheal nam buadh,
　　　　M' uaill agus m' iuil,
　　　　A Mhicheal nam buadh,
　　　　Suamhnas mo shul.

Throughout the Highlands and Islands special cakes were made on the first day of the quarter As in the case of the 'strūan,' a large cake was made for the family and smaller cakes for individual members. So far as can now be ascertained, these cakes were round in form. They were named after their dedications. That baked for the first day of spring was called 'bonnach Bride,' bannock of Bride, that for the first day of summer, 'bonnach Bealltain,' Beltane bannock, that for the first day of autumn, 'bonnach Lunastain,' Lammas bannock, and that for the first day of winter, 'bonnach Samhthain,' Hallowtide bannock. The names of the individual cakes were rendered into diminutives to distinguish them from the family cake, while the sex of the person for whom they were intended was indicated by the termination, as 'Bridean,' masculine diminutive, 'Brideag,' feminine diminutive, after Bride, 'Bealltan,' 'Bealltag,' after Beltane; 'Lunean,' 'Luneag,' after Lammas, and 'Samhnan,' 'Samhnag,' after Hallowmas. The people repaired to the fields, glens, and corries to eat their quarter cakes. When eating them, they threw a piece over each shoulder alternately, saying 'Here to thee, wolf, spare my sheep, there to thee, fox, spare my lambs; here to thee, eagle, spare my goats; there to thee, raven, spare my kids; here to thee, marten, spare my fowls; there to thee, harrier, spare my chickens'

As may be seen from some of the poems, the duty of conveying the souls of the good to the abode of bliss is assigned to Michael. When the soul has parted from the body and is being weighed, the archangel of heaven and the archangel of hell preside at the beam, the former watching that the latter does not put 'crudhean laimhe na spun coise an coir na meidhe,' claw of hand nor talon of foot near the beam. Michael and all the archangels and angels of heaven sing songs of joy when the good in the soul outweighs the bad, while the devil howls as he retreats.

Thou Michael the victorious,
I make my circuit under thy shield,
Thou Michael of the white steed,
And of the bright brilliant blades,
Conqueror of the dragon,
Be thou at my back,
Thou ranger of the heavens,
Thou bright servant of God,
 O Michael the victorious,
 My pride and my guide,
 O Michael the victorious,
 The glory of mine eye

Deanam an cuarta‾
An cluanas mo naomh,
Air machair, air cluan domh,
Air fuar-bheanna fraoch,
Ged shiubhlam an cuan
'S an cruaidh cruinne-ce
Cha deifir domh gu sior
'S mi fo dhidionn do sgeith,
 A Mhicheal nam buadh,
 M' ailleagan cre,
 A Mhicheal nam buadh,
 Buachaille De

Tri Naomh na Gloire
Bhith 'n comhnuidh rium reidh
Ri m' eachraidh, ri m' lochraidh,
Ri cioba cloimh an treud.
Am barr ta fas air raona
No caonachadh an raoid,
Air machair no air mointeach,
An toit, an torr, no an cruach.
 Gach ni tha'n aird no'n iosal,
 Gach insridh agus buar,
 'S le Trithinn naomh na gloire,
 Agus Micheal corr nam buadh.

I make my circuit
In the fellowship of my saint,
On the machair, on the meadow,
On the cold heathery hill,
Though I should travel ocean
And hard globes of worlds,
No harm can e'er befall me
'Neath the shelter of thy shield,
 O Michael the victorious,
 Jewel of my heart,
 O Michael the victorious,
 God's shepherd thou art.

Be the sacred Three of Glory
Aye at peace with me,
With my horses, with my cattle,
With my woolly sheep in flocks
With the crops growing in the field
Or ripening in the sheaf,
On the machair, on the moor,
In cole, in heap, or stack
 Every thing on high or low,
 Every furnishing and flock,
 Belong to the holy Triune of glory,
 And to Michael the victorious.

AN BEANNACHADH STRŪAIN [78]

ACH min tha fo m' chleibh,
  Theid am measgadh le cheil,
  An ainm Mhic De,
    Thug fas daibh.

Bainn us uibheann us im,
Sochair mhath ar cuid fhin,
Cha bhi gainne n'ar tir,
  No n'ar fardraich.

An ainm Mhicheil mo luaidh,
Dh' fhag againn a bhuaidh,
Le beannachd an Uain,
  'S a Mhathar.

Umhlaich sinn aig do stol,
Biodh do chumraig fein oirnn,
Cum uainn fuath, fath, foirn,
  Agus gleidh sinn.

Coisrig toradh ar tir,
Bairig sonas us sith,
An ainm an Athar, an Righ,
  'S nan tri ostal gradhach.

THE BLESSING OF THE 'STRŪAN'

Each meal beneath my roof,   [wattle
They will all be mixed together,
In name of God the Son,
 Who gave them growth.

Milk, and eggs, and butter,
The good produce of our own flock,
There shall be no dearth in our land,
 Nor in our dwelling.

In name of Michael of my love,
Who bequeathed to us the power,
With the blessing of the Lamb,
 And of His Mother

Humble us at thy footstool,
Be thine own sanctuary around us,
Ward from us spectre, sprite, oppression,
 And preserve us.

Consecrate the produce of our land,
Bestow prosperity and peace,
In name of the Father the King,
 And of the three beloved apostles.

Bearnan bride, creamh min,
Lus-mor, glasrach us slim,
Na tri ghroigeanan-cinn,
 Us lus Mairi

Cailpeach ghlas au a buain,
Seachd-mhiarach, seachd uair,
Iubhar-beinne, fraoch ruadh,
 Agus madar.

Cuiream uisge orr gu leir,
An ainm usga Mhic De,
An ainm Mhuire na feil,
 Agus Phadruig

D'uair shuidheas sinn sios,
Gu gabhail ai biadh,
Cratham an ainme Dhia,
 Air na paisdean.

Dandelion, smooth garlic,
Foxglove, woad, and butterwort,
The three carle-doddies,
    And marigold.

Gray 'cailpeach' plucked,
The seven-pronged seven times,   .
The mountain yew, ruddy heath,
    And madder.

I will put water on them all,
In precious name of the Son of God,
In name of Mary the generous,
    And of Patrick.

When we shall sit down
To take our food,
I will sprinkle in the name of God
    On the children.

DUAN AN DOMHNUICH   [79]

This poem was obtained from Janet Currie, Staonabrig, South Uist, a descendant of the Macmhuirichs (corrupted into Currie) of Staoligearry, the famous poet-historians to the Clanranalds. She was a tall, strong, dark-haired, ruddy-complexioned woman, with a clear, sonorous

UAN an Domhnuich, a Dhe ghil,
Firinn fo neart Chriosd a chomhnuidh.

Di-domhnuich rugadh Muire,
Mathair Chriosd an or-fhuilt bhuidhe,
Di-domhnuich rugadh Criosda
      Mar onair dhaoine.

Di-domhnuich, an seachdamh latha,
Dh-orduich Dia gu fois a ghabhail,
Gu cumail na beath-maireannaich,
Gun feum a thoir a damh no duine,
No a creubh mar dheonaich Muire,
Gun sniamh snath sioda no strol,
Gun fuaigheal, gun ghreiseadh ni's mo,
Gun churachd, gun chliathadh, gun bhuain,
Gun iomaradh, gun iomairt, gun iasgaireachd,
Gun dol a mach dh' an t-sliabh sheilg,
Gun snaitheadh deilgne Di-domhnuich,
Gun chartadh taighe, gun bhualadh,
Gun atha, gun mhuileann Di-domhnuich.

THE POEM OF THE LORD'S DAY

voice. Her language was remarkably fluent and copious, though many of her words
and phrases, being obsolete, were unintelligible to the stranger I took down
versions of the poem from several other persons, but they are all more or less corrupt
and obscure Poems similar to this can be traced back to the eighth century

THE poem of the Lord's Day, O bright God,
Truth under the strength of Christ always.

On the Lord's Day Mary was born,
Mother of Christ of golden yellow hair,
On the Lord's Day Christ was born
    As an honour to men.

The Lord's Day, the seventh day,
God ordained to take rest,
To keep the life everlasting,
Without taking use of ox or man,
Or of creature as Mary desired,
Without spinning thread of silk or of satin,
Without sewing, without embroidery either,
Without sowing, without harrowing, without reaping,
Without rowing, without games, without fishing,
Without going out to the hunting hill,
Without trimming arrows on the Lord's Day,
Without cleaning byre, without threshing corn,
Without kiln, without mill on the Lord's Day.

Ge be chumadh an Domhnuch,
Bu chomhnard da-san 's bu bhuan,
Bho dhol fotha greine Di-Sathuirn
Gu eirigh greine Di-luain.

Gheobhadh e feich ga chionn,
Toradh an deigh nan crann,
Iasg air abhuinn fior-ghlan sala,
Sar iasg an ionnar gach abhuinn.

Uisg an Domhnuich blath mar mhil,
Ge be dh' oladh e mar dhibh
Gheobhadh e solas ga chion
Bho gach dolas a bhiodh na char.

Gul an Domhnuich gu ra-luath,
Bean ga dheanadh an an-uair;
Guileadh i gu moch Di-luain,
Ach na guileadh i uair 's an Domhnuch.

Fiodh an Domhnuich gu ra-luadh,
Anns an linnge mar is truagh,
Ge d' thuiteadh a cheann na ghual,
Bhiodh e gu Di-luain na chadal.
Mu thiath-nona Di-luain,
Eiridh am fiodh gu ra-luath,
'S air an dile mhor a muigh
Greas air sgeula mo chuimire,
Gun chnuasachd uan, meile, meinne no minsich
Nach buineadh dh' an Righ anns a bhlagh.
Is ann a nist bu choir a losgadh,
Gun eisdeachd ri gleadhraich nan gall,
No ri dall sgeileireachd choitchinn.

Whosoever would keep the Lord's Day,
Even would it be to him and lasting,
From setting of sun on Saturday
Till rising of sun on Monday

He would obtain recompense therefrom,
Produce after the ploughs,
Fish on the pure salt-water stream,
Fish excelling in every river confluence

The water of the Lord's Day mild as honey,
Whoso would partake of it as drink
Would obtain health in consequence
From every disease afflicting him.

The weeping of the Lord's Day is out of place,
A woman doing it is untimely ;
Let her weep betimes on Monday,
But not weep once on the Lord's Day

The wood of the Lord's Day is too soon
In the pool it is pitiful,
Though its head should fall in char,
It would till Monday be dormant.
About noon on the Monday,
The wood will arise very quickly,
And by the great flood without
Hasten the story of my trouble
Without any searching for lamb, sheep, kid or goat
That would not belong to the King in the cause.
It is now it ought to be burnt,
Without listening to the clamour of the stranger,
Nor to the blind babbling of the public.

Gart a ghleidheadh air cnoc ard,
Leigh a thoir gu galar garga,
Bo chur gu tarbh treun na tana,
Falbh le beothach gu cuthaidh,
Fada no fagasg anns a cheum,
Feumaidh gach creatair umhail.
Eathar a leigeil fo breid-shinil bho thir,
Bho thir gu duthaich a h-aineoil.

Ge be mheoraicheadh mo dhuan,
'S a ghabhadh e gach oidhche Luan,
Bhiodh rath Mhicheil air a cheann,
'S a chaoidh cha bu teann da Irionn.

DOIGHEAN EILE—

Abhuinn sleibh fior bhlasda,
A sior iadhladh gu Iordan,
Is ra mhath chum i a cain,
　　Di-domhnuich ge lan a tuil.

Cha ruith braon ge glan a h-uisge,
An inne na Mara Ruaidh

Fiodh an Domhnuich nis, mo nuar !
An inne na Mara Ruaidh
Ged thuiteadh an ruadh-cheann deth
　　Bhiodh e gu Di-luain na chadal.

Na fagairt mi ni air mo dheigh,
Greis thoir air sgeula mo chumraidh.

To keep corn on a high hillock,
To bring physician to a violent disease,
To send a cow to the potent bull of the herd,
To go with a beast to a cattle-fold,
Far or near be the distance,
Every creature needs attention.
To allow a boat under her sail from land,
From land to the country of her unacquaintance.

Whoso would meditate my lay,
And say it every Monday eve,
The luck of Michael would be on his head,
And never would he see perdition.

ALTERNATIVE VERSIONS—

Hill river is very palatable,
Ever meandering to Jordan,
Right well it retained its tribute
    On the Lord's Day though great its flood

No drop, though pure be its water,
Shall run in the channel of the Red Sea.

The wood of the Lord's Day now, alas!
In the channel of the Red Sea,
Though the red head should fall off
    It would be till Monday asleep.

Let me not leave aught behind,
To talk a while of the redemption.

DUAN AN DOMHNAICH   [80]

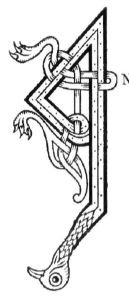

N Domhnach naomha do Dhe
 Tabhair do chre dh' an chinne-daon,
 Do t' athair us do d' mhathair chaomh,
 Thar gach aon 's gach ni 's an t-saoghal.

 Na dean sainn air mhor no bheag,
 Na dean tair air tais no truaigh,
 Fiamh an uile a d' choir na leig,
 Na tabhair 's na toill masladh uair.

 Na deich fana thug Dia duit,
 Tuig gun dail iad agus dearbh,
 Creid direach an Righ nan dul,
 Cuir air chul uidh thoir a dhealbh.

 Bi dileas da d' thighearna-cinn,
 Bi dileas da d' righ 's gach eang,
 Bi dileas duit fein a ris,
 Dileas da d' Ard Righ thar gach dreang.

 Na tabhair toi'eum do neach air bith,
 An earail toi'eum a thoir ort fein,
 'S ged shiubhladh tu cuan us cith,
 Lean cas-cheum Aon-unga Dhe.

HYMN OF THE SUNDAY

On the holy Sunday of thy God
Give thou thine heart to all mankind,
To thy father and thy mother loving,
Beyond any person or thing in the world.

Do not covet large or small,
Do not despise weakling or poor,
Semblance of evil allow not near thee,
Never give nor earn thou shame.

The ten commands God gave thee,
Understand them early and prove,
Believe direct in the King of the elements,
Put behind thee ikon-worship.

Be faithful to thine over-lord,
Be true to thy king in every need,
Be true to thine own self besides,
True to thy High-King above all obstacles.

Do not thou malign any man,
Lest thou thyself maligned shouldst be,
And shouldst thou travel earth and ocean,
Follow the very step of God's Anointed.

DUAN NA DILINN [81]

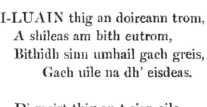

DI-LUAIN thig an doireann trom,
A shileas am bith eutrom,
Bithidh sinn umhail gach greis,
Gach uile na dh' eisdeas.

Di-mairt thig an t-sian eile,
Cradh chridheach, cruaidh pheinneach,
A shileas na gruaidheana glana,
Frasa fala fiona.

Di-ciadain a sheideas gaoth,
Sguaba lom air shrath us raon,
Dortadh oiteag barra theann,
Beithir bheur 's reubadh bheann.

Di-ardaoin a shileas an cith,
Chuireas daoine n'an dalla ruith,
Na 's luaithe na'n duil air an fhiodh,
Mar bharr mhic-Muir air bhalla-chrith.

Di-haoine thig an coinneal dubh,
Is eitiche thaimg fo'n t-saoghal,
Fagar an sluagh braon am beachd,
Fiar agus iasg fo'n aon leachd.

POEM OF THE FLOOD

On Monday will come the great storm
Which the firmament will pour,
We shall be obedient the while,
    All who will hearken.

On Tuesday will come the other element,
Heart paining, hard piercing,
Wringing from pure pale cheeks
    Blood, like showers of wine.

On Wednesday will blow the wind,
Sweeping bare strath and plain,
Showering gusts of galling grief,
    Thunder bursts and rending hills.

On Thursday will pour the element
Driving people into blind flight,
Faster than the foliage on the trees,
    Like the leaves of Mary's plant in terror trembling.

On Friday will come the dool cloud of darkness,
The direst dread that ever came over the world,
Leaving multitudes bereft of reason,
    Grass and fish beneath the same flagstone.

AIMSIRE

Di-sathuirne thig am muir mor,
Ag iomairt air alt aibhne,
Bithidh gach uile mai a shnodh,
    Ag altachadh gu sliabh slighinn

Di-domhnaich a dh' eireas mo Righ,
Lan feirge agus minidh,
Ag eisdeachd ri searbh ghloir gach fir,
    Crois dhearg air gach guala dheis.

On Saturday will come the great sea,
Rushing like a mighty river,
All will be at their best,
    Hastening to a hill of safety.

On Sunday will arise my King,
Full of ire and tribulation,
Listening to the bitter maudlin of each man,
    A red cross on each right shoulder.

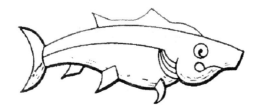

III

OIBRE

LABOUR

BEANNACHADH BEOTHACHAIDH   [82]

THE kindling of the fire is a work full of interest to the housewife. When 'lifting'
the fire in the morning the woman prays, in an undertone, that the fire may be
blessed to her and to her household, and to the glory of

TOGAIDH mi mo theine an diugh,
  An lathair ainghlean naomha neimh,
  An lathair Airil is ailde cruth,
  An lathair Uiril nan uile sgeimh.
  Gun ghnu, gun tnu, gun fharmad.
  Gun ghiomh, gun gheimh roimh neach fo'n ghrein,
  Ach Naomh Mhac De da m' thearmad.
    Gun ghnu, gun tnu, gun fharmad,
    Gun ghiomh, gun gheimh, roimh neach fo'n
      ghrein,
    Ach Naomh Mhac De da m' thearmad.

  Dhe fadaidh fein na m' chridhe steach,
  Aingheal ghraidh do m' choimhearsnach,
  Do m' namh, do m' dhamh, do m' chairde,
  Do 'n t-saoidh, do 'n daoidh, do 'n traille.
  A Mhic na Moire min-ghile,
  Bho'n ni is isde crannachaire,
  Gu ruig an t-Ainm is airde.
    A Mhic na Moire min-ghile,
    Bho 'n ni is isde crannachaire,
    Gu ruig an t-Ainm is airde.

BLESSING OF THE KINDLING

God who gave it The people look upon fire as a miracle of Divine power provided for their good—to warm their bodies when they are cold, to cook their food when they are hungry, and to remind them that they too, like the fire, need constant renewal mentally and physically

I WILL kindle my fire this morning
In presence of the holy angels of heaven,
In presence of Ariel of the loveliest form,
In presence of Uriel of the myriad charms,
Without malice, without jealousy, without envy,
Without fear, without terror of any one under the sun,
But the Holy Son of God to shield me.

    Without malice, without jealousy, without envy,
    Without fear, without terror of any one under the
      sun,
    But the Holy Son of God to shield me

God, kindle Thou in my heart within
A flame of love to my neighbour,
To my foe, to my friend, to my kindred all,
To the brave, to the knave, to the thrall,
O Son of the loveliest Mary,
From the lowliest thing that liveth,
To the Name that is highest of all.

    O Son of the loveliest Mary,
    From the lowliest thing that liveth,
    To the Name that is highest of all.

TOGAIL AN TEINE [83]

OGA mis an tulla
 Mar a thogadh Muire.
 Caim Bhride 's Mhuire
 Air an tulla 's air an lar,
 'S air an fhardraich uile.

 Co iad ri luim an lair ?
 Eoin, Peadail agus Pail.
 Co iad ri bruaich mo leap ?
 Bride bhuidheach 's a Dalt.
 Co iad ri fath mo shuain ?
 Muire ghraidh-gheal 's a h-Uan.
 Co siud a tha na m' theann ?
 Righ na grein e fein a th' ann,
 Co siud ri cul mo chinn ?
 Mac nan dul gun tus, gun linn.

KINDLING THE FIRE

I will raise the hearth-fire
As Mary would
The encirclement of Bride and of Mary
On the fire, and on the floor,
And on the household all.

Who are they on the bare floor?
John and Peter and Paul.
Who are they by my bed?
The lovely Bride and her Fosterling.
Who are those watching over my sleep?
The fair loving Mary and her Lamb.
Who is that anear me?
The King of the sun, He himself it is.
Who is that at the back of my head?
The Son of Life without beginning, without time

SMALADH AN TEINE   [84]

PEAT is the fuel of the Highlands and Islands. Where wood is not obtainable the fire is kept in during the night. The process by which this is accomplished is called in Gaelic smaladh; in Scottish, smooring; and in English, smothering, or more correctly, subduing. The ceremony of smooring the fire is artistic and symbolic, and is performed with loving care. The embers are evenly spread on the hearth—which is generally in the middle of the floor—and formed into a circle. This circle is then divided into three equal sections, a small boss being left in the middle.

A peat is laid between each section, each peat touching the boss, which forms a common centre. The first peat is laid down in name of the God of Life, the second in name of the God of Peace, the third in name of the God of Grace. The circle is then covered over with ashes

N Tri numh

     A chumhnadh,

     A chomhnadh,

     A chomraig

     An tula,

     An taighe,

     An taghlaich,

     An oidhche,

     An nochd,

     O ! an oidhche,

     An nochd,

     Agus gach oidhche,

     Gach aon oidhche.

             Amen.

SMOORING THE FIRE

sufficient to subdue but not to extinguish the fire, in name of the Three of Light. The heap slightly raised in the centre is called 'Tulla nan Tri,' the Hearth of the Three When the smooring operation is complete the woman closes her eyes, stretches her hand, and softly intones one of the many formulæ current for these occasions

Another way of keeping embers for morning use is to place them in a pit at night. The pit consists of a hole in the clay floor, generally under the dresser The pit may be from half a foot to a foot in depth and diameter, with a flag fixed in the floor over the top In the centre of this flag there is a hole by which the embers are put in and taken out. Another flag covers the hole to extinguish the fire at night, and to guard against accidents during the day. This extinguishing fire-pit is called 'slochd guail,' coke or coal-pit. This coke or charcoal is serviceable in kindling the fire.

THE sacred Three
To save,
To shield,
To surround
The hearth,
The house,
The household.
This eve.
This night,
Oh! this eve,
This night,
And every night,
Each single night.
                    Amen.

SMALADH AN TEINE   [85]

AIRIDH mi an tula,
Mar a chaireadh Muire,
Caim Bhride 's Mhuire,
Car an tula 's car an lair,
'S car an fhardraich uile.

Co iad air lian a muigh ?
Micheal grian-gheal mo luin.
Co iad air meadhon lair ?
Eoin, Peadail, agus Pail.
Co iad ri bial mo stoc ?
Moire ghrian-gheal 's a Mac.

Bial Dia dh' orduich,
Aingheal Dia bhoinich,
Aingheal geal an car an tealla,
Go'n tig la geal gu beola.
Aingheal geal an car an tealla,
Go'n tig la geal gu beola.

SMOORING THE FIRE

I will build the hearth,
As Mary would build it
The encompassment of Bride and of Mary,
Guarding the hearth, guarding the floor,
Guarding the household all.

Who are they on the lawn without?
Michael the sun-radiant of my trust.
Who are they on the middle of the floor?
John and Peter and Paul.
Who are they by the front of my bed?
Sun-bright Mary and her Son.

The mouth of God ordained,
The angel of God proclaimed,
An angel white in charge of the hearth
Till white day shall come to the embers
An angel white in charge of the hearth
Till white day shall come to the embers.

BEANNACHD SMALAIDH   [86]

THA mi smaladh an teine,
    Mar a smaladh Mac Moire,
Gu mu slan dh' an taigh 's dh' an teine,
    Gu mu slan dh' an chuideachd uile.

Co siud shios air an lar?
Eoin agus Peadail agus Pal.
Co air am bheil an fhaire nochd?
    Air Moire mhin-gheal 's air a Mac.

Beul De a thubhradh,
Aingheal De a labhradh,
Aingheal an dorus an taighe,
D'ar comhnadh 's d'ar gleidheadh
    Gu 'n tig la geal am maireach.

O! ainghlean Aon Naomha Dhe
Da mo chaimhleachadh fein a nochd,
O! ainghlean Aon Unga Dhe,
Da mo chaim bho bheud 's bho lochd,
    Da mo chaim bho bheud a nochd.

BLESSING OF THE SMOORING

I am smooring the fire
As the Son of Mary would smoor,
Blest be the house, blest be the fire,
    Blest be the people all.

Who are those down on the floor?
John and Peter and Paul.
On whom is the vigil to-night?
    On the fair gentle Mary and on her Son

The mouth of God said,
The angel of God spake,
An angel in the door of the house,
To guard and to keep us all
    Till comes daylight to-morrow.

Oh! may the angels of the Holy One of God
Environ me all this night,
Oh! may the angels of the Anointed One of God
Encompass me from harm and from evil,
    Oh! encompass me from harm this night.

BEANNACHADH SMALAIDH [87]

MALAIDH mis an tula
Mar a smaladh Muire,
Comraig Bhride 's Mhuire,
Air an tula 's air an lar,
    'S air an fhardraich uile.

Co siud air liana mach ?
Muire ghrian-gheal 's a Mac,
Bial Dia dh' iarradh, aingheal Dia labhradh ;
Ainghle geallaidh faire an teallaidh,
    Gu'n tig latha geal gu beallaidh.

SMOORING BLESSING

I will smoor the hearth
As Mary would smoor,
The encompassment of Bride and of Mary,
On the fire and on the floor,
    And on the household all.

Who is on the lawn without?
Fairest Mary and her Son,
The mouth of God ordained, the angel of God spoke;
Angels of promise watching the hearth,
    Till white day comes to the fire.

AN COISRIGEADH SIOIL   [88]

THE preparation of the seed-corn is of great importance to the people, who bestow much care on this work. Many ceremonies and proverbs are applied to seedtime and harvest.

The corn is prepared at certain seasons of the year, which are seldom deviated from. The rye is threshed to allow 'gaoth bhog nan Duldachd,' the soft wind of November and December, to winnow the seed; the oats to allow 'gaoth fhuar nam Faoilleach,' the cold winds of January and February, to winnow the seed; and the bere to allow 'gaoth gheur nam Mart,' the sharp winds of March and

HEID mi mach a chur an t-sioil,
    An ainm an Ti a thug da fas,
    Cuirim m' aghaidh anns a ghaoith,
    Us tilgim baslach caon an aird.
    Ma thuiteas sile air lic luim,
    Cha bhi fuinn aige gu fas;
    Mheud 's a thuiteas anns an uir,
    Bheir an druchd dha a bhi lan.

Di-aoine la nam buadh,
Thig dealt a nuas a chur failt
Air gach por a bha n'an suain,
Bho na thainig fuachd gun bhaigh,
Riamhaichidh gach por 's an uir,
Mar a mhiannaich Righ nan dul,
Thig an fochann leis an druchd,
Gheobh e beatha bho 'n ghaoith chiuin.

Thig mi mu 'n cuairt le m' cheum,
Theid mi deiseil leis a ghrein,
An ainm Airil 's nan aingeal naodh,
An ainm Ghabril 's nan ostal caomh.

THE CONSECRATION OF THE SEED

April, to winnow the seed. All these preparations are made to assist Nature in the coming Spring Three days before being sown the seed is sprinkled with clear cold water, in the name of Father, and of Son, and of Spirit, the person sprinkling the seed walking sunwise the while.

The ritual is picturesque, and is performed with great care and solemnity, and, like many of these ceremonies, is a combination of Paganism and Christianity.

The moistening of the seed has the effect of hastening its growth when committed to the ground, which is generally begun on a Friday, that day being auspicious for all operations not necessitating the use of iron

I WILL go out to sow the seed,
In name of Him who gave it growth ;
I will place my front in the wind,
And throw a gracious handful on high
Should a grain fall on a bare rock,
It shall have no soil in which to grow ;
As much as falls into the earth,
The dew will make to be full.

Friday, day auspicious,
The dew will come down to welcome
Every seed that lay in sleep
Since the coming of cold without mercy,
Every seed will take root in the earth,
As the King of the elements desired,
The braird will come forth with the dew,
It will inhale life from the soft wind.

I will come round with my step,
I will go rightways with the sun,
In name of Ariel and the angels nine.
In name of Gabriel and the Apostles kind.

Athair us Mac us Spiorad Naomh,
Bhi toir fas us toradh maoth
Do gach cail a ta na m' raon,
Go 'n tar an latha caon.

La Fheill-Micheil, la nam buadh,
Cuiridh mi mo chorran cuart
Bun an aibhair mar bu dual,
Togam an ceud bheum gu luath,
Cuirim e tri char mu 'n cuart
Mo cheann, 's mo rann ga luadh,
Mo chulaibh ris an airde tuath,
'S mo ghnuis ri grein ghil nam buadh

Tilgim am beum fada bhuam,
Duinim mo dha shuil da uair,
Ma thuiteas e na aon dual
Bithidh mo chruachan biochar buan,   [mhulain
Cha tig Cailleach ri an-uair
Dh' iarraidh bonnach boise bhuainn,
Duair thig gaillionn garbh na gruaim
Cha bhi gainne oirnn no cruas

Father, Son, and Spirit Holy,
Be giving growth and kindly substance
To every thing that is in my ground,
Till the day of gladness shall come.

The Feast Day of Michael, day beneficent,
I will put my sickle round about
The root of my corn as was wont;
I will lift the first cut quickly,
I will put it three turns round
My head, saying my rune the while,
My back to the airt of the north,
My face to the fair sun of power

I shall throw the handful far from me,
I shall close my two eyes twice,
Should it fall in one bunch
My stacks will be productive and lasting,
No Cailin will come with bad times
To ask a palm bannock from us,
What time rough storms come with frowns
Nor stint nor hardship shall be on us.

BEANNACHADH BUANA　　　　　[89]

The day the people began to reap the corn was a day of commotion and cere-
monial in the townland.　The whole family repaired to the field dressed in their best
attire, to hail the God of the harvest.

Laying his bonnet on the ground, the father of the family took up his sickle,
and, facing the sun, he cut a handful of corn.　Putting the handful of corn
three times sunwise round his head, the man raised the 'Iollach Buana,'
reaping salutation.　The whole family took up the strain
and praised the God of the harvest, who gave them

HE beannaich fein mo bhuain,
　Gach imir, cluan, agus raon,
Gach corran cama, cuimir, cruaidh,
　Gach dias us dual a theid 's an raoid,
　　Gach dias us dual a theid 's an raoid.

Beannaich gach murn agus mac,
　Gach mnui agus miuchainn maoth,
Tiuir iad fo sgiath do neairt,
Us tearmaid ann an teach nan naomh,
　Tearmaid ann an teach nan naomh.

Cuimrich gach mins, ciob, us uan,
Gach ni, agus mearc, us maon,
Cuartaich fein an treuid 's am buar,
Us cuallaich a chon buailidh chaon,
　Cuallaich a chon buailidh chaon.

Air sgath Mhicheil mhil nam feachd,
Mhoire chneas-ghil leac nam buadh,
Bhride mhin-ghil ciobh nan cleachd,
Chaluim-chille nam feart 's nan tuam,
　Chaluim-chille nam feart 's nan tuam.

REAPING BLESSING

corn and bread, food and flocks, wool and clothing, health and strength and peace and plenty

When the reaping was finished the people had a trial called 'cur nan corran,' casting the sickles, and 'deuchain chorran,' trial of hooks. This consisted, among other things, of throwing the sickles high up in the air, and observing how they came down, how each struck the earth, and how it lay on the ground. From these observations the people augured who was to remain single and who was to be married who was to be sick and who was to die, before the next reaping came round

God, bless Thou Thyself my reaping.
Each ridge, and plain, and field,
Each sickle curved, shapely, hard,
Each ear and handful in the sheaf,
 Each ear and handful in the sheaf.

Bless each maiden and youth,
Each woman and tender youngling,
Safeguard them beneath Thy shield of strength,
And gird them in the house of the saints,
 Gird them in the house of the saints.

Encompass each goat, sheep and lamb,
Each cow and horse, and store,
Surround Thou the flocks and herds,
And tend them to a kindly fold,
 Tend them to a kindly fold.

For the sake of Michael head of hosts.
Of Mary fair-skinned branch of grace.
Of Bride smooth-white of ringleted locks,
Of Columba of thegraves and tombs,
 Columba of the graves and tombs.

21

BEANNACHADH BUANA [90]

I-MAIRT feille ri eirigh greine,
Us cul na deise 's an aird an ear,
Theid mi mach le m' chorran fo m' sgeith,
Us buainidh mi am beum an ceud char.

Leigidh mi mo chorran sios,
'S an dias biachar fo mo ghlac,
Togam suas mo shuil an aird,
Tionndam air mo shail gu grad,

Deiseil mar thriallas a ghrian,
Bho 'n airde 'n ear gu ruig an iar,
Bho 'n airde tuath le gluasadh reidh,
Gu fior chre na h-airde deas.

Bheir mi cliu do Righ nan gras,
Airson cinneas barr na h-uir,
Bheir e lon dhuinn fein 's dh' an al
Mar a bhairigeas e dhuinn.

Seumas us Eoin, Peadail us Pal,
Moire ghraidh-gheal lan soluis,
  * * * *

  * * * *

Oidhch Fheill-Micheil agus Nollaig,
Blasaidh sinn uile dhe 'n bhonnach.

REAPING BLESSING

On Tuesday of the feast at the rise of the sun,
And the back of the ear of corn to the east,
I will go forth with my sickle under my arm,
And I will reap the cut the first act

I will let my sickle down,   ,
While the fruitful ear is in my grasp,
I will raise mine eye upwards,
I will turn me on my heel quickly,

Rightway as travels the sun,
From the airt of the east to the west,
From the airt of the north with motion slow
To the very core of the airt of the south.

I will give thanks to the King of grace,
For the growing crops of the ground,
He will give food to ourselves and to the flocks
According as He disposeth to us.

James and John, Peter and Paul,
Mary beloved the fulness of light,
  *   *   *   *

   *   *   *   *

On Michaelmas Eve and Christmas,
We will all taste of the bannock.

BEANNACHADH FUIRIRIDH [91]

WHEN it is necessary to provide a small quantity of meal hastily, ears of corn are plucked and placed in a net made of the tough roots of the yellow bedstraw, bent, or quicken grass, and hung above a slow smokeless fire. The bag is taken down now and again to turn the ears of corn. This net, however, can only be used for bere or barley; rye and oats,

LASAIR leith, chaol, chrom,
Tighinn a toll mhullach nam fod,
A lasair leumrach, leathann, theith,
Na teid le do chleid da m' choir.

Gabhail reidh, sheimh, shuairce,
Tighinn mu 'n cuart mo thetheann,
Teine cubhr, caon, cuana,
Nach dean smur, no smuar, no reubann.

Teasaich, cruadhaich mo shiol miamh,
Chon biadh dha mo leanu-beag,
An ainm Chriosda, Righ nan sian,
Thug duinn iodh, us iadh, us beannachd leis,
     An ainm Chriosda, Righ nan sian,
         Thug duinn iodh, us iadh, us beannachd leis.

THE BLESSING OF THE PARCHING

being more detachable, require the use of a pot or 'tarian' to dry them. This mode of drying corn is called 'fuiireadh,' parching, and the corn 'fuirireach,' parched. The meal ground from the grain is called 'min fhuiiridh,' parched meal. Bread made of meal thus prepared has a strong peaty flavour much relished by the people

> THOU flame grey, slender, curved,
> Coming from the top pore of the peat,
> Thou flame of leaps, breadth, heat,
> Come not nigh me with thy quips.
>
> A burning steady, gentle, generous,
> Coming round about my quicken roots,
> A fire fragrant, fair, and peaceful,
> Nor causes dust, nor grief, nor havoc.
>
> Heat, parch my fat seed,
> For food for my little child,
> In name of Christ, King of the elements,
> Who gave us corn and bread and blessing withal,
> In name of Christ, King of the elements,
> Who gave us corn and bread and blessing withal.

BEANNACHADH BRATHAIN [92]

THE quern songs, like all the labour songs of the people, were composed in a measure suited to the special labour involved. The measure changed to suit the rhythmic motion of the body at work, at times slow, at times fast, as occasion required. I first saw the quern at work in October 1860 in the house of a cottar at Fearann-an-leatha, Skye. The cottar-woman procured some oats in the sheaf. Roughly evening the heads, and holding the corn in one hand and a rod in the other, she set fire to the ears. Then, holding the corn over an old partially-dressed sheep-skin, she switched off the grain. This is called 'gradanadh,' quickness, from the expert handling required in the operation. The whole straw of the sheaf was not burnt, only that part of the straw to which the grain was attached, the flame being kept from proceeding further. The straw was tied up and used for other purposes.

Having fanned the grain and swept the floor, the woman spread out the sheep-skin again and placed the quern thereon. She then sat down to grind, filling and relieving the quern with one hand and turning it with the other, singing the while to the accompaniment of the whirr! whirr! whirr! birr! birr! birr! of the revolving stone. Several strong sturdy boys in scant kilts, and sweet comely girls in nondescript frocks, sat round the peat fire enjoying it fully, and watching the work and listening to the song of their radiant mother.

In a remarkably short space of time the grain from the field was converted into meal, and the meal into bannocks, which the unknown stranger was pressed to share. The bread was good and palatable, though with a slight taste of peat, which would probably become pleasant in time.

The second time I saw the quern at work was in January 1865, in the house of a crofter at Breubhaig, Barra, and it reminded me of Mungo Park's description of a similar scene in Africa. The quern was on the floor, with a well-worn cow-hide under it. Two women sat opposite one another on the floor with the quern between them. The right leg of each was stretched out, while the knee of the other leg formed a

IDHCH Inid

Bi feoil againn,
'S bu choir 'uinn sin
Bu choir 'uinn sin.

Leth-cheann circe,
'S da ghreim eorna,
'S bu leoir 'uinn sin
Bu leoir 'uinn sin.

THE QUERN BLESSING

sharp angle, with the foot resting against the knee-joint of the straight leg A fan containing bere lay beside the women, and from this one of them fed the quern, while the other relieved it of the constantly accumulating meal Each woman held the 'sgonnan,' handle, with which they turned the quern, and as they turned they sang the Quern Blessing here given, to a very pretty air. Then they sang an impromptu song on the stranger, who was hungry and cold, and who was far from home and from the mother who loved him

When mills were erected, the authorities destroyed the querns in order to compel the people to go to the mills and pay multure, mill dues   This wholesale and inconsiderate destruction of querns everywhere entailed untold hardships on thousands of people living in roadless districts and in distant isles without mills, especially during storms   Among other expedients to which the more remote people resorted was the searching of ancient ruins for the 'pollagan,' mortar mills, of former generations   The mortar is a still more primitive instrument for preparing corn than the quern   It is a block of stone about twenty-four inches by eighteen by eight   The centre and one end of this block are hollowed out to a breadth of about six or eight inches, and a depth of four or five, leaving three gradually sloping sides. The grain is placed in this scoop-like hollow and crushed with a stone.   When sufficiently crushed, the meal is thrown out at the open end of the scoop, and fresh grain is put in to follow a similar process   When using the mortar, the woman is on her knees, unless the mortar is on a table

The meal obtained by this process is called 'pronn, pronnt, pronntach, min phronntaidh,' bruised meal, to distinguish it from 'gradan, gradanach, min ghradain,' quick meal, 'min bhrath, min bhrathain,' quern meal, and 'min mhuille,' mill meal The crushed meal of the primitive mortar is similar in character to the crushed meal of modern commerce

The quern and mortar are still used in outlying districts of Scotland and Ireland, though isolatedly and sparingly

> On Ash Eve
> We shall have flesh,
> We should have that
> We should have that
>
> The cheek of hen,
> Two bits of barley,
> That were enough
> That were enough.

Bi bin againn,
Bi beoir againn,
Bi fion againn,
Bi roic agamn.
Meilc us marrum,
Mil us bainne,
Sile fallain,
Meall dheth sin,
Meall dheth sin.

Bi cruit againn,
Bi clar againn,
Bi dus againn,
Bi das againn,
Bi saltair ghrinn,
Nan teuda binn,
'S bi faiichil, righ'nn
Nan dan againn
Nan dan againn.

Bi Bride bhithe, bhana, leinn,
Bi Moire mhine mhathar, leinn.
Bi Micheal mil
Nan lanna hobh,
'S bi Righ nan righ,
'S bi Iosa Criosd
'S bith Spiorad sith
Nan grasa leinn
Nan grasa leinn.

We shall have mead,
We shall have spruce,
We shall have wine,
We shall have feast,
We shall have sweetness and milk produce,
Honey and milk,
Wholesome ambrosia,
Abundance of that,
Abundance of that.

We shall have harp,   (small ?)
We shall have harp,   (pedal ?)
We shall have lute,
We shall have horn. ·
We shall have sweet psaltery
Of the melodious strings
And the regal lyre,
Of the songs we shall have,
Of the songs we shall have.

The calm fair Bride will be with us,
The gentle Mary mother will be with us.
Michael the chief
Of glancing glaves,
And the King of kings
And Jesus Christ,
And the Spirit of peace
And of grace will be with us,
Of grace will be with us.

CRONAN BLEOGHAIN   [93]

THE milking songs of the people are numerous and varied.   They are sung to
pretty airs, to please the cows and to induce them to give their milk.   The cows
become accustomed to these lilts and will not give their milk without them, nor,
occasionally, without their favourite airs being sung to them.   This fondness of
Highland cows for music induces owners of large herds to secure milkmaids
possessed of good voices and some 'go.'   It is interesting and animating to see
three or four comely girls among a fold of sixty, eighty, or a hundred picturesque
Highland cows on meadow or mountain slope.   The moaning and heaving of the

HIG a Bhreannain o'n a chuan,
    Thig a Thorrainn buadh nam fear,
    Thig a Mhicheil mhil a nuas
    'S dilinn domh-sa bua mo ghean.
        Ho m' aghan, ho m' agh gaoil,
        Ho m' aghan, ho m' agh gaoil,
        M' aghan gradhach, bo gach airidh,
        Sgath an Ard Righ gabh ri d' laogh.

    Thig a Chaluim chaoimh o'n chro,
    Thig a Bhride mhor nam buar,
    Thig a Mhoire mhin o'n neol,
    'S dilinn domh-sa bo mo luaidh.
        Ho m' aghan, ho m' agh gaoil.

    Thig am fearan o'n a choill,
    Thig an traill a druim nan stuagh,
    Thig an sionn cha 'n ann am foill,
    A chur aoibh air bo nam buadh.
        Ho m' aghan, ho m' agh gaoil.

MILKING CROON

sea afar, the swish of the wave on the shore, the carolling of the lark in the sky, the unbroken song of the mavis on the rock, the broken melody of the merle in the brake, the lowing of the kine without, the response of the calves within the fold, the singing of the milkmaids in unison with the movement of their hands, and of the soft sound of the snowy milk falling into the pail, the gilding of hill and dale, the glowing of the distant ocean beyond, as the sun sinks into the sea of golden glory, constitute a scene which the observer would not, if he could, forget

Come, Brendan, from the ocean,
Come, Ternan, most potent of men,
Come, Michael valiant, down
And propitiate to me the cow of my joy.
 Ho my heifer, ho heifer of my love,
 Ho my heifer, ho heifer of my love.
 My beloved heifer, choice cow of every sheiling,
 For the sake of the High King take to thy calf.

Come, beloved Colum of the fold,
Come, great Bride of the flocks,
Come, fair Mary from the cloud,
And propitiate to me the cow of my love.
 Ho my heifer, ho heifer of my love.

The stock-dove will come from the wood,
The tusk will come from the wave,
The fox will come but not with wiles,
To hail my cow of virtues
 Ho my heifer, ho heifer of my love.

CRONAN BLEOGHAIN   [94]

IAN a chuir Moire nam buadh,
Moch us anamoch dol dachaidh us uath,
Buachaille Padruig, us banachaig Bride,
D' ar sion, d' ar dion, 's d' ar comhnadh.
    Ho hi holigan, ho m' aighean,
    Ho hi holigan, ho m' aighean,
    Ho hi holigan, ho m' aighean,
        Mo chrodh-laoigh air gach taobh an abhuinn.

Bith buarach chioba air m' aighean siocha,
Bith buarach shioda air m' aighean laoigh,
Bith buarach shugain air crodh na duthcha,
Ach buarach ur air m' aighean gaoil.
    Ho hi holigan, ho m' aighean.

Fhaic thu bho ud air an lianu,
'S a laogh mear aic air a bialu,
Dean a chaomhag mar a rinn i chianu,
Thoir am bainne, a laoigh na Fiannaich.
    Ho hi holigan, ho m' aighean.

MILKING CROON

THE charm placed of Mary of light,
Early and late going to and from home,
The herdsman Patrick and the milkmaid Bride,
Saining you and saving you and shielding you
    Ho hi holigan, ho my heifer,
    Ho hi holigan, ho my heifer,
    Ho hi holigan, ho my heifer,
        My calving kine on each side of the river

A shackle of lint on my elfish heifer,
A shackle of silk on my heifer of calves,
A shackle of straw on the cows of the townland,
But a brand new shackle on my heifer beloved.
    Ho hi holigan, ho my heifer.

Seest thou that cow on the plain,
With her frisky calf before her,
Do, thou lovable one, as she did erstwhile,
Give thou thy milk, O calf of 'Fiannach.'
    Ho hi holigan, ho my heifer

BEANNACHADH BLEOGHAIN　　[95]

HEIR Calum-cille dhi-se piseach,
　Bheir Coibhi cinneil dhi-se fiar,
　Bheir m' aghan ballaidh dhomh-s' am bainne
　'S a laogh bainonn air a bial.
　　　　Ho! m' aghan, m' aghan, m' aghan,
　　　　Ho! m' aghan, caon, ciuin,
　　　　M' aghan caomh, caomh, gradhaidh,
　　　　　　Gur e gaol do mhathar thu.

Seall thu 'n druis ud thall a froineadh,
　'S an druis eil air loin nan smiar,
　Is ionann sin us m' aghan goirridh,
　'S a laogh boirionn air a bial.
　　　　Ho! m' aghan,—

Bheir Bride bhith nan cire geala,
　Li na h-eal am aghan gaoil,
　'S bheir Muire mhin nam mire meala,
　Dhi-se ceal nan cearca-fraoich,
　　　　Ho! m' aghan,—

MILKING BLESSING

COLUMBA will give to her progeny,
Coivi the propitious, will give to her grass,
My speckled heifer will give me her milk,
And her female calf before her.
    Ho my heifer! heifer! heifer!
    Ho my heifer! kindly, calm,
    My heifer gentle, gentle, beloved,
       Thou art the love of thy mother.

Seest yonder thriving bramble bush
And the other bush glossy with brambles,
Such like is my fox-coloured heifer,
And her female calf before her.
     . Ho my heifer!—

The calm Bride of the white combs
Will give to my loved heifer the lustre of the swan,
While the loving Mary, of the combs of honey,
Will give to her the mottle of the heather hen
       Ho my heifer!—

HO HOILIGEAN, HO M' AIGHEAN [96]

UDAIL thu 's thu dh'an chrodh mhara,
  Chra chluasach, bheum chluasach, bheannach,
  Chrathadh fual air cruach do sheanar,
  'S cha tar thu uam-s' a Luan no Sha'urn.
    Ho hoiligean, ho m' aighean!
    Ho hoiligean, ho m' aighean!
    Ho hoiligean, ho m' aighean!
    Mo lochruidh chaomh gach taobh an abhuinn.

Eudail thu 's thu chrodh na tire,
  Bheir thu marrum, bheir thu mis dhomh,
  Bheir thu bainne barr na ciob dhomh,
  'S cha b' e glaisle ghlas an t-siobain.
    Ho hoiligean, ho m' aighean!

Eudail thu 's thu chrodh an t-saoghail,
  Bheir thu bainne barr an fhraoich dhomh,
  Cha bhainne glas air bhlas a chaorain,
  Ach bainne meal 's e air cheal na faoileig.
    Ho hoiligean, ho m' aighean!

Bheir Bride bhinn dhut linn us ograidh,
  Bheir Moire mhin dhut li dha d' chomhdach,
  Bheir Micheal liobha dhut ri dha d' sheoladh,
  'S bheir Iosda Criosda dhut sith us solas.
    Ho hoiligean, ho m' aighean!

HO HOILIGEAN, HO MY HEIFERS

My treasure thou, and thou art of the sea kine,
Red eared, notch eared, high horned,
Urine was sprinkled on the rump of thy grandsire,
And thou shalt not win from me on Monday nor Saturday.
 Ho hoiligean, ho my heifers!
 Ho hoiligean, ho my heifers!
 Ho hoiligean, ho my heifers!
 My kindly kine on each side of the stream.

My treasure thou, and thou art of the land kine,
Thou wilt give me milk produce, thou wilt give me dainty,
Thou wilt give me milk from the top of the club-moss,
And not the grey water of the sand-drift.
 Ho hoiligean, ho my heifers!

My treasure thou, and thou art of the world's kine,
Thou wilt give me milk from the heather tops,
Not grey milk of the taste of the rowan berries,
But honey milk and white as the sea-gull.
 Ho hoiligean, ho my heifers!

The melodious Bride will give thee offspring and young,
The lovely Mary will give thee colour to cover thee,
The lustious Michael will give thee a star to guide thee,
And Christ Jesu will give thee peace and joy.
 Ho hoiligean, ho my heifers!

HO M' AGHAN! [97]

IDHCHE sin bha 'm Buachaill a muigh
  Cha deacha buarach air boin,
  Cha deacha geum a beul laoigh,
  Caoine Buachaill a chruidh,
    Caoine Buachaill a chruidh.

    Ho m' aghan ! ho m' aghan !
    Ho m' aghan ! m' aghan gaoil !
    Chridheag chridh, choir, ghradhaich,
    Air sgath an Ard Righ gabh ri d' laogh.

Oidhche sin bha 'm Buachaill air chall,
Fhuaradh anns an Teampull e.   [thall
Righ na gile thighinn a nall !
Righ na greine nuas a neamh !
    Righ na greine nuas a neamh !

HO, MY HEIFER!

THE night the Herdsman was out
No shackle went on a cow,
Lowing ceased not from the mouth of calf
Wailing the Herdsman of the flock,
    Wailing the Herdsman of the flock.

    Ho my heifer! ho my heifer!
    Ho my heifer! my heifer beloved!
    My heartling heart, kind, fond,
    For the sake of the High King take to thy calf.

The night the Herdsman was missing,
In the Temple He was found.   [yonder
The King of the moon to come hither!
The King of the sun down from heaven!
    King of the sun down from heaven!

THOIR AM BAINNE   [98]

HOIR am bainne, bho dhonn,
    Ce 'n conn ma 'n ceillinn?
    Laogh na ba ud braigh na beinge,
    'S laogh mo ghraidh-sa air graisich eile.
        O ! ho ! graisich eile.

            Thoir am bainne, bho dhonn,
            Thoir am bainne, bho dhonn,
            Thoir am bainne, bho dhonn,
                Trom steilleach.

Ach gheobh mo ghaol-sa laoighean cais-fhionn,
Us buarach caon a theid caomh ma casan,
Cha bhuarach gaoisid, fraoich, no asgairt,
Ach buarach dhaor a bheir daoin a Sasgunn.
        O ! ho ! a Sasgunn.

'S gheobh mo righinn-sa finn na maise
Buarach min a theid sliom ma casan,
Cha bhuarach cioba, lioin, no asgairt,
Ach buarach shiod thig a nios a Sasgunn.
        O ! ho ! a Sasgunn.

'S gheobh mo chiall-sa fiar us fasga,
'S gheobh i aonach, fraoch, us machair,
'S gheobh i mislean, ciob, us fas-bhuain,
'S gheobh i am fian thig 'o shian nan cas-bheann.
        O ! ho ! nan cas-bheann.

GIVE THY MILK

Give thy milk, brown cow,
For what reason should 1 conceal?
The [skin of the] calf of yonder cow on the partition,
While the calf of my love is on another grange.
    Oh! ho ' another grange:

        Give thy milk, brown cow,
        Give thy milk, brown cow,
        Give thy milk, brown cow,
           Heavily flowing.

My beloved shall get white-bellied calves,
And a fetter fine that shall go kindly round her legs,
No fetter of hair, nor of heather, nor of lint refuse,
But a dear fetter that men bring from Saxon land.
    Oh! ho! from Saxon land.

And my queen maiden of beauty shall get
A fetter smooth to go softly round her legs,
No fetter of cord, nor of lint, nor lint refuse,
But a fetter of silk up from Saxon land.
    Oh! ho! from Saxon land.

My beloved shall get grass and shelter,
She shall get hill, heath, and plain,
She shall get meadow-grass, club-rush, and stubble,
And she shall get the wine that comes from the elements of
    the steep bens
    Oh! ho! the steep bens.

A bho dhubh ! a bho dhubh !
Is ionan galar dhomh-s' us dhut,
Thus a gul 's a gal do laoigh,
Mise mo mhac gaoil fo 'n mhuir,
    M' aon mhac gaoil fo 'n mhuir !

O black cow! O black cow!
The same disease afflicts me and thee,
Thou weeping and wailing thy calf,
I my darling son beneath the sea,
    Mine only son beneath the sea!

CRONAN BLEOGHAN   [99]

THIG, a Mhuire, 's bligh a bho,
   Thig, a Bhride, 's comraig i,
Thig, a Chaluim-chille chaoimh,
   'S iadh do dha laimh mu m' bhoin.
     Ho m' aghan, ho m' agh gaoil,
     Ho m' aghan, ho m' agh gaoil,
     Ho m' aghan, ho m' agh gaoil,
     M' aghan cri, coir, gradhach,
       An sgath an Ard Righ gabh ri d' laogh.

Thig, a Mhuire, dh' ios mo bho,
Thig, a Bhride, mhor na loin,
Thig, a bhanachaig Iosda Criosda,
   'S cur do lamh a nios fo m' bhoin.
     Ho m' aghan, ho m' agh gaoil.

An oidhche bha 'm Buachaill a muigh,
Cha deacha buarach air boin,
Cha deacha geum a beul laoigh,
   Caoine Buachaill a chruidh.
     Ho m' aghan, ho m' agh gaoil.

Bo lurach dhubh, bo na h-airidh,
Bo a bha-theach, mathair laogh,
Luban siomain air crodh na tire,
   Buarach shiod air m' aighean gaoil.
     Ho m' aghan, ho m' agh gaoil.

MILKING SONG

Come, Mary, and milk my cow,
Come, Bride, and encompass her,
Come, Columba the benign,
  And twine thine arms around my cow,
    Ho my heifer, ho my gentle heifer,
    Ho my heifer, ho my gentle heifer.
    Ho my heifer, ho my gentle heifer,
    My heifer full of heart, generous and kind,
      For the sake of the High King take to thy calf.

Come, Mary Virgin, to my cow,
Come, great Bride, the beauteous,
Come, thou milkmaid of Jesus Christ,
  And place thine arms beneath my cow.
    Ho my heifer, ho my gentle heifer.

The night the Herdsman was out,
No shackle went on a cow,
Nor ceased lowing from the mouth of calf,
  Wailing the Herdsman of the cattle.
    Ho my heifer, ho my gentle heifer.

Lovely black cow, pride of the sheiling,
First cow of the byre, choice mother of calves,
Wisps of straw round the cows of the townland.
  A shackle of silk on my heifer beloved
    Ho my heifer, ho my gentle heifer

OIBRE

Mo bho dhubh, mo bho dhubh,
Is ionann galar dhomh-s' us dhuit,
Thus a caoidh do luran laoigh,
  Mise mo mhac gaoil fo 'n mhuir,
    Mise mo mhac gaoil fo 'n mhuir.

My black cow, my black cow,
A like sorrow afflicts me and thee,
Thou grieving for thy lovely calf,
   I for my beloved son under the sea,
     I for my beloved son under the sea.

BEANNACHADH BUACHAILLEACHD   [100]

Being a pastoral people, the Highlanders possess much pastoral poetry. The greater part of this is secular with fragments of sacred poetry interspersed. The herding runes are examples of these purely pastoral poems. They are sung by the people as they send their flocks to the pastures, or tend them on the hills, glens, or plains. The customs vary in details in different districts, but everywhere is the simple belief that the King of shepherds watches over men and flocks now as of old—'the same yesterday, to-day, and for ever.'

When a man has taken his herd to the pasture in the morning, and has got a knoll between himself and them, he bids them a tender adieu, waving his hand, perhaps both hands, towards them, saying :—

'Buachailleachd Bride dh' an tan,
Buan us slan dh' an till sibh.

The herding of Bride to the kine,
Whole and well may you return.

'Munachas Mhuire Mhathar dhuibh,
Luth us lan gu'n till sibh.

The prosperity of Mary Mother be yours,
Active and full may you return.

OMRAIG Dhe us Dhomhnuich dhuibh,
Comraig Chriosd a chomhnuidh dhuibh,
Comraig Charmaig 's Chaluim-chille,
Comraig Chairbre, falbh 's a tilleadh,
Us comraig Airighil oirghil oirbh,
Comraig Airighil oirghil oirbh.

Comraig Bhride mhuime dhuibh,
Comraig Mhoire bhuidhe dhuibh,
Iosa Criosda, Mac na sithe,
Righ nan righre, muir us tire,
Us Spioraid siochaint, suthainn, dhuibh,
Spioraid siochaint, suthainn, dhuibh.

HERDING BLESSING

'Cumraig Chalum-chille ma'r casaibh, The sanctuary of Columba around your feet,
Gu mu slan gu'n till sibh dachaidh Whole be your return home

'Micheal min-gheal righ nan aigheal Be the bright Michael king of the angels
D'ar dion,'s d'ar gleidheadh's d'ar comhnadh Protecting, and keeping, and saving you.

'Comraig Dhe us Dhomhnach dhuibh The guarding of God and the Lord be yours
Gu'm faic mise na mo chroilean sibh Till I or mine shall see you again.

'Cobhair Choibhi dhuibh The help of Coivi to you.

'Siubhal coire, siubhal coille, Travelling coire, travelling copse,
Siubhal comhnaird fada sola, Travelling meads long and grassy,
Buachailleachd mhin na Moire The herding of the fair Mary
Bhith mu'r cinn 's mu'r com 's mu'r cobhair ' Be about your head, your body, and aiding you

When these patriarchal benedictions are intoned or chanted, and the music floats over moor and loch, the effect is charming to the ear of the listener.

THE keeping of God and the Lord on you,
The keeping of Christ always on you,
The keeping of Carmac and of Columba on you,
The keeping of Cairbre on you going and coming,
And the keeping of Ariel the gold-bright on you,
 The keeping of Ariel the gold-bright on you.

The keeping of Bride the foster-mother on you,
The keeping of Mary the yellow-haired on you,
Of Christ Jesus, the Son of peace,
The King of kings, land and sea,
And the peace-giving Spirit, everlasting, be yours,
 The peace-giving Spirit, everlasting, be yours.

BEANNACHADH BUACHAILLEACHD [101]

UIRIDH mi an ni seo romham,
Mar a dh' orduich Righ an domhan,
Bride ga'n gleidheadh, ga'n coimhead, 's ga'n comhnadh,
Air bheann, air ghleann, air chomhnard,
 Bride ga'n gleidheadh, ga'n coimhead, 's ga'n
  comhnadh,
 Air bheann, air ghleann, air chomhnard.

Eirich, a Bhride mhin-gheal,
Glac do lion, do chir, agus t' fholt,
Bho rinn thu daibh eolas abhra,
Ga'n cumail bho chall us bho lochd,
 Bho rinn thu daibh eolas abhra,
 Ga'n cumail bho chall us bho lochd.

Bho chreag, bho chathan, bho allt,
Bho chadha cam, bho mhille sluic,
Bho shaighde reang nam ban seanga sith,
Bho chridhe mhi-ruin, bho shuil an uile,
 Bho shaighde reang nam ban seanga sith,
 Bho chridhe mhi-ruin, bho shuil an uile.

Mhoire Mhathair, cuallaich an t-al gu leir,
Bhride nam basa mine, dion domh mo spreidh,
Chaluim chaoimh, a naoimh nan ioma buadh,
Comraig dhomh crodh an ail, bairig dhomh buar,
 Chaluim chaoimh, a naoimh nan ioma buadh,
 Comraig dhomh crodh an ail, bairig dhomh buar.

HERDING BLESSING

I WILL place this flock before me,
As was ordained of the King of the world,
Bride to keep them, to watch them, to tend them,
On ben, on glen, on plain,
    Bride to keep them, to watch them, to tend them,
    On ben, on glen, on plain.

Arise, thou Bride the gentle, the fair,
Take thou thy lint, thy comb, and thy hair,
Since thou to them madest the rich charm,
To keep them from straying, to save them from harm,
    Since thou to them madest the rich charm,
    To keep them from straying, to save them from harm.

From rocks, from drifts, from streams,
From crooked passes, from destructive pits,
From the straight arrows of the slender ban-shee,
From the heart of envy, from the eye of evil,
    From the straight arrows of the slender ban-shee,
    From the heart of envy, from the eye of evil

Mary Mother, tend thou the offspring all,
Bride of the fair palms, guard thou my flocks,
Kindly Columba, thou saint of many powers,
Encompass thou the breeding cows, bestow on me herds,
    Kindly Columba, thou saint of many powers,
    Encompass thou the breeding cows, bestow on me
      herds

BEANNACHADH BUACHAILLEACHD   [102]

IUBHAL beinne, siubhal baile,
    Siubhal featha fada, farsuinn,
    Buachailleachd Mhic De mu'r casaibh,
    Buan us reidh gu'n teid sibh dachaidh,
        Buachailleachd Mhic De mu'r casaibh,
        Buan us reidh gu'n teid sibh dachaidh.

Comraig Charmaig us Chaluim-chille
    Bhith da'r tearmad a falbh 's a tilleadh,
    Agus banachaig nam basa mine,
    Bride nan or chiabh donn,
        Agus banachaig nam basa mine,
        Bride nan or chiabh donn.

HERDING BLESSING

Travelling moorland, travelling townland,
Travelling mossland long and wide,
Be the herding of God the Son about your feet,
Safe and whole may ye home return,
  Be the herding of God the Son about your feet,
  Safe and whole may ye home return.

The sanctuary of Carmac and of Columba
Be protecting you going and coming,
And of the milkmaid of the soft palms,
Bride of the clustering hair golden brown,
  And of the milkmaid of the soft palms,
  Bride of the clustering hair golden brown.

COMRAIG NAM BA [103]

LARAGAN reidh, fada, farsuinn,
   Faileagan feile fo 'r casan,
   Cairdeas Mhic De dh' ar toir dhachaidh
   Gu faiche nam fuaran,
      Faiche nam fuaran.

   Gu'm bu duinte duibh gach slochd,
   Gu'm bu sumhail duibh gach cnoc,
   Gu'm bu clumhaidh duibh gach nochd,
   Am fochar nam fuar-bheann,
      Fochar nam fuar-bheann.

   Comraig Pheadail agus Phoil,
   Comraig Sheumais agus Eoin,
   Comraig Bhride mhin 's Mhuir Oigh,
   Dh' ar comhlach 's dh' ar cuallach,
      O ! comraig gach aon dh' an chomhl
      Dh' ar comhnadh 's dh' ar cuanadh.

THE PROTECTION OF THE CATTLE

PASTURES smooth, long, and spreading,
Grassy meads aneath your feet,
The friendship of God the Son to bring you home
To the field of the fountains,
    Field of the fountains.

Closed be every pit to you,
Smoothed be every knoll to you,
Cosy every exposure to you,
Beside the cold mountains,
    Beside the cold mountains.

The care of Peter and of Paul,
The care of James and of John,
The care of Bride fair and of Mary Virgin,
To meet you and to tend you,
    Oh ! the care of all the band
    To protect you and to strengthen you.

GLEIDHEADH TREUID [104]

U'N gleidheadh Moire min an ciob,
Gu'n gleidheadh Bride bith an ciob,
Gu'n gleidheadh Calum-cille an ciob,
Gu'n gleidheadh Maol-rithe an ciob,
Gu'n gleidheadh Carmag an ciob,
O'n mhi-chu 's o'n mharbh-chu.

Gu'n gleidheadh Odhran an crodh,
Gu'n gleidheadh Modan an crodh,
Gu'n gleidheadh Donnan an crodh,
Gu'n gleidheadh Moluag an crodh,
Gu'n gleidheadh Maolruan an crodh,
Am boglach 's an crualach.

Gu'n gleidheadh Spiorad foir an treud,
Gu'n gleidheadh Mac Moir Oigh an treud,
Gu'n gleidheadh Ti na gloir an treud,
Gu'n gleidheadh an Teoir an treud,
Bho reubain 's bho mhearchall,
    Bho reubain 's bho mhearchall.

GUARDING THE FLOCKS

MAY Mary the mild keep the sheep,
May Bride the calm keep the sheep,
May Columba keep the sheep,
May Maolrithe keep the sheep,
May Carmac keep the sheep,
From the fox and the wolf

May Oran keep the kine,
May Modan keep the kine,
May Donnan keep the kine,
May Moluag keep the kine,
May Maolruan keep the kine,
On soft land and hard land

May the Spirit of peace preserve the flocks,
May the Son of Mary Virgin preserve the flocks,
May the God of glory preserve the flocks,
May the Three preserve the flocks,
From wounding and from death-loss,
    From wounding and from death-loss.

CRONAN CUALLAICH [105]

N crodh an diugh a dol imirig,
    Hill-i-ruin us o h-ug o,
    Ho ro la ill o,
    Hill-i-ruin us o h-ug o,
Dol a dh' itheadh feur na cille,
    Hill-i-ruin us o h-ug o,
    Am buachaille fein ann ga'n iomain,
    Ho ro la ill o,
    Hill-i-ruin us o h-ug o,
Ga'n cuallach, ga'n cuart, ga'n tilleadh,
    Hill-i-ruin us o h-ug o,
Bride bhith-gheal bhi ga'm blighinn,
    Hill-i-ruin us o h-ug o,
Muire mhin-gheal bhi ga'n glidheadh,
    Hill-i-ruin us o h-ug o,
'S Iosa Criosda air chinn an slighe,
    Iosa Criosda air chinn an slighe.
    Hill-i-ruin us o h-ug o.

A HERDING CROON

THE cattle are to-day going a-flitting,
      Hill-i-runn us o h-ug o,
      Ho ro la ill o,
      Hill-i-ruin us o h-ug o,
Going to eat the grass of the burial-place,
      Hill-i-ruin us o h-ug o,
Their own herdsman there to tend them,
      Ho ro la ill o,
      Hill-i-ruin us o h-ug o,
Tending them, fending them, turning them,
      Hill-i-ruin us o h-ug o,
Be the gentle Bride milking them,
      Hill-i-ruin us o h-ug o,
Be the lovely Mary keeping them,
      Hill-i-ruin us o h-ug o,
And Jesu Christ at the end of their journey,
    Jesu Christ at the end of their journey.
      Hill-i-ruin us o h-ug o.

The reciter of this poem, Donald Maclean, was a native of the parish of Small Isles. He emigrated with many others to Canada. After an absence of many years he returned, as he said, ' Feuch am faighinn larach mo dha bhonn a bhothan, agus leathad mo dha shlinnein a dh' uaigh ann am fearann mo dhuthchais agus ann an uir m' aithriche.'—' To see if I could get the site of my two soles of a bothy and the breadth of my two shoulders of a grave in the land of my heredity and in the lair of my fathers.' Not having obtained these in the land of his birth, Donald Maclean returned to the land of his adoption.

Maclean heard this poem, and many other poems and tales, in Canada from a woman called ' Sorcha Chlannradhail,' Clara Clanranald, beside whom he lived for sixteen years. When so many of the small crofts of Uist were converted into large farms, the people removed and not absorbed among the remaining crofters emigrated to Nova Scotia, Prince Edward's Island, and Cape Breton. Clara Clanranald's people had been evicted from Ormacleit, South Uist. She spoke so much of Uist and of the Clanranalds that she came to be known by the name of her loved chief.

When Donald Maclean left Canada, ten or twelve years ago, Clara was 102 years of age. She was still active and industrious, and in the possession of all her faculties, and of all her love for ' the old land.' When Maclean went to bid her good-bye she took his hand in her two hands, and looking him full in the face with her large lustrous blue eyes moist with tears, said :—

'Tha thu falbh a ghaoil a Dhomhnuill agus Dia mor bhi eadar do dha shlinnein.
Bu tu fein an deagh nabaidh agus an caraide caomh.

IRIDH mi moch maduinn Luan,
   Gabhaidh mi mo rann 's mo dhuan,
   Theid mi deiseil le mo chuaich,
   Gu nead mo chearc le beachd na buaidh.

Cuiream mo lamh thoisg ri m' chich,
Mo lamh dheas ri taic mo chridh,
Iarram gliocas graidh an Ti,
Ta pailt an agh, an al 's an ni.

Duineam mo dha shuil air ball,
Mar dhallan-da ni snagan mall,
Sineam mo lamh chli a null
Gu nead mo chire an taobh ud thall.

HATCHING BLESSING

Ma 's a h-e agus gu'n ruig **thu** null fearann do dhuthchais agus duthaich do bhreith,
agus gu'm feumair thu tilleadh a nall dh'an fhonn-sa uthist, tha mise cur mar
bhoid agus mar bhriathar ort, agus mar naoi riaraiche nam bana-sith, thu dhol gu
ruig Cladh Mhicheil ann an Ormacleit, an Uibhist, agus thu thoir as a sin thugam-sa
deannan beag urach a churar air clar mo chridhe-sa la mo bhais

> ' Agus Micheal caomh-gheal, cro-gheal, cra-gheal,
> Ga do dhiona, ga do chaomhna, ga do charamh,
> Le treuin a laimhe, le nimh a ghaise,
> Fo sgaile duilleanach a sgeith '

' Thou art going away, beloved Donald, and may the great God be between thy
two shoulders. Thou thyself wert the good neighbour and the kind friend If it
be that thou reach the land of thy heredity and the country of thy birth, and that
thou shouldst have to come back again to the land of thine adoption, I place it upon
thee as a vow and as a charge, and as the nine fulfilments of the fairy women, that
thou go to the burial-place of Michael at Ormacleit in Uist, and bring to me from
there a little earth that shall be placed upon the tablet of my heart the day
that I die

> ' And may Michael kind-white, strong-white, red-white,
> Preserve thee, protect thee, provide for thee,
> With the might of his hand, with the point of his spear,
> Under the shade of his shimmering shield '

I WILL rise early on the morning of Monday,
I will sing my rune and rhyme,
I will go sunwise with my cog
To the nest of my hen with sure intent.

I will place my left hand to my breast,
My right hand to my heart,
I will seek the loving wisdom of Him
Abundant in grace, in broods, and in flocks.

I will close my two eyes quickly,
As in blind-man's buff moving slowly ;
I will stretch my left hand over thither
To the nest of my hen on yonder side.

2 o

An ceud ugh a bheir mi m' theann,
Cuiream tuathal e air mo cheann,
　　*　　　*　　　*　　　*
　　*　　　*　　　*　　　*

Togam mo lamh thoisg an suas,
Sineam i gun chlos gu luath,
Togam an da ugh an nuas,
Bithidh an uair sin tri 's a chuaich.

Sineam mo lamh dheas a ris,
Togam leath 's a ghreis a tri,
Iarram riaghladh air an Righ,
Bithidh, mo riar, a sia 's an linn.

Lamh mo thoisg an dara h-uair,
Togam ceithir leath an nuas,
An ainm Chriosda Righ nam buadh,
Bithidh an uair sin deich 's a chuaich.

An dorn deas is treasa coir,
Togam leis a dha fo m' mheoir,
Bithidh aig sgur mo ghur gun sgod,
Fo uchd na circe brice moir.

Cuiream suidhe air an da cheann,
Us mi mar bhalbhan balbh 's an am,
An ainm Chruithear mhuir us bheann,
An ainm gach naoimh us ostail ann.

An ainm Thrianailt uile naoimh,
An ainm Chalum-chille chaoimh,
Cuiream iad fo chirc Di-ardaoin,
Thig an t-alach aigh Di-aoin.

The first egg which I shall bring neai me,
I will put it withershins round my head

    ⁂   ⁂   ⁂   ⁂   ⁂

    ⁂   ⁂   ⁂   ⁂   ⁂

I will raise my left hand on high,
I will stretch it without halt quickly,
I will lift the two eggs down hither,
There shall be then three in the cog.

I will stretch my right hand again,
I will lift with it at the time three,
I will seek ruling from the King,
Then verily there shall be six in the clutch.

I will raise my left hand the second time,
I will lift four with it down,
In name of Christ, King of power,
There shall then be ten in the cog.

The right fist of strongest claim,
I will lift with it two in my fingers,
Thus at ceasing my brood will be complete,
Beneath the breast of the speckled big hen.

I will put soot on their two ends,
And I dumb as the dumb the while,
In name of Creator of sea and hill,
In name of saints and apostles all.

In name of the most Holy Trinity,
In name of Columba kindly,
I will set the eggs on Thursday,
The gladsome brood will come on Friday.

COMHARRACHADH NAN UAN　　[107]

The marking of the lambs is done on Thursday, being St. Columba's day. Upon no account would the people mark their lambs on Friday, or in any manner draw blood on that day. Nor till lately would they use iron in any form on Friday.

A blacksmith in Benbecula, a Protestant, an excellent man and an admirable tradesman, never opened his smithy on Friday. He maintained that 'that was the least he could do to honour his Master.'

When the lambs are marked, the people collect the bits taken out of their ears, and carefully bury them beyond the reach of beast or bird. They say that a plant, which they call 'gearra-chluasach,' literally ear-cuts, ear-clips, grows from them. This plant is generally found growing where a carcase has been buried, and when ripe, it is cut, tied up in a bunch, and suspended from the 'casan ceanghail,' couple above the door of the lamb-cot, and dedicated to

| ' Moire mhin-gheal nan grasa buan, | The fair-white Mary of lasting graces, |
| Air shealbh chaorach air ghaol nan.' | For luck of sheep and love of lambs. |

The marks made on the ears of sheep and lambs are varied and descriptive in name, as :—' barr,' ' beum,' ' cluigean,' ' cliopan,' ' cliopadh,'

ITH mo sgian ur, geur, glan, gun mheirg,
　　Mo bhreacan fo m' ghlun le mo luirich dheirg,
　　Cuiream deiseil mo chleibh an ceud bheum gu sealbh,
　　An ath fhear na dheigh leis a ghrein mar ni falbh.

Uan firionn gun ghaoid, air aon dath, gun chearb,
Leig a mach ris an raon, fhuil chraobhach na tearb,
Ma mhaireas a chraobh air an fhraoch le barr dearg,
Bith mo shealbhan gun ghaoid fad 's nach caochail
　　　　mi 'n t-ainm.

An Triuir ta shuas an Cathair nam buadh,
Bhi buachailleachd mo threuid us mo bhuair,
Ga 'n iomachair ri teis ri gaillinn 's ri fuachd,
Le beannachd nam buadh ga 'n saodadh a nuas
Bho 'n tulaich ud shuas gu airidh.

MARKING THE LAMBS

'croean,' 'corran,' 'duile,' 'meaghlan,' 'meangan,' 'sgolta,' 'shos,' 'snathad,' 'sulag,' 'toll' These marks and their modifications are said to number over 250 in the island of Benbecula, in the island of North Uist over 180, and in the island of South Uist over 500 The people know all these marks and modifications at a glance.

When a man marries, it is considered a good omen of the union when the marks on his own sheep and those on the sheep brought him by his wife are nearly alike, and the necessary change easily effected

IARRATAS NA CAOIRE BICE	THE REQUEST OF THE LITTLE SHEEP
Na lom mo cheann,	Do not clip my head,
'S na loisg mo chnamhan '	And do not burn my bones

The small native sheep have a long tuft of wool called 'sguman' coming down the face They are hardy, picturesque little animals, almost wholly free from the innumerable diseases which the larger but softer breeds of sheep have brought in their train. The sheep is regarded with a veneration which is not extended to the cow or other animals

My knife will be new, keen, clean, without stain.
My plaid beneath my knee with my red robe,
I will put sunwise round my breast the first cut for luck,
The next one after that with the sun as it moves

A male lamb without blemish, of one colour, without defect,
Allow thou out on the plain, nor his flowing blood check,
If the froth remains on the heather with red top,
My flock will be without flaw as long as I change not the
    name.

The Three who are above in the City of glory,
Be shepherding my flock and my kine,
Tending them duly in heat, in storm, and in cold,
With the blessing of power driving them down
From yonder height to the sheiling fold.

Ainm Airil is ailne snuadh,
Ainm Ghabril fadh an Uain,
Ainm Raphail flath nam buadh,
Ga 'n cuartach us ga 'n tearnadh.

Ainm Mhuuil us Mhuire Oigh,
Ainm Pheadail agus Phoil,
Ainm Sheumais agus Eoin,
Gach aingheal 's ostal air an toir,
Ga 'n gleidheadh beo le 'n alach,
    Ga 'n gleidheadh beo le 'n alach.

The name of Ariel of beauteous bloom,
The name of Gabriel herald of the Lamb,
The name of Raphael prince of power,
Surrounding them and saving them.

The name of Muiel and of Mary Virgin,
The name of Peter and of Paul,
The name of James and of John,
Each angel and apostle on their track,
Keeping them alive and their progeny,
    Keeping them alive and their progeny.

AM BEANNACHD LOMBAIDH [108]

WHEN a man has shorn a sheep and has set

ALBH lom 's thig molach,
  Beir am boirionn Bealltain,
  Bride mhin a bhi dha d' chonaill,
  Moire gheal dha d' aurais,
     Moire gheal dha d' aurais.

Micheal mil a bhi dha d' dhion
Bho 'n mhi-chu us bho 'n an-chu,
Bho 'n mhac-tir 's bho 'n mhadhan stig,
'S bho ianaibh ineach call-ghobh,
     Bho ianaibh ineach cam-ghobh.

THE CLIPPING BLESSING

it free, he waves his hand after it and says :—

Go shorn and come woolly,
Bear the Beltane female lamb,
Be the lovely Bride thee endowing,
And the fair Mary thee sustaining,
   The fair Mary sustaining thee.

Michael the chief be shielding thee
From the evil dog and from the fox,
From the wolf and from the sly bear,
And from the taloned birds of destructive bills,
   From the taloned birds of hooked bills.

DUAN DEILBH　　　　　　[109]

DURING the winter months the women of Highland households are up late and early at 'calanas'—this comprehensive term embracing the whole process of wool-working from the raw material to the finished cloth. The process is an important factor in the internal economy of a Highland family. The industry of these women is wonderful, performed lovingly, uncomplainingly, day after day, year after year, till the sands of life run down. The life in a Highland home of the crofter class is well described in the following lines:—

' Air oidhche fhada gheamhraidh　　　In the long winter night
　Theid teanndadh ri gniamh,　　　　All are engaged,
　A toir eolas do chloinn　　　　　　Teaching the young
　Bith an seann duine liath,　　　　Is the grey-haired sage,
　An nighean a cardadh,　　　　　　The daughter at her carding,
　A mhathair a sniamh,　　　　　　The mother at her wheel,
　An t-iasgair le a shnathaid　　　While the fisher mends his net
　　A caramh a lian.'　　　　　　　With his needle and his reel.

'Calanas' is an interesting process. The wool is carefully sorted and the coarser parts put aside. It is then washed and laid out to dry, and again examined and teased, and all lumps and refuse taken out.

If the wool is meant to be made into very fine cloth, it is drawn on combs of specially long teeth; if into ordinary cloth, it is carded on the cards without going through the combs. After carding, the wool is made into 'rolagan,' rowans, and spun into thread, which is arranged into hanks. At this stage the thread is generally dyed, although occasionally the wool is dyed after the teasing process and before being carded. The work of dyeing requires much care and knowledge and practical skill. It is done with native plants gathered with patient care from the rocks and hills, moors and fields and lakes, and with certain earths. When it is considered that a thorough knowledge of

AORN nam buadh.

　　Gu deilbh 's gu luadh,
　　Bi ceud gu leth dual
　　　Ri aireamh.

　　Snath gorm gu math caol,
　　Dha gheala ri a thaobh.
　　Agus sgarlaid ri taobh
　　　A mhadair.

THE CHANT OF THE WARPING

plants is necessary, their locality, their colouring properties, whether of root, stem, or leaf, and the stage of growth or decay, it will be understood that those who use them need much intelligence. All Highland women are practical dyers, some more skilful than others. From infancy they are trained in 'calanas,' and in plants and dyeing, the whole clothing, including the blankets, of the household being dependent upon their skill and industry. Are there any other women in any class who can show such widespread skill and intelligence as these Highland women show in wool-working and dyeing operations? Home-made tartans and other fabrics, made many generations, sometimes centuries, ago, are not only wonderfully fine in texture, but all the different colours are still remarkably bright and beautiful.

The Celts must have had an eye for colour in very early times. The Book of Kells is said by experts to be the most beautiful illuminated manuscript in the world. It is believed to have been written in the Columban monastery of Iona, and to have escaped the Norse destruction of mss. and been carried to the Columban monastery of Kells. Not only are the forms of the initial letters in the mss. marvellously intricate and artistic, but the different pigments used in colouring are still bright and beautiful and fresh, while the colouring of copies made during this century is already sickly and faded.

The pattern of the tartan or other cloth to be woven is first designed on a small piece of wood, the thread being placed on the wood according to the design proposed. This is called 'sndheachadh,' setting. It is a work that requires patient care and skill in order to bring out the pattern correctly.

The Chant of the Warping is feelingly intoned by the women in warping the web. When a word or a phrase has struck their minds, they stop singing in order to emphasise the sentiment in a word or a phrase of their own, beseeching Mary's beloved Son to give them strength to observe His laws. These pious interjections and momentary stoppages may not add to the beauty of the singing, but they do to the picturesqueness.

> THURSDAY of beneficence,
> For warping and waulking,
> An hundred and fifty strands there shall be,
> To number.
>
> Blue thread, very fine,
> Two of white by its side,
> And scarlet by the side
> Of the madder

Bi mo dheilbh gu math reidh,
Thoir do beannachd dhomh Dhe,
Us do gach uile fo m' chleith
    'S an fhardraich.

A Mhicheil, aingil nam buadh,
A Mhoire mhin-ghil tha shuas,
A Chriosd, a Bhuachaill an t-sluagh.
Dean bhur beannachd bi-bhuan
    A bhairig.

Do gach neach laigheas sios,
An ainm Athar us Chriosd,
Agus Spiorad na siochaint
    Ghrasmhor

Crath a nuas oirnn mar dhriuchd,
Gliocas caon na ban chiuin,
Nach do dhibir riamh iul
    An Ard Righ.

Cum air falbh gach droch shuil,
Gach uile mhuinntir droch ruin,
Coisrig cur agus dluth
    Gach snathla.

Cur do ghairdean mu 'n cuairt,
Air gach te bhios ga luadh,
Agus dean a tearmad aig uair
    A saruich.

Thoir domh subhailcean mor,
Mar bh' aig Muire ri a lo,
Chum 's gu 'n sealbhaich mi gloir
    An Ard Righ

My warp shall be very even.
Give to me Thy blessing, O God,
And to all who are beneath my roof
    In the dwelling.

Michael, thou angel of power,
Mary fair, who art above,
Christ, Thou Shepherd of the people,
Do ye your eternal blessing
    Bestow.

On each one who shall lie down,
In name of the Father and of Christ,
And of the Spirit of peacefulness,
    And of grace.

Sprinkle down on us like dew
The gracious wisdom of the mild woman,
Who neglected never the guidance
    Of the High King.

Ward away every evil eye,
And all people of evil wishes,
Consecrate the woof and the warp
    Of every thread.

Place Thou Thine arm around
Each woman who shall be waulking it,
And do Thou aid her in the hour
    Of her need.

Give to me virtues abundant,
As Mary had in her day,
That I may possess the glory
    Of the High King.

Bho 'n 's tus a Dhe tha toir fas,
Do gach gne agus gnaths,
Thoir dhuinn olainn thar bharr
    An fheuir ghlais.

Coisng sealbh anns gach ait,
Le 'n uain bheaga bhinne bhath,
Us cuir an lionmhoireachd al
    Ar treudais.

Chum 's gu 'm faigh sinn diubh cloimh,
Bainne sultmhor i'a ol,
Us nach bi gainn oirnn a chomhdach
    Eirigh

Since Thou, O God, it is who givest growth,
To each species and kind,
Give us wool from the surface
    Of the green grass.

Consecrate the flock in every place,
With their little lambs melodious, innocent,
And increase the generations
    Of our herds.

So that we may obtain from them wool,
And nourishing milk to drink,
And that no dearth may be ours
    Of day clothing.

BEANNACHD BEAIRTE [110]

UIDHEAGAN no corr do shuath
Cha do chum 's cha chum mo lamh.

Gach dath a ta 's a bhogha-fhrois
Chaidh troimh mo mheoirean fo na chrois,

Geal us dubh, dearg us madar,
Uaine, ciar-ghlas, agus sgarlaid,

Gorm, us grisionn 's dath na caorach,
'S caoibean cha robh dhith air aodach.

Guidhim Bride bith na faolachd,
Guidhim Muire min na gaolachd,
Guidhim Iosa Criosd na daonnachd,
Gun mi fein dhol eug a 'n aonais,
    Gun mi fein dhol eug a 'n aonais.

LOOM BLESSING

THRUMS nor odds of thread
My hand never kept, nor shall keep,

Every colour in the bow of the shower
Has gone through my fingers beneath the cross,

White and black, red and madder,
Green, dark grey, and scarlet,

Blue, and roan, and colour of the sheep,
And never a particle of cloth was wanting

I beseech calm Bride the generous,
I beseech mild Mary the loving,
I beseech Christ Jesu the humane,
That I may not die without them,
    That I may not die without them

'Imirt,' 'iomairt,' 'iumairt,' 'umairt' is cloth striped lengthwise, not crosswise. While the warp of the 'iomairt' is composed of stripes of various colours, the weft is confined to one—generally light blue, dark blue, or black. This cloth was confined to women's use, in the 'earasaid,' the 'tonnag,' the 'guaileachan,' and the petticoat. Setting the 'iomairt,' like setting other warp, and setting the

N dubh mu'n gheal,
    An geal mu'n dubh,
    An t-uaine meadhon an deirg,
    An dearg am meadhon an duibh,

    An dubh am meadhon an deirg,
    An dearg am meadhon a ghil,
    An geal am meadhon an uaine,
    An t-uaine am meadhon a ghil.

    An geal am meadhon a ghuirm,
    An gorm am meadhon na sgarlaid,
         *   *   *   *
         *   *   *   *

    An sgarlaid ris a ghorm,
    An gorm ris an sgarlaid,
    An sgarlaid ris an dubh,
    An dubh ris an sgarlaid.

Snathla ri da shnathla
Do dha dhath,
Da shnathla dhubh,
Ri aon snathla geal.

Seachd snathla ri coig,
Coig ri tri,
Tri ri dha,
Dha ri aon,
Anns gach oir.

SETTING THE IOMAIRT

eggs, and many other operations of the people, was done on Thursday, that being the day of St Columba Framing the web is a work of much anxiety to the housewife, and she and her maidens are up very early to put the thread in order.

The thread of the 'iomairt,' like that of the tartan, was very fine, hard-spun and double twisted, rendering the cloth extremely durable

THE black by the white,
The white by the black,
The green in the middle of the red,
The red in the middle of the black. ,

The black in the middle of the red,
The red in the middle of the white,
The white in the middle of the green,
The green in the middle of the white.

The white in the middle of the blue,
The blue in the middle of the scarlet,

*   *   *   *
*   *   *   *

The scarlet to the blue,
The blue to the scarlet,
The scarlet to the black,
The black to the scarlet.

A thread to two threads
Of two colours,
Two threads of black
To one thread of white.

Seven threads to five,
Five to three,
Three to two,
Two to one,
In each border.

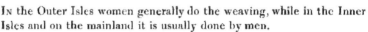

In the Outer Isles women generally do the weaving, while in the Inner
Isles and on the mainland it is usually done by men.

In Uist, when the woman stops weaving on Saturday night she
carefully ties up her loom and suspends the cross or crucifix above the

EANNAICH, a Thriath nam flath fial,
Mo bheirt 's gach sian a ta na m' choir,
Beannaich, mi na'm uile ghniamh
Dean mi tiarninte ri m' bheo.

Bho gach gruagach us ban-shith,
Bho gach mi-run agus bron,
Cuidich mi, a Chuidich-Thi,
Fad 's a bhios mi'n tir nam beo.

An ainm Mhuire mhin nam feart,
Chalum-chille cheart nam buadh,
Coistrig ceithir phuist mo bheairt,
Gu'n am beairtich mi Di-luain.

A casachan, a slinn, 's a spal,
A h-iteachean, a snath, 's a gual,
A crann-aodaich, 's a crann-snath,
Fuidheagan us snath nan dual.

Gach aodach dubh, geal, us ban,
Grisionn, lachdunn, sgaireach, ruadh,
Thoir do bheannachd anns gach ait,
Air gach spal a theid fo dhual.

Mar sin bidh mo bheairt gun bheud,
Gu'n an eirich mi Di-luain ;
Bheir Muire mhin-gheal dhomh dh' a speis,
'S cha bhi eis air nach faigh mi buaidh.

LOOM BLESSING

sleay   This is for the purpose of keeping away the brownie, the banshee, the 'peallan,' and all evil spirits and malign influences from disarranging the thread and the loom. And all this is done with loving care and in good faith, and in prayer and purity of heart.

BLESS, O Chief of generous chiefs,
My loom and everything a-near me,
Bless me in my every action,
Make Thou me safe while I live.

From every brownie and fairy woman,
From every evil wish and sorrow,
Help me, O Thou helping Being,
As long as I shall be in the land of the living.

In name of Mary, mild of deeds,
In name of Columba, just and potent,
Consecrate the four posts of my loom,
Till I begin on Monday.

Her pedals, her sleay, and her shuttle,
Her reeds, her warp, and her cogs,
Her cloth-beam, and her thread-beam,
Thrums and the thread of the plies.

Every web, black, white, and fair,
Roan, dun, checked, and red,
Give Thy blessing everywhere,
On every shuttle passing under the thread

Thus will my loom be unharmed,
Till I shall arise on Monday;
Beauteous Mary will give me of her love,
And there shall be no obstruction I shall not overcome.

COISRIGEADH AN AODAICH [113]

FORMERLY throughout the Highlands and Islands the cloth for the family was made at home. At present home-made clothing is chiefly made in the Islands, and even there to a lesser extent than formerly

After the web of cloth is woven it is waulked, to thicken and strengthen and brighten it. The frame on which the cloth is waulked is a board some twelve to twenty-four feet long and about two feet broad, grooved lengthwise along its surface The frame is called 'cleith,' wattle, and 'cleith-luaidh,' waulking-wattle, probably from its having been originally constructed of wattle-work. The waulking-frame is raised upon trestles, while the waulking-women are ranged on seats on either side, about two feet of space being allowed to each woman. The web is unrolled and laid along the board. It is then saturated with ammonia, warm water, and soap-suds, and the women work it vigorously from side to side across the grooves of the frame, slowly moving it lengthwise also, that each part of the cloth may receive due attention. The lateral movement of the cloth is sunwise. Occasionally the waulking-board is laid on the ground instead of on trestles, and the women work the cloth with their feet instead of with their hands

Generally the waulking-women are young maidens, a few married women of good voice being distributed among them. They sing as they work, one singing the song, the others the chorus. Their songs are varied, lively, and adapted to the class of work. Most of them are love-songs, with an occasional impromptu song on some passing event—perhaps on the casual stranger who has looked in, perhaps a wit combat between two of the girls about the real or supposed merits or demerits of their respective lovers. These wit combats are much enjoyed, being often clever, caustic, and apt

A favourite subject at these waulkings is Prince Charlie, and a favourite song is 'Morag'—little Marion—the endearing term under which the Prince is veiled The words of the song are vigorous and passionate, and the air stirring, while the subject is one to fire the hearts and imaginations of the people even at this distance of time, and notwithstanding the spoliations, oppressions, and butcheries inflicted on their fathers through their adherence to 'Morag'

The song begins as follows:—

CHORUS   'Agus ho Mhorag,   And ho ro Mòrag,
         Ho ro na ho ro gheallaidh,   Ho ro na ho ro darling,
         Agus ho Mhorag   And ho ro Morag

Mhorag chiatach a chul dualaich,   Beauteous Morag of the clustering locks,
'S e do luaidh tha tighinn air m' aire   To sing of thee is my intent

THE CONSECRATION OF THE CLOTH

Ma dh' imich thu null thar chuan
Gu mu luadh thig thu dachaidh.

If thou art gone beyond the sea,
Prithee hasten home to me.

Cuimhnich thou leat bannal ghruagach,
A luaidheas an clo-ruadh gu daingeau '

Remember, bring a band of maidens,
Who will waulk the red cloth firmly

When the women have waulked the cloth, they roll up the web and place it on end in the centre of the frame. They then turn it slowly and deliberately sunwise along the frame, saying with each turn of the web :—

' Cha 'n ath-aodach seo.

This is not second clothing

Cha 'n thaoigh seo

This cloth is not thigged

Cha chuid cleir no sagairt seo '

This is not the property of cleric or priest

Another form is —

' Roinn a h-aon, roinn a dha, roinn a tri, roinn a ceithir, roinn a coig, roinn a sia, roinn a seachd, roinn a seachd

Division one, division two, division three, division four, division five, division six, division seven, division seven

' Cha'n aodach seo do shagairt no chleir,
Ach 's aodach e do mo Dhomhllan caomhach fein,
Do m' chombanach graidh 's do dh' Iain an aigh,
'S do Mhuiril is aillidh sgeimh '

This is not cloth for priest or cleric,
But it is cloth for my own little Donald of love,
For my companion beloved, for John of joy,
And for Muriel of loveliest hue.

Each member of the household for whom the cloth is intended is mentioned by name in the consecration The cloth is then spat upon, and slowly reversed end by end in the name of Father and of Son and of Spirit till it stands again in the centre of the frame The ceremony of consecrating the cloth is usually intoned, the women, hitherto gay and vivacious, now solemn and subdued, singing in unison The woman who leads in the consecration is called 'coisreagan,' consecrator or celebrant. After the cloth is waulked and washed it is rolled up. This is called 'coilleachadh '—stretching,—'coilleachadh an aodaich '—stretching the cloth,—a process done with great care in order to secure equal tension throughout the web.

The operation of waulking is a singularly striking scene, and one which High-landers cherish wherever situated.

COISRIGEADH AN AODAICH

S math a ghabhas mi mo rann,
  A teurnadh le gleann ;
      Aon rann,
      Da rann,
      Tri rann,
      Ceithir rann,
      Coig rann,
      Sia rann,
      Seachd rann,
      Seachd gu leth rann
      Seachd gu leth rann.

Nar a gonar fear an eididh,
Nar a reubar e gu brath,
Cian theid e 'n cath no 'n comhrag,
Sgiath chomarach an Domhnach da,
Cian theid e 'n cath no 'n comhrag,
Sgiath chomarach an Domhnach da.

Cha 'n ath-aodach seo, 's cha'n fhaoigh e,
'S cha chuid cleir no sagairt e.

Biolair uaine ga buain fo lic,
'S air a toir do mhnai gun fhiosd,
Lurg an fheidh an ceann an sgadain,
'S an caol chalp a bhradain bhric.

THE CONSECRATION OF THE CLOTH (*continued*)

WELL can I say my rune,
Descending with the glen;
 One rune,
 Two runes,
 Three runes,
 Four runes,
 Five runes,
 Six runes,
 Seven runes,
 Seven and a half runes,
 Seven and a half runes.

May the man of this clothing never be wounded,
May torn he never be;
What time he goes into battle or combat,
May the sanctuary shield of the Lord be his.
What time he goes into battle or combat,
May the sanctuary shield of the Lord be his.

This is not second clothing and it is not thigged,
Nor is it the right of sacristan or of priest.

Cresses green culled beneath a stone,
And given to a woman in secret.
The shank of the deer in the head of the herring,
And in the slender tail of the speckled salmon

BEANNACHADH SEILG   [114]

A YOUNG man was consecrated before he went out to hunt. Oil was put on his head, a bow was placed in his hand, and he was required to stand with bare feet on the bare grassless ground. The dedication of the young hunter was akin to those of the 'maor,' the judge, the chief, and the king, on installation. Many conditions were imposed on the young man, which he was required to observe throughout life. He was

HO m' leasraidh ghineadh thu a mhic,
    Seolaim thu an t-iul tha ceart,
    An ainm naomh nan aon ostal deug,
    An ainm Mhic De chaidh a reubadh leat.

An ainm Sheumais, Pheadail, agus Phail,
    Eoin bhaistidh, us Eoin ostail tha shuas,
    Lucais leigh, agus Steafain a chraidh,
    Mhuiril mhin, us Mhoire mathair Uain.

An ainm Phadra naoimh nam feart,
    Agus Charmaig nan ceart 's nan tuam,
    Chaluim chaoimh, 's Adhamhnain nan reachd,
    Fhite bhith, us Bhride bhliochd us bhuar.

An ainm Mhicheil mil nan slogh,
An ainm Airil og nan snuadh,
An ainm Uiril nan ciabhan oir,
Agus Ghabrail fadh Oigh nam buadh.

An trath a dhuineas tu do shuil,
Cha lub thu do ghlun 's cha ghluais,
Cha leon thu lach bhios air an t-snamh,
Chaoidh cha chreach thu h-alach uaip.

HUNTING BLESSING

not to take life wantonly He was not to kill a bird sitting, nor a beast lying down, and he was not to kill the mother of a brood, nor the mother of a suckling. Nor was he to kill an unfledged bird nor a suckling beast, unless it might be the young of a bird, or of a beast, of prey It was at all times permissible and laudable to destroy certain clearly defined birds and beasts of prey and evil reptiles, with their young

FROM my loins begotten wert thou, my son,
May I guide thee the way that is right,
In the holy name of the apostles eleven
In name of God the Son torn of thee

In name of James, and Peter, and Paul,
John the baptist, and John the apostle above,
Luke the physician, and Stephen the martyr,
Muriel the fair, and Mary mother of the Lamb

In name of Patrick holy of the deeds,
And Carmac of the rights and tombs,
Columba beloved, and Adamnan of laws,
Fite calm, and Bride of the milk and kine.

In name of Michael chief of hosts,
In name of Ariel youth of lovely hues,
In name of Uriel of the golden locks,
And Gabriel seer of the Virgin of grace.

The time thou shalt have closed thine eye,
Thou shalt not bend thy knee nor move,
Thou shalt not wound the duck that is swimming,
Never shalt thou harry her of her young.

Eala bhan a ghlugaid bhinn,
Odhra sgaireach nan ciabh donn,
Cha ghear thu it as an druim,
Gu la-bhrath, air bharr nan tonn.

Air an ite bitheadh iad a ghnath
Mu 'n cuir thu lamhaidh ri do chluais,
Us bheir Moire mhin-gheal dhut dha gradh,
Us bheir Bride aluinn dhut dha buar.

Cha 'n ith thu farasg no blianach,
No aon ian nach leag do lamh,
Bi-sa taingeil leis an aon-fhear,
Ge do robh a naodh air snamh.

Eala shith Bhride nan ni,
Lacha shith Mhoire na sith

The white swan of the sweet gurgle,
The speckled dun of the brown tuft,
Thou shalt not cut a feather from their backs,
Till the doom-day, on the crest of the wave.

On the wing be they always
Ere thou place missile to thine ear,
And the fair Mary will give thee of her love,
And the lovely Bride will give thee of her kine.

Thou shalt not eat fallen fish nor fallen flesh,
Nor one bird that thy hand shall not bring down,
Be thou thankful for the one,
Though nine should be swimming.

The fairy swan of Bride of flocks,
The fairy duck of Mary of peace

COISRIGEADH NA SEILG   [115]

This hymn was sung by the hunter when he went away in the

N ainm na Trianailt, mar aon,
  Ann am briathar, an gniomh 's an smaon,
  Ta mi 'g ionn mo lamha fein,
  Ann an sionn 's an sian nan speur.

    A dubhradh nach till mi ri m' bheo
    Gun iasgach, gun ianach ni 's mo,
    Gun seing, gun sithinn nuas a beinn,
    Gun sul, gun saill, a muigh a coill.

O Mhoire mhaoth-gheal, chaomh-gheal, ghradh-gheal,
Seachainn orm-s' am bradan tarra-gheal marbh air sala,
Lach le h-alach na'm b'e b'aill leat,
Nead ri beul an uisge far nach traigh e.

An liath-chearc air bharr nan stuc,
Us coileach-dubh an tuchain truim,
An deigh laighe luth na greine,
Seachainn, o seachainn orm fein an eisdeachd.

O Mhoire, mhathair chubhr mo Righ,
Crun-sa mi le crun do shith,
Cuir do bhrat rioghach oir dha m' dhion,
Us comhnuich mi le comhnadh Chriosd,
    Comhnuich mi le comhnadh Chriosd.

CONSECRATING THE CHASE

morning, and when he had bathed his hands and face in the junction of the first
three streams he met

In name of the Holy Three-fold as one,
In word, in deed, and in thought,
I am bathing mine own hands,
In the light and in the elements of the sky.

Vowing that I shall never return in my life,
Without fishing, without fowling either,
Without game, without venison down from the hill,
Without fat, without blubber from out the copse.

O Mary tender-fair, gentle-fair, loving-fair,
Avoid thou to me the silvery salmon dead on the salt sea,
A duck with her brood an it please thee to show me,
A nest by the edge of the water where it does not dry.

The grey-hen on the crown of the knoll,
The black-cock of the hoarse croon,
After the strength of the sun has gone down,
Avoid, oh, avoid thou to me the hearing of them.

O Mary, fragrant mother of my King,
Crown thou me with the crown of thy peace,
Place thine own regal robe of gold around me,
And save me with the saving of Christ,
    Save me with the saving of Christ.

ORA TURAIS　　　　　　[116]

This hymn was sung by a pilgrim in setting out on his
pilgrimage.　The family and friends joined the traveller

ITH a bhi na m' bhial,
　　Bladh a bhi na m' chainn,
　　Blath na siri na mo bhile,
　　Gu 'n an tig mi nall.

　　An gaol thug Iosa Criosda
　　Bhi lionadh gach cridhe domh,
　　An gaol thug Iosa Criosda
　　Da m' lionadh air an son.

Siubhal choire, siubhal choille,
Siubhal fraoine fada, fas,
Moire mhin-gheal sior dha m' chobhair,
Am Buachaill Iosa m' dhion 's a chas,
Moire mhin-gheal sior dha m' chobhair,
Am Buachaill Iosa m' dhion 's a chas.

PRAYER FOR TRAVELLING

in singing the hymn and starting the journey, from which too frequently, for
various causes, he never returned

LIFE be in my speech,
Sense in what I say,
The bloom of cherries on my lips,
Till I come back again.

The love Christ Jesus gave
Be filling every heart for me,
The love Christ Jesus gave
Filling me for every one.

Traversing corries, traversing forests,
Traversing valleys long and wild.
The fair white Mary still uphold me,
The Shepherd Jesu be my shield,
The fair white Mary still uphold me,
The Shepherd Jesu be my shield.

BEANNACHD IASGAICH [117]

On Christmas Day the young men of the townland go out to fish. All the fish they catch are sacred to the widows and the orphans and to the poor, and are distributed among them according to their necessities.

There is a tradition among the people of the Western Isles that Christ required Peter to row 707 strokes straight out from the shore when He commanded him to go and procure the fish containing the tribute-money. Following this tradition, the old men of Uist require the young men to row 707 strokes from the land before casting their lines on Christmas Day. And whatever fish they get are cordially given to the needy as a tribute in the name of Christ, King of the sea, and of Peter, king of fishermen. This is called 'dioladh deirc,' tribute-paying, 'deirce Pheadair,' Peter's tribute, 'dioladh Pheadail,' Peter's payment, and other terms. This tribute-paying on Christmas Day excites much emotional interest, and all try to enhance the tribute and in various ways to render the alms as substantial as possible.

The whiting and the haddock of the same size bear a strong resemblance to one another. There are differences, however. The haddock has a black spot on each side of its body above the pectoral fin, while the head of the whiting is more elongated than that of the haddock. Children and strangers are taught to differentiate between the two thus :—

| 'Ball dubh air an adaig, | A black spot of the haddock, |
| Gob fad air a chuideig.' | A long snout on the whiting. |

A na soillse thainig oirnn,
Rugadh Criosda leis an Oigh.

Na ainm-san cratham am burn
Air gach cail a ta na m' churt.

A Righ nam feart 's nan neart tha shuas,
Do bheannachd iasgaich dort a nuas.

Suidhim sios le ramh na m' ghlac,
Imirim a seachd ceud 's a seachd.

FISHING BLESSING

The people of Uist say that the haddock was the fish in whose mouth Peter found the tribute-money, and that the two black spots are the marks left by Peter's fingers when he held the fish to extract the money from its mouth   The crew of young men who get most haddocks on Christmas Day are looked upon during the year as the real followers of the king of fishers.   There is, therefore, considerable emulation among the different crews.

The haddock is called 'iasg Pheadail,' Peter's fish, and 'iasg Pheadair runaich,' the fish of loving Peter; and a family of birds 'peadaneach,' 'peitnich'—Peter-like, petrels, because in their flight they seem to be walking on the sea

The tradition as to rowing 707 strokes is curious and interesting.   The only other similar tradition which I know is of the wars between the Fomorians and the Milesians in Ireland   Both were invaders.--the Milesians earlier, the Fomorians later   When the Fomorians landed in Ireland the Milesians were already established, and the result was a long-continued war, till both sides were exhausted and tired of the strife   During a temporary truce it was agreed that the Fomorians should retire to the sea and row straight out 707 strokes from land, and if they succeeded in landing again they were to be allowed to remain and enjoy their hard-won honours   Whether for good or for ill to Ireland, the Fomorians effected a landing a second time, and settled in the south and west of the island

The Irish were Pagan at the time, and the tradition of the 707 strokes being imposed by Christ on Peter must have been inserted in the Fomorian tradition after Ireland became Christian.

THE day of light has come upon us,
Christ is born of the Virgin

In His name I sprinkle the water
Upon every thing within my court.

Thou King of deeds and powers above,
Thy fishing blessing pour down on us.

I will sit me down with an oar in my grasp,
I will row me seven hundred and seven [strokes].

Tilgidh mi mo dhubhan sios,
'S an ciad iasg a bheir mi nios,

An ainm Chriosda, Righ nan sian,
Gheobh an deoir e mar a mhiann.

Us righ nan iasgair, Peadair treun,
Bheir e bheannachd dhomh na dheigh.

Airil, Gabril, agus Eoin,
Raphail baigheil, agus Pol,

Calum-cille caomh 's gach cas,
'S Muire mhin-gheal leis a ghras.

Siubhlaibh leinn gu iola cuain,
Ciuimbh dhuinne barr nan stuagh.

Righ nan righ ri crich ar cuart,
Sineadh saoghail us sonais buan.

Crun an Righ o'n Tri tha shuas,
Crois Chriosda d'ar dion a nuas.
    Crun an Righ o'n Tri tha shuas,
    Crois Chriosda d'ar dion a nuas.

I will cast down my hook,
The first fish which I bring up,

In the name of Christ, King of the elements,
The poor shall have it as his need.

And the king of fishers, the brave Peter,
He will after it give me his blessing.

Ariel, Gabriel, and John,
Raphael benign, and Paul,

Columba, tender in every distress,
And Mary fair, the endowed of grace.

Encompass ye us to the fishing-bank of ocean,
And still ye to us the crest of the waves.

Be the King of kings at the end of our course,
Of lengthened life and of lasting happiness.

Be the crown of the King from the Three on high,
Be the cross of Christ adown to shield us,
　　The crown of the King from the Three above,
　　The cross of Christ adown to shield us.

BEANNACHADH CUAIN [118]

SEA prayers and sea hymns were common amongst the seafarers of the Western Islands   Probably these originated with the early Celtic missionaries, who constantly traversed in their frail skin coracles the storm-swept, strongly tidal seas of those Hebrid Isles, oft and oft sealing their devotion with their lives.

Before embarking on a voyage the voyagers stood round their boat and prayed to the God of the elements for a peaceful voyage over the stormy sea   The steersman led the appeal, while the swish of the waves below, the sough of the sea beyond, and the sound of the wind around blended with the voices of the suppliants and lent dignity and solemnity to the scene.

There are many small oratories round the West Coast where chiefs and clansmen were wont to pray before and after voyaging   An interesting example of these is in the island of Grimisey, North Uist.   The place is called Ceallan, cells, from 'ceall,' a cell   There were two oratories within two hundred yards of one another   One of the two has wholly disappeared, the other nearly.   The ruins stand on a ridge near the end of the island looking out on the open bay of Ceallan and over the stormy Minch to the distant mountains of Mull and Morven   The oratory is known as 'Teampull Mhicheil,' the temple of St Michael.   The structure was simple but beautiful, while the remains are interesting and touching from their historical associations.   Tradition says that the oratory was built by 'Eibhric'—Euphemia or Amie, sole daughter and heiress of Ruaraidh, the son of Alan, High Chief of Lorn.

Amie, the daughter of Ruaraidh, married in 1337 John of Islay, Lord of the Isles   The two being related, they were granted a dispensation by Pope Benedict XII.   The Lady Amie had three sons.

About the year 1358 John of Islay discarded Amie, and married Margaret, daughter of Robert Steward, and granddaughter of Robert Bruce   When the Lord of the Isles came south to celebrate his marriage with the Lady Margaret, one hundred and eight ships full of kinsmen and clansmen, chiefs and chieftains, came in his train   Such a sight had never been seen in Scotland before, and people came to the Clyde from long distances to see this large fleet   The power and influence indicated by this enormous retinue created much comment and envy among the nobles of the south and even at the court

The Lord of the Isles retained possession of the extensive territories of the Lady Amie, disposing of them afterwards to his several sons.

The discarded lady took to a religious life, building and restoring oratories, churches, nunneries, monasteries, and castles throughout her ancestral lands   Saint Michael's Temple at Ceallan was one of these.   In this little sanctuary built for the

THE OCEAN BLESSING

purpose the Lady Amie offered prayers and sacrifice before and after voyages to her kindred in Lorn

John, Lord of the Isles, was a man of much munificence, like all those princely Macdonalds He gave largely to the Church, earning for himself from the priests of the period the name of 'The Good John of Islay' He was buried in Iona in the year 1386, in splendour and magnificence never surpassed, if ever equalled, in the case of the many kings of the five nationalities buried there

About two years after his father's death, Ranald, the eldest surviving son of the Lady Amie, handed over the lordship of the Isles to Donald, eldest son of the Lady Margaret, who afterwards fought the battle of Harlaw The ceremony of installing a Lord of the Isles usually took place at Loch Finlaggan in Islay, the principal seat of the Macdonalds, where the ruins of their castle, chapel, and other buildings are still to be seen, as well as the stone with the footmarks cut in it upon which the chief stood when, before the 'gentlemen of the Islands' and Highlands, he was proclaimed 'Macdonald' and 'High-prince of the seed of Conn' But it was at Kildonan in the island of Eigg that Ranald gave the sceptre into the hand of Donald, who thus became eighth Lord of the Isles. The account given of the ceremony by Hugh Macdonald, the Seanchie of Sleat, is interesting as representing the usual manner of installing a king, chief, or other dignitary among the Celts :—'At this the Bishop of Argyll, the Bishop of the Isles, and seven priests were sometimes present, but a bishop was always present, with the chieftains of all the principal families and a Ruler of the Isles. There was a square stone seven or eight feet long, and the tract of a man's foot cut thereon, upon which he stood, denoting that he should walk in the footsteps and uprightness of his predecessors, and that he was installed by right in his possessions He was clothed in a white habit to show his innocence and integrity of heart, that he would be a light to his people and maintain the true religion The white apparel did afterwards belong to the poet by right Then he was to receive a white rod in his hand intimating that he had power to rule, not with tyranny and partiality, but with discretion and sincerity. Then he received his forefathers' sword, or some other sword, signifying that his duty was to protect and defend them from their enemies in peace or war, as the obligations and customs of his predecessors were The ceremony being over, mass was said after the blessing of the Bishop and seven priests, the people pouring their prayers for the success and prosperity of their new-created lord When they were dismissed, the Lord of the Isles feasted them for a week thereafter, and gave liberally to the monks, poets, bards, and musicians. You may judge that they spent liberally without any

exception of persons.' Other accounts differ but slightly from the above, as when
Martin says that 'the young chief stood upon a cairn of stones, while his followers
stood round him in a circle, his elevation signifying his authority over them, and
their standing below their subjection to him, also that

HI tha chomhnadh nan ard,
   Tiuirich duinn do bheannachd aigh,
   Iomchair leinn air bharr an t-sal,
   Iomchair sinn gu cala tamh,
   Beannaich ar sgioba agus bat,
   Beannaich gach acair agus ramh,
   Gach stadh us tarruinn agus rac,
   Ar siuil-mhora ri crainn ard
   Cuin a Righ nan dul na'n ait
   Run 's gu 'n till sinn dachaidh slan ;
Suidhidh mi fein air an stiuir,
Is e Mac De a bheir domh iuil,
Mar a thug e Chalum ciuin,
'N am dha stadh a chur ri siuil.

Mhuire, Bhride, Mhicheil, Phail,
Pheadair, Ghabriel, Eoin a ghraidh,
Doirtibh oirnn an driuchd o'n aird,
Bheireadh oirnn 's a chreideamh fas,
Daingnibh sinn 's a Charraig Ail,
Anns gach reachd a dhealbhas gradh,
Run 's gu 'n ruig sinn tir an aigh,
Am bi sith us seirc us baigh
Air an nochdadh duinn tre ghras ;
Chaoidh cha'n fhaigh a chnoimh n' ar dail,
Bithidh sinn tearuint ann gu brath,
Cha bhi sinn an geimhlibh bais,
Ge do tha sinn do shiol Adh.

immediately after the proclamation the chief druid or bard performed a rhetorical
panegyric setting forth the ancient pedigree, valour, and liberality of the family as
incentives to the young chieftain and fit for his imitation.' Martin speaks of this
ceremony of installing a chief as prevalent in the eighteenth century.

O Thou who pervadest the heights,
Imprint on us Thy gracious blessing,
Carry us over the surface of the sea,
Carry us safely to a haven of peace,
Bless our boatmen and our boat,
Bless our anchors and our oars,
Each stay and halyard and traveller,
Our mainsails to our tall masts
Keep, O King of the elements, in their place
That we may return home in peace ;
I myself will sit down at the helm,
It is God's own Son who will give me guidance.
As He gave to Columba the mild
What time he set stay to sails.

Mary, Bride, Michael, Paul,
Peter, Gabriel, John of love,
Pour ye down the dew from above
That would make our faith to grow,
Establish ye us in the Rock of rocks,
In every law that love exhibits,
That we may reach the land of glory,
Where peace and love and mercy reign,
All vouchsafed to us through grace ;
Never shall the canker worm get near us,
We shall be safe there for ever,
We shall not be in the bonds of death
Though we are of the seed of Adam

La Fheill Micheil, La Fheill Mairt,
La Fheill Andrais, bann na baigh,
La Fheill Bride, la mo luaidh,
Tilg an nimhir sios an chuan,
Feuch an dean e slugadh suas ;
La Fheill Paruig, la nam buadh,
Sorachair oirnn an stoirm o thuath,
Casg a fraoch, maol a gruam,
Diochd a gairge, marbh a fuachd.

La nan Tri Righrean shuas,
Ciuinich dhuinne barr nan stuadh,
La Bealltain thoir an driuchd,
La Fheill Sheathain thoir an ciuin,
La Fheill Moire mor nan cliar,
Seachainn oirnn an stoirm o 'n iar,
Gach la 's oidhche gach stoirm us fiamh,
Bi thusa leinn, a Thriath nan triath,
Bi fein duinn a' d' chairt-iuil,
Biodh do lamh air failm ar stiuir,
Do lamh fein, a Dhe nan dul,
Moch us anamoch mar is iul,
    Moch us anamoch mar is iul

On the Feast Day of Michael, the Feast Day of Martin,
The Feast Day of Andrew, band of mercy,
The Feast Day of Bride, day of my choice,
Cast ye the serpent into the ocean,
So that the sea may swallow her up ;
On the Feast Day of Patrick, day of power,
Foreshow to us the storm from the north,
Quell its wrath and blunt its fury,
Lessen its fierceness, kill its cold.

On the Day of the Three Kings on high,
Subdue to us the crest of the waves,
On Beltane Day give us the dew,
On John's Day the gentle wind,
The Day of Mary the great of fame,
Ward off us the storm from the west ;
Each day and night, storm and calm,
Be Thou with us, O Chief of chiefs,
Be Thou Thyself to us a compass-chart,
Be Thine hand on the helm of our rudder,
Thine own hand, Thou God of the elements,
Early and late as is becoming,
    Early and late as is becoming.

BEANNACHADH CUAIN　　　[119]

HE, Athair uile-chumhachdaich, chaoimh,
Ios a Mhic nan deur agus na caoidh,
Le d'chomh-chomhnadh, O! a Spioraid Naoimh.

Thrithinn bhi-bheo, bhi-mhoir, bhi-bhuain,
Thug Clann Israil tri na Muir Ruaidh,
Us Ionah gu fonn a bronn miol-mhor a chuain,

Thug Pol agus a chomhlain 's an long,
A doruinn na mara, a dolais nan tonn,
A stoirm a bha mor, a doinne bha trom.

D'uair bhruchd an tuil air Muir Ghailili,
　　※　　　※　　　※　　　※　　　※
　　※　　　※　　　※　　　※　　　※

Seun agus saor agus naomhaich sinne,
Bi-sa, Righ nan dul, air ar stiuir a' d' shuidhe,
'S treoirich an sith sinn gu ceann-crich ar n-uidhe.

Le gaotha caona, caomha, coistre, cubhr,
Gun fhaobhadh, gun fhionnsadh, gun fhabhsadh,
Nach deanadh gniamh fabhtach dhuinn.

Iarramaid gach sian a Dhe,
A reir do rian 's do bhriathra fein.

OCEAN BLESSING

God the Father all-powerful, benign,
Jesu the Son of tears and of sorrow,
With thy co-assistance, O! Holy Spirit.

The Three-One, ever-living, ever-mighty, everlasting,
Who brought the Children of Israel through the Red Sea,
And Jonah to land from the belly of the great creature of the ocean,

Who brought Paul and his companions in the ship,
From the torment of the sea, from the dolour of the waves,
From the gale that was great, from the storm that was heavy.

When the storm poured on the Sea of Galilee,
  *   *   *   *   *   *
  *   *   *   *   *   *

Sain us and shield and sanctify us,
Be Thou, King of the elements, seated at our helm,
And lead us in peace to the end of our journey.

With winds mild, kindly, benign, pleasant,
Without swirl, without whirl, without eddy,
That would do no harmful deed to us.

We ask all things of Thee, O God,
According to Thine own will and word

RIAGHLAIR NAN SIAN [120]

LANN Israil us Dia da 'n gabhail,
  Troimh 'n Mhuir Ruaidh fhuair iad rathad,
Is ann a fhuair iad casg am pathaidh,
  An creag nach d' fhaodadh le saor a shnaidheadh.

Co iad air falm mo stiuir
  Deanamh falbh da m' iubhraich shoir ?
Peadail, Pal, us Eoin mo ruin,
  Triuir da 'n talmaich fiu us foir.

Co 'n croil an coir mo stiuir ?
  Peadail, Poil, us Eoin Baistidh,
Criosda na shuidh air mo stiuir,
  Deanamh iuil da 'n ghaoith a deas.

Co da 'n criothnaich guth na gaoith?
  Co da 'n caonaich caol us cuan ?
Iosa Criosda, Triath gach naoimh,
  Mac Moire, Friaimh nam buadh,
  Mac Moire, Friaimh nam buadh.

RULER OF THE ELEMENTS

The Children of Israel, God taking them,
  Through the Red Sea obtained a path,
They obtained the quenching of their thirst
  From a rock that might not by man be sculptured.

Who are they on the helm of my rudder,
  Making joyance to my eastern barge?
Peter and Paul and John the beloved,
  Three to whom are due obeisance and laud.

Who are the group near to my helm?
  Peter and Paul and John the Baptist;
Christ is sitting on my helm,
  Making guidance to the wind from the south.

To whom does tremble the voice of the wind?
  To whom become tranquil strait and ocean?
To Jesus Christ, Chief of each saint,
  Son of Mary, Root of victory,
  Son of Mary, Root of victory.

URNUIGH MHARA   [121]

STIURADAIR   Beannaicht an long.   [Beannaichteadh
SGIOBA   Beannaicheadh Dia an t-Athair i

              Beannaicht an long.
              Beannaicheadh Dia am Mac i.

              Beannaicht an long
              Beannaicheadh Dia an Spioiad i.

UILE   Dia an t-Athair,
              Dia am Mac,
              Dia an Spiorad,
                  Beannaicheadh an long.

STIURADAIR   Ciod is eagal duibh
              Us Dia an t-Athair leibh ?

SGIOBA   Cha 'n eagal duinn ni.   [aoin

              Ciod is eagal duibh
              Us Dia am Mac leibh ?

              Cha 'n eagal duinn ni.

              Ciod is eagal duibh
              Us Dia an Spiorad leibh ?

              Cha 'n eagal duinn ni.

SEA PRAYER

HELMSMAN	Blest be the boat	[Blessed
CREW	God the Father bless her	

Blest be the boat.
God the Son bless her.

Blest be the boat
God the Spirit bless her.

ALL God the Father,
God the Son,
God the Spirit,
    Bless the boat.

HELMSMAN What can befall you
And God the Father with you?

CREW No harm can befall us.   [Not one thing

What can befall you
And God the Son with you?

No harm can befall us.

What can befall you
And God the Spirit with you?

No harm can befall us.

UILE

Dia an t-Athair,
Dia am Mac,
Dia an Spiorad,
  Leinn gu sior

STIURADAIR

Ciod is fath bhur curam
Us Ti nan dul os bhur cinn ?

SGIOBA

 Cha churam dhuinn ni.

Ciod is fath bhur curam
Us Righ nan dul os bhur cinn ?

 Cha churam dhuinn ni.

Ciod is fath bhur curam
Us Spiorad nan dul os bhur cinn ?

 Cha churam dhuinn ni.

UILE

Ti nan dul,
Righ nan dul,
Spiorad nan dul,
Dluth os ar cinn,
  Suthainn sior.

ALL   God the Father,
God the Son,
God the Spirit,
    With us eternally.

HELMSMAN   What can cause you anxiety
And the God of the elements over you?

CREW   No anxiety can be ours.

What can cause you anxiety
And the King of the elements over you?

No anxiety can be ours.

What can cause you anxiety
And the Spirit of the elements over you?

No anxiety can be ours.

ALL   The God of the elements,
The King of the elements,
The Spirit of the elements,
Close over us,
    Ever eternally.

EDINBURGH: T. AND A. CONSTABLE, PRINTERS TO HER MAJESTY